PRAISE
RONALD KESSLER
and
INSIDE THE CIA

Revealing the Secrets of the World's Most Powerful Spy Agency

"Writing with the cooperation of active and retired personnel, Kessler offers a working portrait of the contemporary CIA. His background in journalistic study of intelligence, augmented by an unusual array of other resources, enables him to provide an account unique for balance, perspective, clarity of writing, and the large amount of factual material."

—*Booklist*

"An appraisal of the Central Intelligence Agency in as much detail as the organization and the law will allow. . . . Kessler is quite clear that the Agency violated its charter in times past, and suspects it might do so again, given the proper circumstances. . . . INSIDE THE CIA . . . does lift the veil of secrecy just a tad, and that is all for the better."

—*Salem Press* (Pasadena, CA)

Books by Ronald Kessler

Inside Congress*
The Sins of the Father
Inside the White House*
The FBI*
Inside the CIA*
Escape from the CIA*
The Spy in the Russian Club*
Moscow Station*
Spy vs. Spy*
The Richest Man in the World
The Life Insurance Game

*Published by POCKET BOOKS

INSIDE THE CIA

RONALD KESSLER

POCKET BOOKS

New York   London   Toronto   Sydney

POCKET BOOKS, a division of Simon & Schuster, Inc.
1230 Avenue of the Americas, New York, NY 10020

Copyright © 1992 by Ronald Kessler

All rights reserved, including the right to reproduce
this book or portions thereof in any form whatsoever.
For information address Pocket Books, 1230 Avenue
of the Americas, New York, NY 10020

ISBN 13 : 978-0-671-73458-9
ISBN 10 : 0-671-73458-X

First Pocket Books paperback printing February 1994

20 19 18 17 16 15

POCKET and colophon are registered trademarks of
Simon & Schuster, Inc.

Cover art by Tom Cushwa

Printed in the U.S.A.

For Pam, Rachel, and Greg Kessler

Contents

PART I
The Directorate of Operations

Contents

PART II
The Directorate of Science and Technology

PART III
The Directorate of Intelligence

PART IV
The Directorate of Administration

Contents

PART V
The Office of the Director
of Central Intelligence

Acknowledgments

My editor, Paul D. McCarthy of Pocket Books, came up with the idea for this book, provided strong encouragement throughout the project, guided me through difficult decisions about organization, and brilliantly edited the manuscript. An editor with his range of talents is rare. I owe him a tremendous debt.

In the early stages, people who were particularly helpful were Col. Russell J. Bowen, Dr. Lee S. Houchins, David D. Whipple, the late John A. Bross, and several others who cannot be named.

As explained in the author's note, once the book was well under way, William H. Webster, then director of Central Intelligence, gave approval for limited CIA cooperation—the first time the CIA has cooperated on a book about the agency. He and Joseph R. DeTrani, E. Peter Earnest, and Gwen Cohen of the CIA public affairs office are due special thanks.

A number of former employees of each CIA directorate,

of the office of the director of Central Intelligence, and of the Senate Select Committee on Intelligence, read portions of the manuscript. While some cannot be named, they include Herbert F. Saunders, Robert R. Simmons, Nancy D. McGregor, John B. Bellinger, Russell J. Bruemmer, and Roland Inlow. The fact that they read portions of the book does not mean that they agree with everything in it. However, by investing their time and energy, they helped to make it a richer and more accurate book.

My wife, Pamela Kessler, applied her sharp editing eye to the manuscript and improved the quality of the book. My friend Daniel M. Clements also read the manuscript and came up with insightful advice on themes and organization.

By being both friend and professional colleague, Pam Kessler did more than anyone to make this book a reality. My children, Greg V. Kessler and Rachel Kessler, now pursuing their own careers, have been a source of pride that helped sustain me.

The book would never have been written without the valuable time devoted to it by those who consented to be interviewed. While all of them cannot be named, those who were interviewed or who helped in other ways include:

John (Jay) T. Aldhizer; Moria Arsenault; John P. Austin; Dr. William Bader; William M. Baker; Howard T. Bane; Isabella Bates; Sean Beeny; David W. Belin; Bestor T. Bell; John B. Bellinger III; Abram Bergson; Igor Birman; Richard M. Bissell, Jr.; Nancy H. Blanchet; Sylvia Blanchet; Lane Bonner; Col. Russell J. Bowen; the late John A. Bross; Russell J. Bruemmer; Dino A. Brugioni; Coralie Marcus Bryant; Donald F. Burton; and Plato Cacheris.

Vincent M. Cannistraro; Leo Carl; Francis D. Carter; Douglass Cater; David Chavchavadze; Walter M. Clark; John Clarke; Dr. Ray S. Cline; Gwen Cohen; William E. Colby; George C. Constantinides; Elizabeth M. Cooke; Alexandra Costa; Robert T. Crowley; James Currie; Kenneth E. deGraffenreid; Joseph R. DeTrani; John T. Downey; E. Peter Earnest; Walter N. Elder; Stephen Engelberg; Andrew T. Falkiewicz; David E. Faulkner; Richard G. Fecteau; Horace Z. Feldman; and Charles Fenyvesi.

Acknowledgments

Harry E. Fitzwater; Dr. Harold P. Ford; Gary E. Foster; Thomas B. Fricke; Graham E. Fuller; Robert M. Gates; Clair E. George; Cathie Gill; Lt. Gen. Daniel O. Graham; John K. Greaney; James W. Greenleaf; Howard W. Gutman; Samuel Halpern; Howard P. Hart; William T. Hassler; Richard Helms; Allan Bruce Hemmings; Herbert E. Hetu; William Hood; Eugene J. Horan; John B. Hotis; Dr. Lee S. Houchins; Lawrence R. Houston; Col. David L. Huxsoll; and Roland Inlow.

Adm. Bobby R. Inman; Donald F. B. Jameson; Louise R. (Lisa) Jameson; F. Peter Jessup; Paul Joyal; D. Barry Kelly; Charles M. Kerr; Richard J. Kerr; William Kucewicz; Conrad E. LaGueux; George V. Lauder; William T. Lee; Stanislav Levchenko; Arthur C. Lundahl; Douglass S. Mackall II; Henry C. Mackall; Andrew W. Marshall; John L. Martin; Linda McCarthy; Rep. Dave McCurdy; Nancy D. McGregor; John N. McMahon; Clayton E. McManaway, Jr.; and Ann Medinger.

Cord Meyer; Herbert E. Meyer; William G. Miller; Judge William H. Orrick; Phillip A. Parker; Thomas Polgar; Edward W. Proctor; Oliver (Buck) Revell; Juan Antonio Menier Rodriguez; Steven Rosefield; Henry S. Rowen; Jim Sanborn; Richard Sandza; Herbert F. Saunders; Daniel F. Sheehan; Joe Shimon; Rear Adm. Donald M. "Mac" Showers; Rep. Bud Shuster; Rep. Robert R. Simmons; Russell Jack Smith; L. Britt Snider; Bruce Solie; Mary Spaeth; Judge Stanley Sporkin; Sol Stern; Gen. Richard G. Stilwell; Philip Stoddard; Lawrence B. Sulz; John E. Taylor; and Eric Tobias.

Adm. Stansfield Turner; Robert N. Walewski; John S. Warner; Doris Webb; Lynda Jo Webster; William H. Webster; David D. Whipple; John Wiant; Donald Wortman; F. Mark Wyatt; Dr. Keith R. Yamamoto; Roger S. Young; and Norman A. Zigrossi.

They have my gratitude.

Author's Note

My introduction to the spy business came in the fall of 1986, when *Regardie's,* a Washington magazine, asked me to write a piece about an espionage case that had been investigated by the FBI. Having written off and on about the FBI for twenty years, I knew a good deal about the bureau but nothing about its counterintelligence program, which entails catching spies.

To my surprise, the FBI's Washington Metropolitan Field Office allowed me to interview the agents who had worked on the spy case and go out in their cars as they checked out Soviet establishments. From the agents, I learned firsthand how intelligence and counterintelligence really work.

The world of spies was entirely different from anything I had encountered. It was not at all like the portrait that emerges from most spy novels. While just as exotic, it was governed by rules understood by both sides. Unlike murder or drug cases, intelligence cases were pursued by the super-powers of the world, not by punk drug dealers.

I expanded the magazine piece into *Spy vs. Spy,* a book about the FBI's counterintelligence program. To round out the picture, I interviewed the other side—Karl Koecher, a Czech Intelligence Service officer who became a mole in the CIA. After he had been caught, he was traded for Anatoly Shcharansky.

I went on to write other spy-related books—*Moscow Station,* about the security breaches at the American embassy in Moscow; *The Spy in the Russian Club,* about a Navy spy who defected to Moscow and committed suicide there; and *Escape from the CIA,* about the 1985 defection and redefection of KGB officer Vitaly Yurchenko. For that book, I again obtained the other side's view by interviewing Yurchenko for fourteen hours in Moscow.

Each of the books touched in some way on the CIA. Most of the references painted the agency in an unfavorable light. In Yurchenko's case, I wrote that the CIA had treated him coldly and as a prisoner; William J. Casey, then CIA director, had leaked stories about his defection to the press. In the area of counterintelligence, I wrote that James J. Angleton, the CIA's chief spy hunter, was an amateur at catching spies and in fact, had never caught one in the U.S. Moreover, Angleton had paralyzed the agency with his paranoid theories.

Like those of most Americans, my impressions of the CIA had been formed during the 1975 and 1976 Church Committee hearings, which depicted agency officers as bumblers who were a law unto themselves, administering LSD to unknowing subjects. FBI counterintelligence agents, who were in natural competition with the agency, reinforced those impressions. The only other notion I had was that the agency was adrift —paralyzed by the devastating impact of the Church Committee hearings and weighed down by bureaucracy.

These impressions came from secondhand or thirdhand accounts. Until I was well into the book about Yurchenko, I had never spent any time with a modern-day CIA officer. That was soon to change.

When I finished the Yurchenko book, my editor, Paul D.

McCarthy, senior editor at Pocket Books, suggested as my next book *Inside the CIA*. The book would tell what the agency is all about—its failures, successes, and secrets—and depict CIA officers and what they are like.

No book like this had ever been done before. John Ranelagh's *The Agency: The Rise and Decline of the CIA* was an excellent and authoritative history. But it did not really tell what the CIA does and how it does it.

Victor Marchetti and John D. Marks's 1974 book, *The CIA and the Cult of Intelligence,* had attempted to give an inside view of the CIA. But because Marchetti had previously worked for the agency, the book had been censored by the CIA. It was one-sided and was now out of date.

Other books by former CIA directors and officers, while exceptionally well done, had had to go through prepublication review by the agency. As a result, they could reveal little of the CIA's operations. Moreover, most of the books had focused on one or another of the CIA's directorates, or on personalities within the CIA. None had portrayed in detail how the directorates work together.

At first, the idea seemed overwhelming. Each directorate was a book in itself. How would I penetrate each of these areas in an agency where practically everything is, after all, classified? But having developed CIA sources in researching the book on Yurchenko, I decided that I could do it.

After discussing the idea further with Paul McCarthy and with retired CIA officers, I decided to focus primarily on the modern agency—the CIA since the Church Committee hearings. The last detailed look at the CIA's operations came during the Church Committee hearings. What had the agency done since 1976? At the same time, by referring to past events, the book would serve as a history of the agency.

In the spring of 1990, I set up a lunch with E. Peter Earnest, the CIA's deputy director of public affairs. I let him know what I was doing and elicited the agency's cooperation. While the book would be done regardless, the CIA's help would enable me to write a more complete account.

Meanwhile, I approached people who are politically well connected in the spy world—for example, David D. Whipple, the former CIA officer who heads the Association of Former Intelligence Officers. I wanted to give them a feel for the types of questions I would be asking. At the same time, I began interviews with other former CIA officers I had come to know while writing the Yurchenko book and the previous spy books.

Most of the interviews were with people who had been in the field—the officers who had recruited spies overseas, placed bugs in embassies, directed overhead surveillance, prepared intelligence estimates, and debugged the offices of the CIA director. Some of them gave up weeks of their time to give me a feel for the agency and what it does. I also made it a point to interview nearly all the living former directors of the CIA and deputy directors.

During this time, I kept in touch with the CIA's public affairs office. Joseph R. DeTrani, the CIA's new chief of public affairs, invited me to have lunch in his office on September 14, 1990. As with Peter Earnest, I went over with him what I was attempting to do: present an honest and fair picture of what the CIA does, portraying both its weaknesses and strengths. I also gave him an idea of the sorts of people I would like to interview at the agency and the issues I would be exploring.

A few weeks later, DeTrani told me that the first interview had been approved. It was to be with analysts who work on the Soviet economy. After the interview, DeTrani said that William H. Webster, the director of Central Intelligence, had personally approved CIA cooperation on the book—the first time the CIA had ever cooperated on a book about the agency.

For the next nine months, I conducted interviews at the agency, including with Webster and his deputy, Richard J. Kerr. The interviews were on such diverse subjects as the CIA's counternarcotics effort, the President's Daily Brief, the agency's employment program, and the future of the agency. In addition, when they could, DeTrani and Earnest answered my questions.

I was allowed to tour the CIA building, eat lunch in one of its cafeterias, see offices where the President's Daily Brief is prepared, and sit in on a Career Training Program session, where potential spies are recruited to work at the agency. Meanwhile, I continued to interview recently retired CIA officers in an effort to penetrate the more sensitive areas that the agency's public affairs office could not discuss.

Some of these former officers asked the public affairs office for guidance on whether to talk to me. They were given a favorable account of what I was doing and told to "use your judgment." I also learned that Webster had given the go-ahead to former aides—and even to his wife, Lynda Webster—to submit to interviews.

Later, DeTrani would say that the decision to cooperate was based on my reputation and on the fact that the CIA knew I already had a substantial amount of knowledge of the agency anyway. Still, it took guts for Webster and DeTrani to approve even limited cooperation. Traditionally, the CIA has dealt with the media by paying someone to say "no comment" when reporters call. While the CIA under Webster had come a long way from that posture, cooperating on a book that would undoubtedly contain criticism of the CIA and give away secrets required a longer-term vision of where the public interest lies.

As with any sensitive subject, most of the interviews were conducted on a background or not-for-attribution basis. Under these ground rules, the information can be used but the source cannot be quoted. However, an account can usually be given of what the individual did or what the individual said to others. This same information may have been obtained from other parties to a conversation, or from people to whom the individuals later related the incident.

Where possible, the notes at the end of the book cite people interviewed and the date of the interview. If they help illuminate the subject and are believed by the author to be accurate, publications are also cited in the notes. Confidential interviews are not cited in the notes because such references would not shed more light on the subject or help the reader to judge the veracity of the information.

Any sensitive information was verified by at least two people. This is the same standard used generally by the media for investigative or exclusive stories where the source cannot be disclosed. In addition, former employees of each of the CIA's directorates, of the office of director of Central Intelligence, and of the Senate Select Committee on Intelligence read portions of the manuscript for accuracy. While they could not vouch for all the information and do not necessarily agree with everything in the book, their suggested changes lent an additional layer of authenticity to the finished book.

Introduction

For William H. Webster, the day began routinely enough. A heavily armed Central Intelligence Agency car equipped with three telephones picked him up at his home in Bethesda, Maryland, and drove him to the White House. Just before eight A.M., he met with President Bush to present the President's Daily Brief, a top-secret document that contains the most sensitive secrets in Washington. At eight-thirty A.M., Webster arrived at Langley in McLean, Virginia, taking his private elevator to his seventh-floor suite of gray-carpeted offices.

At ten A.M., Webster met with John L. Helgerson, the Central Intelligence Agency's deputy director for intelligence. It was Helgerson's job to make sense of all the agency's reports from human spies, billion-dollar satellites, and eavesdroppers on communications, and to predict the most likely course of events. This was one of their regular meetings, but they spent most of their time talking about the Iraqi threat to Kuwait. Helgerson warned that, based on the latest information, Saddam Hussein would most likely invade Kuwait within a matter of days. The only question was how much of Kuwait he would take and whether he would go on to invade Saudi Arabia.

Webster later conferred with Richard J. Kerr, the deputy director of Central Intelligence, and with Richard F. Stolz, the deputy director for operations. Stolz had the job of directing the agency's human-spy operations, along with covert action. That was the area that had gotten the CIA into so much trouble—for example, in the abortive invasion of Cuba at the Bay of Pigs, and more recently in the Iran-contra affair.

At twelve-thirty P.M., Webster had lunch with Donald Graham, publisher of the *Washington Post,* in the director's dining room. He then met with officials from the CIA's National Collection Division. Among other things, the division—now merged into a new Domestic Resources Division—interviews businessmen and other travelers after they return from overseas trips. The officials told Webster that they were starting to obtain plans for Iraqi chemical and biological weapons factories from the companies that had built the plants.

Just after six-thirty P.M., Webster took the elevator back to the CIA's underground garage, where his CIA car and a chase car were waiting to return him to his red brick home on a secluded street off Bradley Boulevard.

During the day, the Office of Security guards who drove him back and forth remained in a glass-enclosed cubicle lined with closed-circuit television monitors across from his office. Technicians from the Office of Security swept his office for bugs every few months and installed special devices on his windowpanes to prevent possible KGB eavesdropping using laser beams.

At first, Webster had refused to allow the security guards to stay in his home at night. Later, he had relented. In any case, the house was protected by alarms that would bring CIA guards, FBI agents, and Montgomery County police officers running.

Webster had just fed a biscuit to his basset hound, Babs, when the white phone in his study rang. The phone was a

direct, secure link to the White House. It was seven-thirty
P.M. on Wednesday, August 1, 1990.

Brent Scowcroft, the President's assistant for national affairs, was on the other end. Scowcroft had been getting scattered, unconfirmed reports that Iraqi forces might be surging
over the Kuwaiti border. Scowcroft wanted to know what else
Webster knew about it.

Ever since November 1989, the CIA had been warning in
top-secret reports that Saddam Hussein had aggressive intentions and wanted to dominate the Middle East. But the CIA
predicted it would take three years before the Iraqi leader
recovered enough from the costs of the Iran-Iraq war to take
action. On July 23, 1990, the CIA reported that Saddam
Hussein was moving troops toward Kuwait and that an invasion was possible. A few hours before Scowcroft called
Webster, CIA deputy director Kerr had told the State Department, based on intercepted communications, that an invasion would occur within the next twenty-four hours.

Webster told Scowcroft he would find out what was new
and get back to him. He called the CIA's operations office,
a communications center at Langley that is manned twenty-
four hours a day. The center had gotten the same reports.
Webster called Scowcroft back and told him he knew nothing
further.

By eight that evening, the invasion had begun, setting into
motion a chain of events that would culminate with Iraq's
defeat by American and allied forces by February 27, 1991.
In the intervening months, the CIA would generate most of
the intelligence needed to evaluate Saddam Hussein's intentions and then to prosecute the war. Before the war began
on January 16, 1991, the agency would send some five hundred
reports to the White House on the effect of economic sanctions against Iraq, on Saddam Hussein's preparations for war,
and on the Iraqi leader's character and personality. Through
Webster's control of the National Reconnaissance Office committee that assigns satellite coverage, the CIA would position
satellites over the Middle East so that the military could see
their targets on television monitors in real time. The agency
would obtain the engineering and architectural plans of key

Iraqi targets. It would assess Iraqi troop strength and morale. It would predict in the President's Daily Brief that Saddam Hussein would unleash an oil spill on the Persian Gulf and that he would use other scorched-earth tactics before withdrawing from Kuwait. The CIA would coordinate propaganda efforts such as distribution of leaflets and establishment of a clandestine radio station urging Iraqi soldiers to surrender. And it would help to free some of the Americans taken hostage by Saddam Hussein in the early stages of the conflict.

While the CIA would make some mistakes, such as over-estimating the number of Iraqi troops in Kuwait, its record overall during the Persian Gulf War would be impressive.

By midnight, Webster was back behind his mahogany desk in his office at the CIA, surrounded by four telephones, six in-boxes, and fifteen direct "hot lines" to the CIA's senior officials. On his walls were dozens of mementos of his career as a lawyer, judge, and director of the Federal Bureau of Investigation and then the CIA: a photo of Webster with President Bush and two of Millie's puppies romping on the White House lawn; a photo of Webster giving President Reagan a pistol that could be used to pull off riding boots; a copy of a painting of President Lincoln signing the Emancipation Proclamation, given to Webster, a Civil War buff, by the Society of Former Special Agents of the FBI.

At sixty-six, Webster had an ageless face, thin lips, and a high forehead. His slightly graying black hair was always immaculately combed. He was a study in contrasts, an austere man who liked to be called "judge" to emphasize his separation from the agency and the abuses that had occurred in the past, who surrounded himself with brilliant young lawyers as if he were still in his judge's chambers, and who wore Brooks Brothers suits, monogrammed button-down shirts, and gold tie clips. At the same time, Webster was then dating—and would soon marry—Lynda Jo Clugston, a highly attractive thirty-four-year-old blonde who was director of sales and marketing at the Watergate Hotel in Washington. Webster had dated a number of attractive women, from tennis pro Kathy Kemper to syndicated columnist Karen Feld, since the death of his wife, Drusilla, in 1984. Webster was a highly competitive tennis player who recognized that "tennis diplomacy" could win more support in Washington than the most eloquent testimony before congressional oversight committees. He had played with everyone from George Bush when Bush was vice president to Zsa Zsa Gabor.

Despite his stern demeanor, Webster had a sense of humor, occasionally signing letters to friends "00-14," doubling James Bond's code number because he was the fourteenth director of Central Intelligence. One of Webster's most treasured possessions, given to him by an assistant at the FBI, was a two-foot-high brown bear dressed in judicial robes, tennis shoes, an FBI T-shirt, and pin-striped pants, its hands clutching a tennis racket.

As he prepared to meet representatives of Middle East intelligence services to exchange views at one A.M. on August 2, Webster was feeling good about the CIA and the role it played. To be sure, he still found some offices lacking. But when he first became director of Central Intelligence on May 26, 1987, he was shocked to find that agency officials on more than one occasion had failed to tell him the truth. Not that they lied outright; they were too smart for that. But by telling only half the story, by answering questions precisely, by not addressing the real intent of Webster's questions, they had misled him, just as some CIA officers had misled the agency's inspector general and the presidentially appointed Tower Commission when they had investigated the CIA's role in the Iran-contra affair.

Moreover, Webster had found that the CIA's methods for making decisions were woefully inadequate. Plans for undertaking covert action were approved rather informally, and the hard questions were often not addressed: What would happen if it became public? Would it make sense to the American people? Does it conform with American law? Above all, Webster was a lawyer, a man who wanted facts to be backed up and procedures to be followed. Too often he found that when he asked the source of a statement, the answer was "Johnny Smith on the third floor told me." As a judge, first on the district court level and then on the appeals court level, his opinions had been replete with citations. He wanted the same documentation to back up reports at the CIA.

Webster found the attitude of some CIA officials about Congress and the congressional oversight process infuriating. "They're not entitled to know that; we don't have to tell them that," some of them said. In briefing books presented to him before he testified on Capitol Hill, CIA officials prepared expected questions with suggested answers. Repeatedly, Webster found, the answers did not tell the whole truth.

At least in part, the attitude was a holdover from Webster's predecessor, William J. Casey, who had developed nonresponsiveness to oversight into an art form. The Senate Select Committee on Intelligence had even built a special amplifying system into its bug-proof hearing room in an effort to make Casey's muttering intelligible. What the senators did not realize was that, when he wanted to be understood, Casey spoke as clearly as John F. Kennedy. That kind of arrogance had gotten the agency involved in the Iran-contra mess in the first place.

Not long after Webster took over the agency in 1987, stories began appearing in the press that he was about to be replaced. Even though Bush had asked Webster to continue to head the agency after Bush became president, the stories persisted, saying he was not doing a good job, that Bush was dissatisfied with him, that he spent all his time playing tennis, and that he would not last another month. The fact that Webster remained in office years after the stories had appeared did not prevent new ones from being published. Meanwhile, rumors circulated that the CIA was drifting, that it had become bloated by bureaucrats, that morale was bad, that it had stopped doing anything worthwhile.

Clearly, some of the people around Bush were unhappy with Webster. He was a lawyer and a former judge who had been brought in to impose order on the CIA. He was not a foreign policy expert and felt uncomfortable posing as one. But Bush had no problems with him, and each time one of the stories appeared, Bush called Webster on the phone, dropped him a note, or took him aside after their almost daily morning meetings. The president would crack some joke about the media and assure him that he was fully satisfied with his performance and wanted him to stay on. Several times, Webster offered to resign, and Bush had insisted that he remain.

The disparity between the public perception and the reality could be a metaphor for the CIA itself, for no agency of government is so little understood or so misunderstood. That, of course, is the way the founders of the agency had wanted it—men such as William J. ("Wild Bill") Donovan, Allen W. Dulles, John A. McCone, and Richard Helms. They were the men who kept the secrets and were proud of it. They saw no conflict in running a secret intelligence organization within a free society. Nor did they see any reason to let the rest of America know what they were doing. They asked only—as Helms asked the American Society of Newspaper Editors in 1971—to take it in part on faith that "we, too, are honorable men devoted to her [the nation's] service." Even the most devastating charges, from accusations of drug running to murder, were met by a stoic—some would say masochistic—"no comment."

Aided and abetted by a Congress that shirked its oversight duties, "the company," as it was called in its early days, was answerable only to the president. It had a "can do" spirit, a willingness to tackle any problem in an era when the United States legitimately felt threatened by the advancing armies of the Soviet Union and the Cold War.

Then came Watergate and Vietnam, when the government lied about the progress of the war and President Nixon covered up White House involvement in the break-in at Democratic National Committee headquarters. When Seymour Hersh of the *New York Times* broke the story in December 1974 that the CIA had violated its charter by spying on Americans who were against the war, Congress could no longer look the other way.

In 1975, a committee headed by the late Sen. Frank Church, an Idaho Democrat, began an investigation that would profoundly alter the way the CIA did business. The committee and a president's commission chaired by Vice President Nelson A. Rockefeller found that the CIA for twenty years had illegally intercepted and opened mail between the United States and the Soviet bloc; had kept dossiers on thousands of American citizens and indexed the names of 300,000 American citizens who had no connection with espionage; had infiltrated dissident groups in the Washington, D.C., area; had experimented with LSD on unsuspecting Americans, leading to one suicide; and had unsuccessfully attempted to kill at least five foreign leaders, including Cuban premier Fidel Castro.

Most of these actions had been approved if not ordered by the presidents at the time. Most were known to cabinet officers as well, including attorneys general. Most of the abuses had stopped by the time they were exposed. And nearly all the abuses had been uncovered by the CIA itself. James R. Schlesinger, as director of Central Intelligence, had ordered CIA employees in 1973 to report any activities that might be "outside the legislative charter of this agency."[1] The result was the "family jewels," 693 pages of single-spaced documents that William E. Colby brought to the attention of Congress after he had been nominated as CIA director. Once he became director of Central Intelligence, Colby confirmed for Hersh the basic points of his story, giving the *Times* greater confidence about running it.

To be sure, the agency reflected the prevailing norms. The FBI performed illegal break-ins and wiretaps, police departments routinely brutalized blacks, and trustees of nonprofit hospitals kept millions of dollars of hospital funds in interest-free accounts at banks where they were officers.

But that was no excuse. The abuses were not only improper and illegal, they betrayed a lack of understanding of what America was all about. For what was the CIA for, if not to help preserve American freedoms? Aside from their impropriety, many of the abuses betrayed a dismaying lack of competence. The CIA had enlisted the Mafia to assassinate Castro, which was not only outrageous but stupid. And the agency plotted to humiliate Castro with his own people by trying to get his beard to fall off—something that only someone whose level of maturity had not advanced beyond kindergarten could have dreamed up.

Introduction

"The attempts to kill Castro were absurd, just absurd," said John N. McMahon, deputy director of Central Intelligence under Casey. "I guess we're embarrassed because it's like the gang that couldn't shoot straight. But that's bush league."[2]

The Church hearings led to tighter control of covert action by Congress and establishment of permanent intelligence committees to oversee the CIA and related agencies in 1976 and 1977. For most Americans, this was the last glimpse they would have of the CIA and what it does. CIA officers repeated their catechism: "Our failures are publicized; our successes are not."

The old saw happened to be correct. Like a shimmering oasis, the agency is usually not what it seems to be. Even something as basic as the CIA's complement of employees is routinely understated in the press as 16,000. The true number—which is classified—is 22,000, not including 4,000 contract and part-time employees.

To find out what the CIA is really like, and how CIA officers think and act, one must probe into each of the agency's five components—four directorates and the office of the director of Central Intelligence. For each directorate has its own mission, its own culture and mores. Each reports to the director of Central Intelligence (DCI) only grudgingly, fearful that its own turf will be infringed upon or that its secrets will be shared with the other directorates.* Like opposing sports teams, each component is in silent competition with the others, certain that its work is most important, vying for available funds, attention, and status.

It is the Directorate of Operations that does the human spying. *Operations* refers to covert operations. The Directorate of Science and Technology uses satellites and other

---

* The title *director of Central Intelligence* signifies that the DCI is director not only of the CIA but of the intelligence community, a dozen agencies including military intelligence, the National Security Agency, and the counterintelligence component of the FBI, whose budgets are submitted to Congress by the director of Central Intelligence.

technical means to spy; it also conducts research into technological innovations. The name of the directorate implies that it collects intelligence through technical means. The Directorate of Intelligence brings together all the available information—80 percent of it from overt sources such as publications—and analyzes it. The information is used to prepare memos and estimates that go to the president. The Directorate of Administration holds it all together by providing computers, security, communications, and the like.

"The Directorate of Science and Technology feels that it collects as much intelligence and therefore is as important as the Directorate of Operations," Herbert F. Saunders, a former CIA officer, said. "On the other hand, the Directorate of Operations, always cocky, says, 'We got all the action. We make the world go around. Satellites can't tell you what people are going to do.' The logistics people in the Directorate of Administration say, 'Without vehicles, you guys couldn't get anything done.' The security people say, 'Without us, you'd have no secrets.' The analytical people in the Directorate of Intelligence think that what it all comes down to is their work—the analysis, publication, and delivery to the consumer. And they have a point, too," Saunders said. "They say, 'That's the name of the game, to bring information to the country's leaders to let them make decisions.' "[3]

Even within each directorate, there are separate components with their own unique character—the Office of Technical Service, within the Directorate of Science and Technology, which provides lock-pickers, installs bugging devices, and makes spy equipment ranging from disguises and speech-altering devices to papers used for secret writing; the Office of Security, within the Directorate of Administration, which participates in espionage investigations with the FBI and sweeps the CIA's offices for electronic bugs; the Office of Financial Management, within the same directorate, which not only issues paychecks but launders money for clandestine operations; the Office of Logistics, also within Administration, which arranges for overseas homes for CIA officers and also buys weapons for use in faraway wars; the Counternarcotics Center, within the Directorate of Intelligence, which employs satellites to spot fields planted with coca plants and ships laden with cocaine; and the Counterterrorism Center, which traces terrorists' bank accounts using satellites that intercept electronic bank transfers.

Besides an original and a new building at its headquarters on Dolley Madison Boulevard in McLean, Virginia, the CIA has its own printing plant on the compound that turns out routine classified documents as well as the President's Daily Brief, the top-secret document presented to the president every morning. The document—usually eight to nine pages—comes off the press at six A.M. A double-wrapped copy is delivered to the director's home so he can read it on the way to the White House. A CIA briefer gives a second copy to the president around eight A.M.

Hidden in the basement of the new building is another secret printing plant that prints forged documents—phony birth certificates, foreign passports, and driver's licenses for use in the CIA's clandestine work. The plant also prints books and other publications in foreign languages to be distributed abroad, and leaflets to be dropped on countries such as Iraq for their propaganda value.

The agency maintains twenty-two other offices throughout the Washington area. One building houses the CIA's Foreign Broadcast Information Service, which monitors and translates broadcasts throughout the world, including television programs in forty-seven countries. Other offices throughout Washington are leased through phony companies and used to recruit KGB officers to turn on their own country and spy for the United States. Still another building in Rosslyn, Virginia, is used by the CIA to recruit the agency's own spies—the staff officers who will live overseas under cover and recruit agents who will risk their lives to help the U.S. For it is the CIA's role to collect foreign intelligence, not to collect information on the U.S., and for that it maintains stations in 130 countries of the world.

If the CIA is fascinating, it is also secretive—sometimes foolishly so. In late 1990, the members of the CIA's Employee Activity Association decided that the group's store on the ground floor of CIA headquarters in McLean should sell CIA commemorative mugs, T-shirts, and baseball hats. They pointed out that Cassel's Sports & Awards a mile and a half away did a booming business in the souvenirs. Why shouldn't CIA employees be able to buy the mugs at headquarters?

Each of the powers at the CIA weighed in with his views. The deputy director for administration, Raymond Huffstutler, opposed the mugs. The CIA's effectiveness depended on keeping a low profile. How could undercover officers take home CIA hats and shirts for their kids? Richard Kerr, the agency's deputy director, had the same reservations. It went against the CIA's grain to advertise itself, he argued.

Others said undercover officers should not be working for the CIA if they were dumb enough to take home CIA mementos. It was an example of CIA paranoia. Anyone could buy the items in the center of McLean, Virginia. Why all the fuss?

The issue made its way up to what is known as the front office, where William Webster decided against selling the mugs. Webster was puzzled by the controversy. Covert employees were not supposed to take such items home anyway, and it was difficult for him to understand how CIA officers could be so insistent on remaining unseen. But Webster was also sensitive to tradition. If selling memorabilia went against past practice, it was not worth making an issue of it.

As this vignette illustrates, the CIA would like to remain as invisible as a pane of glass. Practically everything that goes on at the agency is classified. Even newspaper clippings have been stamped "secret." Employees must sign pledges when they begin and leave employment that anything they write about their work will be submitted first to CIA censors. Polygraph tests that are supposed to be conducted every five years act as a deterrent against secrets being revealed.

Every employee accepts this code of silence, a pact that prohibits employees from telling even spouses what they are doing in any detail. It is a code that pervades the CIA's environment, from the front entrance—where no signs proclaim that this is the fabled agency—to a building at the rear of the CIA's 258-acre compound, where top-secret documents that are no longer of value are shredded and treated with chemicals to remove any writing.

The CIA is a relatively new agency, established in 1947. Because the legislation that set it up gave it little guidance, the agency has had to invent itself along the way. There have been many false starts and many mistakes.

Today, the CIA is a mature organization, one that is very different from the agency of just fifteen years ago. Despite the breakup of the Soviet Union, the CIA's mission of finding out what potential adversaries are doing remains critically important, as illustrated by the agency's role in the events leading up to the invasion of Kuwait by Iraq, and America's subsequent war against Iraq. To this day, the Russian Republic continues to spy on the U.S., and the U.S. through the CIA continues to spy on the Russian Republic. Despite its importance, the CIA to most Americans remains a perplexing cipher. To some, it represents a threat to American freedoms. To others, it is a protector of those same freedoms. Both glorified and vilified throughout the world, it is more closely identified with the United States than is any other institution.

To separate myth from reality, one must examine each of the agency's parts. For the modern CIA is not so much a single entity as a mosaic, each square filled with secrets.

Director of Central Intelligence

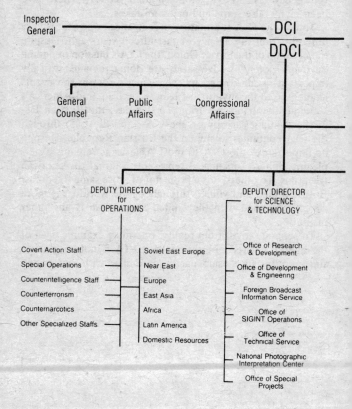

Inspector General — DCI

DDCI

General Counsel   Public Affairs   Congressional Affairs

DEPUTY DIRECTOR for OPERATIONS

Covert Action Staff — Soviet East Europe
Special Operations — Near East
Counterintelligence Staff — Europe
Counterterrorism — East Asia
Counternarcotics — Africa
Other Specialized Staffs — Latin America
Domestic Resources

DEPUTY DIRECTOR for SCIENCE & TECHNOLOGY

Office of Research & Development
Office of Development & Engineering
Foreign Broadcast Information Service
Office of SIGINT Operations
Office of Technical Service
National Photographic Interpretation Center
Office of Special Projects

Command Responsibilities*

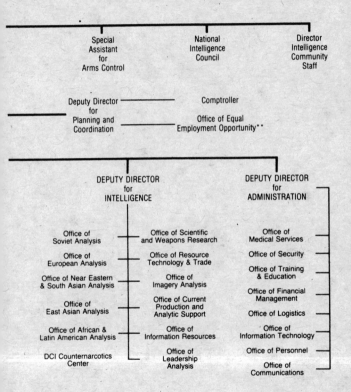

| Special Assistant for Arms Control | National Intelligence Council | Director Intelligence Community Staff |

Deputy Director for Planning and Coordination — Comptroller

Office of Equal Employment Opportunity**

DEPUTY DIRECTOR for INTELLIGENCE

DEPUTY DIRECTOR for ADMINISTRATION

Office of Soviet Analysis	Office of Scientific and Weapons Research	Office of Medical Services
Office of European Analysis	Office of Resource Technology & Trade	Office of Security
Office of Near Eastern & South Asian Analysis	Office of Imagery Analysis	Office of Training & Education
Office of East Asian Analysis	Office of Current Production and Analytic Support	Office of Financial Management
Office of African & Latin American Analysis	Office of Information Resources	Office of Logistics
DCI Counternarcotics Center	Office of Leadership Analysis	Office of Information Technology
		Office of Personnel
		Office of Communications

*DCI Counterintelligence Center, DCI Counterterrorist Center and DCI Counter-
narcotics Center.
**Also serves as Special Assistant to the DCI for Affirmative Employment

PART I

The Directorate of Operations

1 | The Real CIA

WHEN MOST PEOPLE THINK OF THE CIA, THEY THINK OF the Directorate of Operations, the spy side of the house that is also known as the clandestine service. Consisting of some 5,000 of the CIA's 22,000 full-time employees, the Directorate of Operations is the most secretive CIA component and the proudest, the one that takes the greatest risks and the one that gets the CIA into the most trouble. Given its mission, this is understandable. The Directorate of Operations commits espionage in other countries, seeking out information that is usually classified.*

---

* The CIA's four directorates are abbreviated DO for Directorate of Operations, DS&T for Directorate of Science and Technology, DI for Directorate of Intelligence, and DA for Directorate of Administration. Each is headed by a deputy director of the agency, referred to as the DDO for deputy director for operations, DDS&T for science and technology, DDI for intelligence, and DDA for administration.

By definition, it is the job of this directorate to break the laws of other countries. In that respect, the directorate's mission differs from that of the State Department, which seeks information that is overt and can therefore be obtained legally. Moreover, it is the Directorate of Operations that undertakes covert action—attempts to influence or overthrow foreign governments or political parties or leaders through secret funding, training, paramilitary operations, and propaganda.

Like the CIA's other directorates, the Directorate of Operations is chauvinistic about its work, convinced that its role is the most important one.

"The covert side is the real CIA," a former CIA operations officer said.* "The DS and T [Directorate of Science and Technology] people are relatively new and work in research. The DI [Directorate of Intelligence] people are paper pushers."

"In my experience, the most important thing in intelligence is people," Thomas Polgar, a former CIA officer, said. "There is no substitute for having your own reporting sources in the field who can tell you what is going on."[4]

People decide to join the clandestine side of the house for any number of reasons. The ones given by David D. Whipple, a former chief of station in Finland, Cambodia, Portugal, Switzerland, and the former Belgium Congo, are as representative as any.

"It suited my spirit of adventure, I would be dedicating myself to one thing, the idea of living abroad in a very challenging situation appealed to me. As a youngster, I had a desire to experience as many things as I could before I die,"

In conversation, the abbreviations are frequently confused, with DDO used to refer interchangeably to the deputy director for operations and to the directorate itself.
* An operations officer is a staff employee of the CIA and works for the Directorate of Operations, the human-spying side of the agency. The term is synonymous with *case officer*. The Directorate of Operations is also referred to as the clandestine service or the covert side of the CIA.

Whipple said. "Patriotism was involved. When you give something to your country, you become more attached to your country."[5]

When the CIA was started, Ivy League graduates tended to fill the top jobs. William J. Donovan, the director of the Office of Strategic Services, was a lawyer who had graduated from Columbia College and Columbia University Law School. As far back as George Washington, government officials have recruited spies from among people they know. Donovan was no different. Those he knew were the Eastern establishment. Many of the same people formed the nucleus of the CIA. But the CIA was never primarily a cloister of the Ivy League—Walter Bedell Smith, director of Central Intelligence from 1950 to 1953, never graduated from college.[6]

"I went around the table at the morning meeting with twelve senior people of the agency, and I said, 'Let's get this straight. How many of you are Ivy League?' " William Colby, director of Central Intelligence from 1973 to 1976, recalled. "There were three. Two hadn't gone to college."[7]

Before being sent to spy overseas, CIA operations officers—known colloquially as spies—are trained at Camp Peary, the legendary center outside Williamsburg, Virginia, whose existence is still supposed to be a secret. There, members of the Career Trainee program are given courses in the detection of explosives, surveillance and countersurveillance, how to write reports, how to shoot a variety of weapons, and how to run counterterrorism, counternarcotics, and paramilitary operations. Most important, they are taught how to recruit and run agents, the foreign nationals who provide CIA officers with secret information.

In the spy business, the distinction between *officers* and *agents* is crucial: the CIA officers are staff employees who are patriots in their own country; the agents are the people recruited by the CIA officers to betray their own countries. Invariably, the press mixes up the two, calling anyone who works for the CIA an agent.

Paramilitary training is conducted at Harvey Point, North Carolina, and in such places as Panama or the mountains of Arizona, where officers must hike through snake-infested swamps or freeze during overnight treks. Each year, the CIA bangs up hundreds of old cars in a defensive-driving course that teaches officers what to do if terrorists set up blockades on the road.

The training in running agents is designed not only to teach officers tradecraft but also to make them think. For example, in one role-playing exercise, a CIA employee pretending to be an agent arranged to meet a female trainee in a movie theater. During the movie, he placed his hands on her dress and tried to kiss her. The female officer objected. The man persisted. She finally got up and left.

A subsequent critique criticized her because she had made no plans to get in touch with the agent again. Moreover, officers are not supposed to meet agents in a movie theater. It's dark, and an officer cannot take notes.

In another exercise, the CIA trainees kidnap other trainees and take them to a secret location to get them to break down and confess to being CIA officers.

"You are in your apartment at two A.M.," a former operations officer said. "Someone knocks on your door. You are in your pajamas. Three or four big guys grab you and wrap you in a sheet, put you in a van, take you to a site near National Airport, put you in a plane, and fly you off."

The trainee is untied in a cell and interrogated. Unknown to him, the questioning is done by other trainees undergoing their final exercise. Days go by, and the trainee is given little sleep. He is allowed out of his cell only to take a cold shower. Some trainees become distraught, break down, and confess they work for the CIA. Others do not. Nothing happens to those who confess: it's just a training exercise. CIA officers are taught that faced with torture, they will eventually spill the beans anyway.

Including assignments to different directorates to gain experience, the training takes a year.

Usually, CIA operations officers work under government cover. Most often they pose as State Department officers. They may also masquerade as military officers or civilians or as other government employees. They never use the Peace Corps as a cover. In most cases, CIA officers have diplomatic immunity, meaning that if one of them is caught spying, he can only be declared persona non grata and expelled by a foreign government. However, host governments often rough them up before releasing them, claiming they were not aware they had diplomatic immunity.

The CIA also fields several hundred operations officers who work under commercial cover, meaning they pose as entrepreneurs or employees of private companies. Called nonofficial cover, this is a far riskier assignment than working under government cover, since CIA officers without diplomatic immunity can be arrested and imprisoned for spying. It is also far more expensive to maintain a CIA officer in this capacity. While they usually use their real names, their true affiliations are concealed. Elaborate cover stories must be devised to establish their false backgrounds. The top officer of a company knows they are with the CIA. Depending on the size of the company, one or two others may know their true identity. Ideally, the CIA officer is the company's only representative in a given geographic area. That way, he has no supervisors who are aware of what the officer is doing each day. Sometimes, CIA officers under commercial cover do so well in their jobs that the companies offer them real jobs at double what the CIA was paying.

Decades ago, CIA officers under commercial cover were used to spot and recruit agents. That was far too risky and not always necessary. Today, they are used more to communicate with agents who have already been recruited, particularly sensitive ones who should not be handled by anyone connected with the local embassy.

"It's a program that has never been enthusiastically supported," a former operations officer said. "You go to the trouble of getting someone into a company, and it costs a lot of extra money. . . . Only in the last twenty years has there been a shift to using them for sensitive people who cannot have contact with Americans."

Besides staff employees, the CIA maintains contract employees, who are typically employed for two years with salary and benefits. They may be hired to perform specific tasks such as undertaking paramilitary activities. Together with part-time employees, the CIA has 4,000 such employees in addition to its 22,000 regular employees. Retired CIA people are often rehired for specific projects as well. They are called independent contractors or annuitants and are usually paid on a daily basis as consultants. All must sign a secrecy agreement.

The job of operations officers is to recruit people—known as agents or assets—in foreign countries to spy for the CIA. Typically, 10 to 15 percent of a station's overall budget goes to pay agents.

In the old days, even CIA officers who did not work for the clandestine service were told that, if asked, they should say only that they work "for the government." Everyone in Washington knew what that catch phrase meant.

When Sen. Patrick J. Leahy was elected to the Senate in 1974, he rented a town house in McLean, Virginia. Because he did not want his children to put on airs now that their father was a senator, he told them that if anyone asked, they should say their father worked for the U.S. government.

Soon, his Vermont license plates, "Senate 2," arrived in the mail. A few days later, Leahy pulled into the driveway of his home just as a neighbor whose children played with Leahy's children was returning from work. The man came over and looked at the plate, then looked at Leahy.

"Boy, you must have one hell of a cover!" he said.[8]

Nowadays, unless they work under cover, employees of the noncovert directorates may acknowledge they work for the CIA.

Undercover operations officers who say they work for a particular agency such as the Defense Department are given cover telephone numbers, a briefing on their cover, and a written description of the office they allegedly work for. For example, if they are based in Washington, they may have a cover office that sounds like a real Pentagon unit but does not actually exist. They are given telephone numbers with Pentagon exchanges that are answered at the CIA. There, special operators pretend to be secretaries for the officers and take messages for them.

Often, CIA officers who work under government cover are suspected by friends, neighbors, and family of being in the

CIA. Whether that is good or bad depends on their neighbors' perceptions of what the CIA does. A 1979 Opinion Research Corp. poll found 62 percent of all Americans had a favorable opinion of the CIA, while 24 percent had an unfavorable opinion. Fourteen percent had no opinion. Unfavorable opinions were highest among Americans who were college educated and had higher incomes.

Simply not knowing what someone else does can lead to negative reactions. In America, said Robert R. Simmons, a former CIA officer who is now a Connecticut state representative, "Americans as a people generally are open about things—especially good things. So something secret is considered something bad. We as a country want to be a city on a hill for all to see. If something is secret, we assume it must be immoral or illegal."[9]

CIA officers must also be willing to break the laws of other countries and lie.

"Violating laws in other countries has never bothered me," David D. Whipple said. "Violating their laws is part of our business. Laws in America are violated every day by foreign agents. Therefore, it's important that we collect information in this way. You need clandestine information to go with the other information we collect. It's very necessary for us to understand situations in other countries—the motivation of people, why are they doing it, what their intentions are. That's not easy to collect by open, legal means. It's not the whole story, but it is an important ingredient.

"We don't think of it as living a lie. We think of it as a necessary thing," Whipple said. "You have to protect your identity in order to remain effective. It is necessary that others cooperate with you in protecting your identity. It's as if you were a slightly different person."[10]

Most people think the Directorate of Operations spies only on hostile targets, such as the former Soviet Union. When the Cold War ended, dozens of commentators began questioning whether the CIA now had any purpose. They did not realize that even at the height of the Cold War, only 10 percent to 12 percent of the CIA's budget—excluding development of satellites and other technical systems—was devoted to the Soviet Union and the East Bloc.

Even more important, the commentators did not understand a crucial fact about the CIA—that it spies in friendly countries as well as in hostile ones. By agency policy, CIA operations officers may commit espionage in any country of the world. The only exceptions are Great Britain, Australia, and Canada. By CIA thinking, no country is completely friendly. Any country may turn against the U.S. and its interests or may have elements within it that may turn against the U.S. Thus France has engaged in stealing American technology from the European branches of such companies as IBM and Texas Instruments, even breaking into hotel rooms of American businessmen in Paris to copy corporate documents.[11] And Israel, one of America's closest allies, recruited Jonathan J. Pollard to obtain an entire roomful of classified documents for the Jewish state. The fact that Iraq, which was supported by the U.S. during its war with Iran, could so quickly threaten American interests by seeking to control more than half the world's supply of oil illustrates why the CIA needs to know what is going on in every country.

"They [other countries] have their own priorities, their own view of the world, and it often doesn't coincide with ours," a former operations officer said. He quoted Charles de Gaulle: "A state worthy of the name has no friends—only interests."

"Espionage is illegal basically in most places," a former CIA officer said. "So you have to break the law, as long as it's not your own law. . . . When I recruit a citizen of that country, he accepts the idea he will break his laws.

"You're after classified information," the former officer said. "Or paying off a minister. . . . One thing you don't do, whatever country you're in, is you don't worry about the local laws. If you did that, you basically wouldn't function." He added, "Almost every country in the world has government people on the payroll of the CIA. Some countries we don't care about."

"The CIA has to violate the laws of any country," said Thomas Polgar, a former CIA station chief in Saigon, Mexico City, and Buenos Aires and a former consultant to the Senate

Select Committee on Intelligence. "Every country has laws against espionage and conspiracy, and our job is to engage in a conspiracy to get secrets which the foreign government wants to protect. You do it through false pretenses, you do it by encouraging treason. In effect, you direct a conspiracy for the purpose of stealing something. . . . If you are an officer under diplomatic cover, you are protected. But the local [agent] who gets caught is not."[12]

The types of crimes committed by CIA officers overseas range from paying a local telephone company employee to hand over long-distance toll records to breaking into an embassy to steal the codes to its communications. The CIA keeps carefully hidden the fact that it spies in friendly countries. In most cases, CIA officers are not caught. On those few occasions when they are caught, the matter is usually disposed of without any publicity or punitive action. The officer may be quietly expelled, and a complaint filed with the State Department. Often, both countries are too embarrassed to do anything.

"Usually, you have sort of a gentleman's agreement," Polgar said. " 'You do it to us, and we do it to you, and if we have an operational accident, we settle it in a friendly way without anyone getting hurt too badly.' "

"When they break the laws of friendly countries, it's always handled in an ad hoc way," a former National Security Council staff member said.

" 'Does this name mean something?' 'Yeah.' 'We have reason to believe . . .' 'Of course, he would be a renegade.' 'We know you wouldn't.' 'Of course not,' " a former CIA officer said in describing how such an incident would be handled.

One of the CIA's goals in friendly countries is to determine if they are developing nuclear, chemical, or biological weapons. Nearly forty countries currently have these weapons or are trying to develop them. Once the CIA learns that a country is engaged in such a program, diplomatic or economic pressure can be applied to stop it.

The amount of attention paid to a country depends on its importance and the current orientation of its government. African or Scandinavian countries get relatively little attention. France, because of its frequent opposition to U.S. policies, gets more attention. Japan, as a major economic competitor, is a target as well. Israel gets some attention. When James Angleton was in charge of the CIA's counterintelligence program, he also acted as liaison with Israeli intelligence. Spying in Israel was then off limits, but not anymore.

"It's okay to recruit Israelis, mostly military officers, meaning paying them," a former operations officer said. "That began gingerly after Angleton."

The reason is the CIA wants to make sure that Israel is not taking steps that might suck the U.S. into a war.

Besides recruiting a key agent with critical information, the greatest success an operations officer can have is penetrating the communications of a country, either by bugging an embassy or obtaining the codes to its communications. Usually these are team efforts, and the plaudits go to many. Soviet successes in penetrating U.S. communications have been well publicized—the bugging of the new and old American embassies in Moscow and the recruitment of former Navy warrant officer John A. Walker, Jr., who provided the Soviets with codes to classified naval communications.

But what of CIA successes? There have been a number of them, most of them secret. Over the years, the CIA has planted bugs in or obtained the codes of a number of Soviet and Soviet-bloc embassies, as well as the codes of embassies of other countries, to cite just one category. For all the rivalry among the directorates, when cooperation is really needed, they work well together.

"The goal was to bug all the embassies [of hostile countries]," said a former CIA officer who was involved in providing technical assistance for these jobs. "You try to get it while it's building. If it is not possible to penetrate an embassy electronically, the next best thing is to recruit someone—the cleaning force or whatever—and have them bring you material from the embassy. A break-in at the embassy would be stupid. If you jimmy the safe and it is discovered, they are alerted. You find someone who has access to it and bring it out each day. That way, life goes on."

In penetrating these communications, the CIA has learned of diplomatic initiatives before they are broached, the plans of KGB officers, and identities of Americans working for the KGB.

Usually, a break-in at a local embassy is directed by the local station chief. The Office of Technical Service within the Directorate of Science and Technology supplies the bugging devices or other technical paraphernalia needed to do the job—the tools of the spy trade. For example, the CIA may break into an embassy and photograph the key cards that are used each day to decrypt secret messages. In this case, the Office of Technical Service may supply the cameras, lock-pickers, and installers of bugging devices. But for all the technical skill required, the most important ingredients for an operation of this kind are resourcefulness and courage, demonstrated when the CIA bugged a Chinese Communist mission.

2 | *Bikinis*

WHEN THE CHINESE COMMUNISTS AND THE SOVIETS EACH decided to open new missions in Asia, the Directorate of Operations assigned Howard T. Bane to find a way to bug the new offices. Bane is as far removed from the original Ivy League image as one can get. Standing five feet nine and a half inches and weighing 172 pounds, Bane has a florid complexion and a raspy voice. His temper is legendary. He chews tobacco and smokes a cigar. Bane attended Georgetown University but flunked out, then went to a junior college to get his grades up. He eventually graduated from George Washington University with a degree in government and international relations.

Bane had an exceptional operational mind, intelligence lingo meaning he was a phenomenally good spy. He had intelligence, imagination, common sense, and an ability to foresee problems, solve them, and go on to the next job. He could recognize opportunities when they arose and create them when he needed them. Because of his exploits, he received the CIA's Distinguished Intelligence Medal.

Like many officers who joined the CIA during the Korean War, Bane did not give his decision a lot of thought. Bane had been a diver in the Navy, and a CIA recruiter considered this useful background for operating in the war. Bane began in 1950 as a GS-5 filing clerk. The CIA soon sent him to Korea as an operations officer under military cover. There, he ran operations aimed at rescuing pilots who had been shot down.

Bane served in India and Bangkok and was chief of station in Ghana, Kenya, and Amsterdam. Later, he became chief of operations for Africa, special assistant to the CIA's deputy director for operations, and finally chief of counterterrorism.

Not every CIA officer is big on bugging. It takes a tremendous amount of time to plan an operation, operations that can be extremely risky and sometimes yield paltry results. In one infamous effort to install a bug in an embassy in Southeast Asia, the CIA got only the sounds of birds chirping. Nor are telephone taps—as opposed to bugs that pick up sounds in rooms—particularly useful. Often, the local intelligence service helps the CIA by placing wiretaps. They may give an idea of the daily activity of opposing intelligence officers or which ones are vulnerable to recruitment, but they seldom provide much in the way of secrets. Soviets, in particular, tend to be not very gabby, although their wives may be.

With either bugs or wiretaps, the tapes take time to transcribe. Usually, a translator on site gives a rapid assessment of what is being said, but the tapes are sent to Washington for transcription. Yet for all the trouble, if well placed, a bug—known in CIA lingo as an audio operation, an audio op, or a technical penetration—can do wonders to let the CIA know just what the other side is up to.

When he was based in Washington, Bane agreed to try to bug the new missions. Since the Soviets and Chinese planned to rent or buy existing buildings, the key would be to determine in advance which properties they might acquire. Bane would then try to bug the buildings before the diplomats moved in.

Pretending to be a State Department administrative official looking for space for the U.S. consulate, Bane came up with a list of a dozen buildings the Soviets and Chinese might be interested in. Meanwhile, Bane arranged for a "quick plant"—a temporary, easily installed bug—to go in the hotel rooms where the Chinese and Soviet officials who were looking for their new quarters would stay. That way, Bane was confident, he would hear them discussing their plans.

Bane decided the diplomats would have to stay in one of five major hotels in the city.* He and an officer from the Office of Technical Service stayed in each one and waited until maids left their master keys in guests' doors. The two CIA men made an impression of the keys and sent them to a CIA Office of Technical Service location in Europe. There, technical officers fabricated a master key for each of the five hotels. Using the keys, Bane entered guest rooms and helped himself to lamps from each hotel. He sent the lamps to the office in Europe, which made replicas of the lamps with transmitting devices concealed inside.

When the Soviet and Chinese diplomats checked into one of the five hotels, Bane exchanged the lamps in their rooms for the bugged replicas. But the effort did not work. Bane could listen to the diplomats' conversations, but the diplomats never discussed which specific site they would like to acquire for the new missions.

Meanwhile, Bane had gotten in touch with a local real estate broker whose business included office buildings for diplomats. Bane told him what he wanted and agreed to pay him for the information. Thus, the man became an agent of the CIA.

Taking no chances, Bane also decided to bug the house of a KGB officer who had come to town posing as a *Pravda* correspondent. The man spent most of his time helping the Soviet diplomats look for a suitable location.

When the KGB officer was out, a CIA technical officer surreptitiously entered his house and scraped a sample of paint from the wall in his living room. Later, the technical officer

---

* Because it could still compromise people who aided the effort, neither the city nor the date of the bugging is included here.

returned and installed a transmitter inside a wall. To conceal the sound of drilling, the officer used a "silent drill" developed by the CIA to mute the sound of drilling with a minute spray of water.

The CIA officer connected the listening device to an electrical switch in the wall, so it derived its power from house current. After he installed the device, the officer plastered over the hole in the wall and painted it, matching the old paint perfectly. A pinhole made after the wall was painted conveyed sound to the microphone in the transmitter, which beamed its signal to a nearby listening post.

As it turned out, this failed also. To Bane's consternation, the KGB officer usually conducted his business outside his home and said nothing useful while on the air.

Before each bug was installed, CIA headquarters approved the plan. Sometimes the CIA decides such an effort is too risky and vetoes the idea. The agency also rules on the level of sophistication for the bugging device. Usually, this depends on how important and sensitive the operation is. The more important, the more likely the most advanced device will be approved.

With the help of the local real estate agent who was now on the CIA payroll, Bane decided that the Soviets and Chinese would most likely settle on two buildings. One was a fifteen-room private home owned by an Asian. The other was an office building next to a golf course.

Bane decided that both buildings should be bugged. By this time, the real estate agent Bane had recruited was working with the Chinese and Soviets almost daily to help them find a place. Bane told him he should push the two locations.

Meanwhile, Bane arranged to meet the son of the owner of the house by having an intermediary introduce them at a bar. Bane knew that the man liked to go to good restaurants, so he invited him to an evening out with his wife. After they had become regular companions over a period of weeks, the man introduced Bane to his father and mother, the owners of the house. Bane began wining and dining them as well.

The CIA approved Bane's proposal to bug the fifteen-room house, but decided the British should be given the task of bugging the office building. Because a British company owned the building, CIA headquarters figured MI-6 would be in a better position to do the job.

By now, Bane had recruited the son of the owner of the house as an agent, paying him $1,000 in cash as a start. He was ready to pull off what he hoped would be a major success for the CIA. Bane told the son to tell his father that Bane had a friend who was an Italian movie director. The movie director wanted to rent the place for a week so he could polish a screenplay. He would be bringing a couple of movie stars with him. Bane offered to pay the man's father and mother to move to a hotel for a week. In addition, Bane would pay $5,000 for renting the compound.

As the man conveyed the offer to his parents, Bane alerted Office of Technical Service officers in Europe. He sent them photographs of the inside of the house. Seven officers were assigned to the job.

The owners of the home agreed to the offer. When they moved out, the CIA people moved in. Bane replaced the padlock on the front gate with a CIA lock. Bane also arranged a code with the real estate agent. If anyone was coming to look at the home, he was to phone and say a prearranged phrase. As it turned out, just before the officers were to leave, the Chinese wanted to visit the home. The agent called Bane and gave the signal. Horrified, Bane told him not to let them in.

The Chinese drove up to the home in limousines. The agent tried to open the lock on the gate but found his key would not work. The Chinese would have to come back the next day.

After working steadily throughout the week, the CIA officers had outfitted the entire mansion for sound. The transmitters beamed their signals to a listening post three hundred yards away. Some of the bugs worked off house current, while others had long-lasting batteries. They could be turned on and off remotely to conserve power and further conceal them. If they heard any indication that a sweep might be in progress, the monitors turned them off.

To add a little credibility to the cover story, Bane left the bottoms of two bikinis on the clothesline—evidence that the Italian movie stars had stayed at the home.

After the Chinese finally saw the home, they agreed to rent it. Meanwhile, the Soviets took the office building. The British, however, had done a poor job of bugging the building. The bugs did not work, and the effort was a failure.

Bane set up a listening post some one hundred and fifty yards from the Chinese Communist compound. For the next several years—until the Chinese found a new location—the CIA was able to listen to every conversation in the mission, including those in the code room.

The information was a treasure trove for the CIA. Unlike the Soviets, the Chinese tended to share overall strategies with their embassies. The CIA was able to learn in advance of the Chinese Communist government's diplomatic overtures and plans, as well as relationships the Chinese had with local officials and with the Soviets.

This is the kind of success that thrills CIA operations officers and wins them awards—the kind that only rarely becomes known. It is one reason CIA officers repeat the maxim "Our failures are publicized; our successes are not."

If there is any success that surpasses bugging a sensitive diplomatic post, it is recruiting a high-level official or intelligence officer who is willing to continue to work for his own country. That gives the CIA the benefit of being able to instruct the agent to obtain information according to the CIA's needs. Short of recruiting a high-level official in the Kremlin, nothing could be more sensitive than recruiting a KGB officer in the Soviet embassy in Washington.

3 | *Courtship*

THE BROWN BRICK OFFICE BUILDING AT 6551 LOISDALE
Court in Springfield, Virginia, is hardly the sort of place where
James Bond would make his headquarters. With tiny vertical
windows, it is the plainest of structures, the lobby decorated
with thin, slate-blue carpeting and cheap blondwood doors.
Known as the Spring Mall Building, the structure could not
be more inconspicuous or less inviting—which is the point.
For it was from this building that the CIA and the FBI re-
cruited the first KGB officer inside the Soviet embassy in
Washington.

Under the CIA's charter, the agency may not exercise law
enforcement or police powers or undertake internal security
functions. But that does not mean it cannot operate within
the United States. Obviously, in order to operate at all, the
CIA must have a headquarters in the U.S. and train people
in the U.S. The CIA's charter does not specifically say the
CIA may not gather intelligence in the U.S. Rather, the his-

tory of the legislation makes it clear the CIA may gather intelligence within the United States so long as the target is foreign.[13] That understanding was codified by Executive Order 12333, which President Reagan signed on December 4, 1981. It says the CIA may operate domestically in order to collect "significant" foreign intelligence, so long as the effort does not involve spying on the domestic activities of Americans.

The CIA's internal regulations—most of them classified—make this clearer. They say that if a CIA officer intends to recruit a U.S. citizen or enlist the cooperation of a U.S. firm, he must identify himself as being with the CIA.

For years, through what used to be called the Foreign Resources Division within the Directorate of Operations, the CIA has operated within the U.S. by recruiting foreigners visiting in the U.S.—diplomats of other countries, for example, or visiting scientists. The greatest percentage of these recruits who become agents or spies for the CIA are military personnel being trained in the U.S. When they return home, these agents continue to work for the CIA. As a side benefit, they may also report on foreign targets of interest—for example, what is happening within the Chinese Communist embassy in Washington—while they are stationed in the U.S.

The very existence of the Foreign Resources Division—now called a branch within a new Domestic Resources Division—is a closely guarded secret. Usually, the only references in the press to domestic operations of the CIA are to what was previously called the National Collection Division, now a branch within the Domestic Resources Division. Also located within the Directorate of Operations, this component operates overtly, asking Americans who travel overseas to report on what they see once they return. During the war in the Gulf, the domestic collection office obtained plans for Iraqi targets from American and other businessmen who had helped build them.

The two components—the National Collection Branch and the Foreign Resources Branch—maintain separate offices in major cities throughout the country. The offices operate under commercial cover. That means the offices purport to be private companies. For example, in the 1980s, the Foreign Resources office for the Washington area was identified only as a consulting firm in the Air Rights Building at 7101 Wisconsin Avenue in Bethesda, Maryland. Here, in a building sheathed with brown-tinted glass, the station chief, deputy station chief, and a communicator maintained their offices. In addition, three other nearby offices, also operating as national companies, targeted people from the Soviet bloc, East Asia, and the Third World. A lawyer was recruited to act as a front man for the companies.

Each CIA officer in the Washington office had three aliases used in conducting his work—one as a businessman, one as an ordinary government employee, and one as a CIA official. Meetings were never conducted at the office. Rather, the CIA officers arranged to meet contacts at lunch or in other social settings.

Besides the one in Washington, the CIA maintains FR stations—formerly known as bases—in such cities as Boston, New York, Chicago, St. Louis, Houston, Miami, San Francisco, Los Angeles, and Seattle. The two biggest stations are in Washington, which has some thirty officers, and New York, which has nearly forty.

The Domestic Resources Branch has more offices and a larger staff. Even though it operates under commercial cover, its activities are more open. Identifying themselves as CIA officers, its staff members ask American businessmen and university professors for information they pick up on their travels.

By contrast, the Foreign Resources Branch recruits foreigners to become agents or spies. In deciding which foreigners to recruit, each station has a wish list. The list ranks the importance of each target country, from one to five. Traditionally, the Soviets have been number one and still are within FR. But with the end of the Cold War, the Chinese, Japanese, and Cubans were given higher priority in many overseas locations.

In recruiting people, the CIA officers in the FR office go to receptions and parties where foreign diplomats may show up. They strike up conversations with them and try to gauge their susceptibility. Pretending to be employees of private companies, they invite them to lunch or dinner. Eventually, they make a pitch, offering a steady income if they agree to spy for the U.S. The amount varies with the country and the status of the individual being recruited. Typically, it is a few hundred dollars a month. Money is seldom a motivating factor with Soviets or Communist Chinese. Rather, they agree to spy for ideological reasons or disagreements with their bosses.

Each year, FR recruits two hundred to three hundred people as CIA agents or spies. Over the years, FR has recruited Czech, Hungarian, Polish, and other Soviet-bloc diplomats as spies.

During the early 1980s, roughly half of those recruited accepted money and training and then vanished once they returned home. Yet case officers and station chiefs still received credit for the recruitments.

"What was happening," a former operations officer said, "was FR officers would recruit these guys, they would go back, and the local station couldn't find them. They would arrange to meet on the third Thursday of the month, and they wouldn't show. Or they would show up and wouldn't be cooperative."

To improve performance, the CIA put a new system into effect. No one would get credit for a recruitment until the agent had produced useful intelligence or had cooperated over a period of time.

If the fact that the CIA recruits spies in the U.S. sounds surprising, the idea of the CIA teaming up with the FBI to do so, given the historic relationship between the two agencies, is even more astonishing. Under the long reign of FBI director J. Edgar Hoover, the FBI and the CIA were frequently at loggerheads. At one point, Hoover actually forbade FBI agents to communicate with the agency, forcing them to meet with CIA officers clandestinely.

That changed dramatically when William H. Webster became FBI director, succeeding Clarence M. Kelley. In 1980, the CIA and the FBI created a secret joint operation to recruit Soviet spies in Washington—a move that would have been unthinkable under Hoover. The operation, in the form of a squad within the FBI's Washington metropolitan field office, was the idea of George Kalaris, who had been chief of the CIA's counterintelligence staff, and James Nolan, the FBI's deputy assistant director in the counterintelligence division. In part, it represented an effort to overcome the historical enmity between the two agencies.

Normally, the CIA recruits agents in the U.S. so they can spy overseas. It is the FBI that is charged, as part of its counterintelligence program, with developing agents to engage in counterspying within the U.S. But Nolan and Kalaris, who had become friends in the course of work, decided it made sense to pool the knowledge and resources of the FBI and the CIA to recruit Soviets to work for the intelligence agencies while still stationed on American soil.

Code-named COURTSHIP, the joint operation is designated squad CI-11 within the FBI's Washington metropolitan field office. Besides secretaries and an administrative officer, the squad consists of nine professional employees—five FBI agents and four CIA officers. The squad is headed by an FBI agent whose deputy is a CIA officer. Each of the CIA officers and FBI agents assigned to the squad has three different covers. They could pose as employees of another government agency, as employees of a private company, or as FBI or CIA officers—under aliases. To back up their cover stories, they have VISA cards, social security numbers, and driver's licenses, all in false names. The credit limit on the VISA cards was only $1,000 until FR objected, and the limit was raised to $2,000.

Until recently, the squad was based in the Loisdale Court building behind the Hilton Inn off exit 57 on Interstate Route 95 in Springfield, Virginia. In contrast to the spartan appearance of the building and its lobby, COURTSHIP's suite was lavishly furnished with Oriental rugs and screens confiscated during raids. A receptionist sat behind a glass window inside a reception area. Only the members of the squad could enter the inner offices. At the time COURTSHIP was recruiting a KGB officer in the Soviet embassy in Washington, it was operating out of the Springfield office building, behind the sign of a consulting firm.

As its name implies, the purpose of the squad is to court

Soviet spies—either officers of the KGB or the GRU, the Soviet military intelligence organization. Normally, when a Soviet is assigned to work in Soviet establishments in the United States for the first time, one of the FBI's counterintelligence squads is assigned to watch him. For a year, the FBI studies his activities to determine if he is an intelligence officer. If the FBI decides he is, the FBI assigns him to an appropriate counterintelligence squad for further observation and possible recruitment. Each of the twenty squads specializes in a particular intelligence service and division within that service. Even if the FBI decides he is not a spy, he is still assigned to a squad for observation.

Under the rules established by the FBI and CIA, the COURTSHIP squad has first choice in picking the intelligence officers that appear most susceptible to recruitment. Once an intelligence officer is recruited by COURTSHIP, he is reassigned to the appropriate FBI squad based on his KGB or GRU affiliation.

In determining which KGB officers would most likely agree to spy for the U.S., the COURTSHIP squad consults with psychologists from the CIA and the FBI and reviews all the available information about him. Each officer looks for different signs of receptivity. Some are interested in Soviets who have never been outside the Soviet Union before, who dress well, and who seem to be interested in American society. Others swear these qualities bear no relation to whether a Soviet will agree to be recruited. As a rule, the squad targets only one Soviet at a time. If the recruitment effort fails, they assign the Soviet to the appropriate FBI squad and target another individual.

The squad never uses outright blackmail or other forms of coercion. It is an article of faith within the U.S. intelligence community that blackmail never works. The CIA once spent months trying, to no avail, to recruit a KGB officer in Southeast Asia who was believed to be a homosexual. However, a vulnerability such as cheating on an expense account or becoming involved in repeated car accidents with an embassy vehicle may be used to coax a prospective agent into cooperating.

Money is one way to recruit an agent. It also contributes to compromising agents in case they later have second thoughts about cooperating. But even large sums do not work if a prospective agent does not already have misgivings or complaints about his situation.

Just before he was to be sent home in 1982 after a lengthy tour in the United States, the FBI sought to recruit Dmitri I. Yakushkin, the KGB resident or station chief in Washington. For the purpose, the FBI had been authorized to offer $20 million—a reasonable figure when one considers that Yakushkin could have revealed almost every detail of the KGB's operations against the U.S.

Shortly before Yakushkin was to leave for Moscow, two FBI agents approached him when he and his wife, Irina, were shopping at the Safeway on Wisconsin Avenue in Washington's Georgetown section. As Irina went off in another direction and Yakushkin was fondling the oranges, an FBI agent approached him.

"I am a special agent of the FBI, and I wondered if I could have an opportunity to talk to you," the FBI man said. He asked Yakushkin if he would agree to meet with the special agent in charge of the Washington field office.

"What is your name?" the KGB man asked.

The agent gave a false name.

"May I see your ID to prove you are an FBI agent?"

Sheepishly, the agent showed it to Yakushkin. The KGB officer saw that the FBI agent had given a phony name.

"I'm sorry; I kind of made that up," the agent said.

"Yeah, I know how it is."

"Would there be a way to arrange an appointment for our SAC [special agent in charge] to speak to you?" the agent persisted.

"Sure, have him come by the embassy anytime," Yakushkin said, smiling.

"Well, actually, I was hoping for a less formal environment, if that would be okay."

"I don't really think I'd be interested in that."

It was clear the conversation was going nowhere, so the agent decided to take a chance and make the offer on the spot. He offered Yakushkin $20 million to work for the U.S.

"Young man, I appreciate the offer," Yakushkin said. "If I were twenty years younger, I'd give it serious consideration."

"It was nice meeting you," the KGB officer said, then adjusted his beret and walked off toward the meat section to find his wife.

It was a CIA officer assigned to the Foreign Resources Branch who first spotted the KGB officer later recruited by COURTSHIP in late 1982. The man was attending a professional conference in Washington. To the CIA officer, he seemed susceptible to recruitment. The CIA officer had a hunch that the man was more interested in American life than other KGB officers. For one thing, he spoke English better than others. He was also more eager to please the Americans he met than other Soviets. All reports of contacts by FR officers are seen by COURTSHIP, which decided to single him out for recruitment.

Pretending to be a private consultant, a member of the COURTSHIP squad befriended the KGB officer, taking him to dinner and letting him know that he had access to military secrets. Once satisfied that the man would likely agree to work for the American side, the COURTSHIP officer revealed his true affiliation. For a number of years, squad members met with the KGB officer at least once a week.

The meetings with the KGB officer were alternately held in two safe houses, both apartments in the Washington area. To give the KGB officer an alibi for taking time away from his regular duties, the squad passed him information obtained from a man who was in the defense consulting business. Acting as a double agent, the man pretended to work for the Soviets but really was working for COURTSHIP. Occasionally, the squad members let the KGB officer meet with the man himself. Anything the man told the KGB officer or the Soviets was cleared by the U.S. government first.

The squad members instructed the KGB officer to engage in elaborate "dry cleaning"—driving into dead ends, speeding up to seventy miles per hour, then slowing to twenty miles per hour—before he met with them. They wanted to make sure he was not being followed. Because it is a precaution the man should have taken anyway in the normal course of his spy work, the "dry cleaning" would not raise any suspicions if the Soviets noticed it.

Even before they asked him for any information, the squad members asked the KGB officer what he had been doing for the past several hours. They wanted to make sure he had protected himself. The next order of business was to agree on the location for the next meeting—one of the two safe houses rented just for meeting with the KGB man. Then the squad members debriefed him on the latest developments within the embassy and the KGB's plans. Without his knowledge, the squad members videotaped the sessions, which lasted an hour to an hour and a half.

To make sure he was genuine, the squad members asked the KGB officer a series of questions the answers to which they already knew. He passed with flying colors.

It was the first recruitment of a KGB officer from the Soviet embassy in Washington. In the view of CIA and FBI officials, that one recruitment alone justified the existence of COURTSHIP.*

The COURTSHIP squad paid the KGB officer $200 for each meeting, plus $1,000 a month placed directly in a special bank account in his name. Because the squad members were worried that the man would call attention to himself, they asked him near the beginning of each meeting what he had done with the money he'd previously received.

Only a few months after the man had been recruited, an FBI squad succeeded in recruiting a second KGB officer within the embassy. Besides this source, the FBI had previously recruited a KGB officer assigned to the Soviet United Nations delegation in New York. With the help of the CIA, the FBI had also recruited another KGB officer assigned to the Soviet consulate in San Francisco. However, the two recruitments in Washington were by far the most important.

The KGB man recruited by COURTSHIP provided the

---

* Because doing so could jeopardize the man's life, his identity and details of his assignments are not revealed here. The author has made it a point not to learn his identity.

CIA and FBI with a road map to how the KGB worked in Washington. He gave away identities and duties of KGB and GRU officers, biographical data on Soviet diplomats, and plans for recruiting Americans as spies. The KGB officer knew the locations of listening devices the KGB had planted and the details of how other electronic devices operated. For example, he revealed that the KGB supplies its agents with devices that propel themselves underwater. When they surface, they send coded messages in bursts to satellites for transmission to Moscow. They thus conceal the location of the agent using the transmitter.

From the KGB officer, the CIA and FBI learned how the KGB protects itself just before its officers pick up classified documents from dead drops in tree stumps in the Washington area. A KGB officer drives around the area with a monitor that picks up FBI radio transmissions. If everything is safe, he switches on a green light visible through his windshield. If FBI transmissions are detected, he switches on a red light and the pickup is called off.

The KGB officer revealed how the Soviets intercepted microwave calls to and from U.S. government offices from a secret listening post at Mount Alto, their new compound in Washington. Thanks to gross bureaucratic ineptitude, the State Department had allowed the Soviets to build the compound on the second-highest elevation in Washington.

"They were trying to isolate CIA recruiting offices," an American intelligence officer said. "They intercepted a call from someone in North Carolina who was calling a recruiting office. If the Soviets got their names and they showed up somewhere, they would conclude they are CIA. . . . The KGB officer said the Soviets targeted Langley, the White House, and State, but he never knew of anything good that came out."

According to the KGB officer, the KGB supplies its officers with a wish list of technology or other information it would like to obtain. The list ranges from plans for the Strategic Defense Initiative, known as Star Wars, to inside information on who would most likely win the next presidential election. The KGB officer relayed these lists to the COURTSHIP squad members. In addition, when he returned to Moscow periodically, the officer reported back on the latest changes in the leadership of the Soviet intelligence organization and the KGB's plans worldwide.

At one point, the KGB man handed over copies of the formal plans of the KGB in Washington for the next year, including specific plans to sow disinformation by distributing fraudulent documents.

As an example of how the KGB worked, the officer related that KGB headquarters—known as the center—periodically sent a tasking document that instructed each officer to mention the same piece of information to every American with whom they met. The information might relate to Soviet plans for arms reduction talks, for example, or how many missiles the Soviets had.

"So you had a hundred guys saying the same sentence. Everyone agrees it must be true. In fact, it's a lie," the KGB officer involved in the operation said.

From the officer's account, the squad gathered that the KGB was not having quite as much success as the FBI and CIA had thought. Often, KGB officers sent reports to Moscow claiming to have obtained secret information that they actually got from the newspapers.

"One guy wrote a ten-page report on a conversation he allegedly had with Caspar Weinberger [when he was secretary of defense]," a former officer involved in the operation said. "Actually, all he did was shake his hand in a receiving line."

Understandably, there was much that the KGB man did not have access to. For example, he did not know of any recruitments of Americans in Washington, even though former Navy warrant officer John A. Walker, Jr., was then working for the Soviets there. But the information he did provide enabled the CIA and FBI to anticipate KGB moves and, where possible, counteract the KGB's schemes. He also identified Americans who were working for the Soviets but not necessarily providing them with classified information that would result in prosecution for espionage.

It was a counterintelligence officer's dream—to be able to

find out from the inside what the opposition was planning to do before it did it.

"We knew everything," said an individual who read the material from the debriefings. "Stuff wouldn't happen unless we knew about it."

The fact that the recruitment occurred in Washington, where numerous sensitive agencies are prime KGB targets, made it even more important. The recruitment is but one of hundreds of similar CIA successes, most of them still secret. In some cases, KGB officers recruited by the CIA have retired in place without their country's ever knowing that for most of their careers, they were traitors. Nearly all of them were recruited not in Washington but in the CIA's stations overseas.

4 | *Falling in Love*

THE CIA HAS STATIONS IN 130 COUNTRIES. THEY RANGE IN size from one-person stations in some African countries to sixty-person posts—including support employees—in such cities as Tokyo and Rome. About 15 percent of the CIA's employees are stationed overseas.

Depending on their size, CIA stations may have a chief of support, a finance officer, a communications officer, a logistics officer, and a personnel officer. Large stations may have branches that focus on internal political affairs, Soviet matters, terrorism, narcotics, nuclear weapons, and liaison with local intelligence and internal-security services.

Through liaison, the CIA obtains information on people of interest to the agency. In exchange, the CIA usually gives the host country information it wants—perhaps the location of a fugitive. Besides providing useful intelligence, the CIA may supply the host intelligence service with funds to help it combat a local communist or terrorist problem. But the CIA plays it both ways. The agency recruits members of the local intelligence service to find out what that country is trying to do to penetrate or thwart the CIA, and to obtain other information the local security services do not want to share with the CIA. Often, the CIA's liaison with local services is a pretext to enable CIA officers to get close to individuals in the local services and recruit them. In a reversal of that, Ghana recruited Sharon M. Scranage, a CIA support employee, to find out what the agency was doing in that country.

The primary role of the stations is to recruit agents to tell the CIA what the host government is doing and to report on the activities of diplomats from other countries—such as the Soviet Union or Communist China—that are of interest to the CIA. Depending on how sensitive he or she is, a CIA officer may choose to receive information from an agent over lunch or in microfilm left in dead drops in tree stumps or holes in telephone poles. To further protect the agent, a seemingly chance encounter known as a brush pass may be arranged. The agent passes documents or film to a CIA officer inside a briefcase or some other article as they pass each other. Coded transmissions by radio or by satellite are commonly used. Laser beams aimed at office buildings are used to carry messages as well. The only way a laser communication can be intercepted is if a receiver is placed in the path of the laser beam.

Since most have official cover, CIA officers must perform their normal State Department or military duties on weekdays and then carry out CIA operations evenings and weekends.

"If you wanted to know who was CIA, look at the embassy sign-in log on Sunday. With the possible exception of the ambassador, only CIA people showed up on Sunday," Herbert F. Saunders, a former CIA officer, said.

The CIA officers are paid through the State Department or military, with funds secretly provided by the CIA. If a letter is sent to an undercover officer at Langley, it is returned. Likewise, the CIA switchboard operator, if asked, would say there is no listing for the employee.

A CIA officer may fill any State Department position overseas except that of ambassador or deputy chief of mission, the second-in-command at an embassy. Thus when former CIA director Richard Helms became ambassador to Iran, he could not serve as a CIA officer. In practice, the rank of counselor—used for higher-ranking diplomats who are often in charge of a section—is never used either.

CIA officers recruit agents the same way salesmen or lawyers go looking for business or journalists go looking for sources. If an officer in Mexico City, for example, is interested in recruiting a military officer, he might ask for recommendations from the U.S. military attachés stationed at the embassy, attend functions and conferences where military personnel show up, go to bars where they might hang out, and take advantage of other opportunities to meet the sort of person he is after. If an officer is interested in recruiting diplomats, he might attend diplomatic functions or go to diplomatic clubs, many of which were started by the CIA for that purpose.

Once the officer has spotted a likely prospect, he cables CIA headquarters for "traces"—a search of CIA files for information on the person. Most of the information is stored in computers. He may also call for help from the Office of Technical Service, which provides the tools of the spy trade, such as radio transmitters and secret-writing papers.

CIA headquarters may provide information on the individual's interests, such as tennis, and the CIA officer may suggest that they play. Or the CIA officer may learn that the prospect has a health problem.

In the case of a key Soviet ambassador in Africa, CIA officer Howard Bane knew that he had a heart problem. In the days when the machines were still new, Bane arranged to lend him an EKG machine. When it came time to pick up the machine, Bane picked it up himself. Then Bane made his pitch. He showed the ambassador a *Time* magazine article about some recent developments in treating heart problems in the U.S.

"We could arrange for you to have all of this," he said. "Nobody would know about it."

In this case, the pitch didn't work, but often it does. After the CIA officer has struck up a friendship, he usually offers money to become a CIA agent and spy for the U.S. After each meeting with a "developmental"—an individual targeted for recruitment—or an agent already recruited, the CIA officer writes a contact report. It says where and when the meeting took place, whether any money was exchanged, whether documents were received, and what was discussed. Any security problems are also noted. A reports officer in the station decides if the contact report is worth sending to Washington.

If the case officer believes he has learned valuable intelligence that should be relayed to Washington, he writes it up as an intelligence report. The reports officer decides how it is to be sent and to whom. When transmitted to Washington, the report has two parts. The first page includes the cryptonym of the source and is for internal CIA use only. Depending on the information it conveys, the rest of the report is sent to such other agencies as State, the FBI, or NSA within the intelligence community. It gives a general idea of the source of the information and an indication of his reliability. If the information in the report is extremely sensitive, the general description may be altered to further conceal the source.

The real name of the agent is kept at the Mexico City station in a safe. Next to the agent's name is a number. Another safe contains a list that links each number to a cryptonym. To find out the real name behind a cryptonym, an officer in Mexico City would have to have the combinations to both safes and match both lists, or he would have to obtain it from the agent's case officer. Headquarters has his real name as well.

Every report from Mexico City and each of the CIA's 129 other stations carries an addressee line that gives its destination, followed by a slug line. The slug line directs the way the report is to be disseminated within the CIA and to outside agencies. One code means the report should not be disseminated to other agencies without first consulting the division responsible for that area of the world—in this case, Latin America.

In nearly all cases, the material is transmitted electronically and stored in computers. Each communication has a designated level of importance. The most important level is *critic*, followed by *flash, immediate, priority,* and *routine*. The first two designations, while rarely used, give a cable precedence over other cables and require immediate transmittal.

Most intelligence reports go to the Directorate of Intelligence, which prepares estimates and other memos through the National Intelligence Council on the likely shape of future events in the world—the possibility that a given country will develop nuclear weapons or that Iraq will invade Kuwait. These go to the president, often in the President's Daily Brief.

The value of the reports from the stations is later graded by a reports staff within the appropriate area division at headquarters. In some cases, the grades are influenced by reactions of other agencies such as State or Defense that read the reports as well. Twenty is the best and ten is very good. A minus five means it should never have been sent. At the end of the month, each station gets a score. The more reports with high grades, the better the score for the station. Most operations officers think the average grades are meaningless.

The Evaluation and Plans Staff within the Directorate of Operations assesses the effectiveness of the operations, keeps track of the money for budgeting purposes, and tries to assign dollar values to the information obtained after consulting with those who use it.

Meanwhile, an elaborate financial accounting system keeps track of the money being spent by each station. The CIA has a rigid system of financial controls that has made theft and fraud rare. The most common form of fraud is when CIA officers claim they have paid a local agent and actually kept the money themselves. While agents are required to sign receipts, it is easy to forge such documents. Yet CIA officers in Vietnam routinely paid out $100,000 in cash each month to local officials to distribute to their men, and there were few allegations of internal theft.

"I think that the CIA has the tightest control over every dollar spent of any government agency," Dr. John M. Clarke, a former comptroller and associate deputy director of the CIA, said. "While attending the Harvard Advanced Management Program, I had occasion to compare the financial practices of fifty of America's largest corporations and financial firms. None had tighter controls than the CIA. That isn't to say an agent in the field never stole any money. The auditors in the finance department uncovered fraud or theft perhaps a dozen times a year. Once in a while there was a large one."[14]

"CIA is by no means a rogue elephant," Whipple, a former CIA officer who is executive director of the Association of Former Intelligence Officers, said. "There isn't anything independent about the CIA. We are asked to do these things under legal authority. Everything we do is under strict controls. Everything we spend has closer controls on it than in any other element of the government."

Occasionally, an officer claims he has obtained information from agents who do not exist. Often, this is uncovered when the officer is sent to another station. His replacement expects to be introduced to the agent and finds he has vanished. Or if he meets with him, the agent appears to know nothing about any secret arrangement with the CIA.

"It's a problem in rare cases," a former operations officer said. "You replace somebody, he says, 'Here are my agents,' and the guy says, 'What do you mean? I never agreed to do that. What do you mean you want me to be a spy?' "

Eventually, deceptions like these catch up with officers, and they are fired.

"There's a perception from the outside that CIA case officers, or operations officers, are loose cannons, free to operate with little or no supervision," former CIA officer Saunders said. "In reality, there are a multitude of checks and balances. If nobody's heard from you for eight hours, you'd better have an explanation when you surface. 'This is where I've been, and this is what I've been doing.' "

"When you undertake a covert or political action, you never do it without authority from Washington," former CIA officer Whipple said. "I don't know of any case where any of us undertook a covert action we were not ordered to do."

As a rule, there is a degree of friction between State Department and CIA officers assigned to a post. The CIA officers look at State Department officers as softheaded errand boys. The State Department looks at CIA officers as bumbling troublemakers.

"You need intellectuals on the DI [Directorate of Intelligence] side. You need scientists. But the agency is not about intellectuals. The agency is about hard-nosed covert operators," a former operations officer said. "That's why the State Department doesn't get along very well with the agency. They think the CIA is full of uncultured thugs. The CIA thinks the State Department is all pussies. And they are, most of them. They'll never be able to work in great harmony."

In part, the frictions stem from the fact that the two agencies have different roles.

"The State Department guys are expected to talk to people at their level in the host government. They take at face value what they are told," a former operations officer said. The CIA, on the other hand, recruits agents who will obtain classified information or reveal confidential conversations. They are quizzed over and over again to make sure they are telling the truth.

"The name of the game is getting agents who tell you what people are doing," he said. "The State Department is paid to hang out at receptions and ask diplomats, 'What are you doing these days?' A covert agent is a backup. The diplomat says one thing and the covert agent says, 'Bullshit.' They're doing the opposite."

For their part, diplomats insist the information they pick up is often more valuable than what the CIA learns because it is attributable to responsible government officials. They often look down their noses at CIA officers.

"They [CIA officers] were not of the same caliber as we were," a former U.S. consul general in Leningrad said. "To be a Foreign Service officer, you practically have to be a Ph.D., and the exams were rigorous. The same was not true of other agencies. Frequently people who couldn't get into Foreign Service went into the others. I was offered a job by the CIA at twenty-five percent more salary. But I wasn't interested."

Problems develop when the CIA and the State Department both wind up dealing with the same individual, or when an ambassador wants to know everything the CIA is doing. Some ambassadors think they have a right to know who the CIA's agents are in his country. They do not, and often they have to be told that by State.

"Once in a while, you recruit somebody who may be a contact of someone in the embassy. That's when you run into trouble," a former CIA officer said. "There's no reason ever to tell anyone, except maybe the ambassador or deputy chief of mission, this is our agent.

"There are always some jealousies because of the usually incorrect assumption that because you are CIA, you have extra privileges [such as better housing]," the former CIA officer said. "That somehow you get more than they do, which isn't the case at all. This is usually based on the belief that the CIA doesn't pay for what it gets and is thus a drain on the embassy's budget. In fact, the CIA provides State with more than enough money to pay for each of its officers overseas. State comes out ahead, but it remains a source of friction."

As in any organization, there is always some friction between headquarters and the field.

"In every government agency, and especially in the CIA, there is continuing competition, and perhaps a touch of resentment, between headquarters and field personnel," Saunders said. "The field officer thinks that headquarters is staffed by idiots who do nothing but attend meetings and don't understand squat. The headquarters guy thinks the field person is narrow. The ironic thing is that when they switch places, as inevitably they will, they will both conclude that they have now entered the big time, where they have all the action and all the answers."

"It [the Directorate of Operations] is a fraternity," William Colby said. "People who work closely together with a sense of discipline. There are mutual loyalties. When you live in a station overseas, there is a tendency for the families to stay together."

While the CIA moved under William Webster to hire and promote more women and minorities, the Directorate of Operations remains a backwater. Many older operations officers think women cannot relate properly to males in Latin America or the Middle East—a similar prejudice that existed, until recently, about female police officers. There has never been a female division chief and only a few female station chiefs in the CIA.

"They say there are certain countries where you can't operate. For example, how can a woman operate in the Middle East?" Robert R. Simmons, a former CIA officer, said. "Sometimes, some of the best officers there have been women. In some cases, it may make it easier to go against what people expect in an area. A female officer may have a reason for being there. You can hold hands. He [an agent] can give you flowers. Inside is a secret message. You can kiss him on the cheek and put something in his pocket. You can go together and not draw attention."

Because of the stress of working under cover, marriages between CIA operations officers are common.

"You can tell your wife that you work for the CIA," Saunders said. "You can say that you're going to Singapore on a delicate operational assignment, but you don't add that you're going to tap so-and-so's telephone. The security constraints sometimes have the effect of encouraging marriage among CIA people; there are many husband and wife teams in the CIA. A spouse who works, or formerly worked, for the agency is more likely to be sensitive to the security requirements and the stress associated with the work. He or she won't ask what you're doing and won't be offended if you don't offer the information."

If both spouses are CIA officers, things are a little easier. While in theory they should not talk about sensitive operational matters unless they are both assigned to the same operation, in practice they usually wind up freely talking about their daily activities.

For the most part, the job of a CIA operations officer is not as dangerous as that of a police officer. Most CIA officers operate under diplomatic immunity, and most governments do not want to risk retaliation against their own intelligence officers by harming a CIA officer. Yet a number of CIA officers have been killed in the line of duty—fifty-three at last count.

Richard Welch, the CIA station chief in Athens, was one

of the more well-known casualties. On November 25, 1975, the English-language *Athens News* published his name and home address. His name had first appeared in 1967 in the East German publication *Who's Who in the CIA*. Other publications, such as *CounterSpy,* later listed him as well. The Athens publication urged action against Welch and other CIA officers. On December 23, 1975, Welch was shot to death on his doorstep in Athens.

Because the more recent listing had been in *CounterSpy,* many CIA officers blamed the publication for Welch's death. However, some of the CIA officers assigned to Athens at the time said Welch's identity and his home address were well known before they were published.

"He was living in a house that had been occupied by his predecessor," one of the officers assigned to Athens said. "It was careless. You get comfortable. The climate is benign. It was convenient. He didn't have to go looking for a house. Everybody knows the chief of station. You can't do your job as chief of station if they don't know."

On March 16, 1984, William Buckley, the CIA station chief in Beirut, was kidnapped. On June 3, 1985, he died in captivity after being brutally tortured.

Despite claims that morale has suffered since the Church Committee hearings, most operations officers say their mood depends more on what they are doing than who heads the agency or what investigations are going on.

"Morale is about the same," said a recently retired operations officer who was with the agency for several decades. "Everything depends on who you work for. Maybe you're working for a gem, but the one above him is a son of a bitch. Any station overseas is happy if it's successful and knows it's successful. Any organization becomes more bureaucratic. Now they standardize the car for each defector. They're not taking into account the fact one is more valuable to you. That's bureaucracy at work."

For officers who perform well, the CIA provides monetary awards and intelligence medals, along with promotions. The most prized officers are those who can recruit almost anyone, yet they are not necessarily good managers. Many of the best spies do not want to work in headquarters.

"If a CIA officer recruits a lot, it doesn't mean he is a leader," a former CIA officer said. "You have very good case officers who can recruit a tree. But they may not be chief-of-station material. Sometimes you find people who say they only want to be case officers. But most want more power. You often don't know if he can recruit.

"Somebody who can be recruited by one person can't be by another," the former officer said. "Some people can be recruited by anybody. That person may see CIA and begin imagining money. Others are not interested in money but feel they can't do much in their own system and so they try the CIA as a way of trying to change their own government."

Usually, CIA officers woo potential agents for several weeks or months before they make a pitch. The KGB, on the other hand, tends to be more patient and sometimes works on developing a relationship for years before making a move. The KGB also tends to focus more on people who can reveal specific secrets, rather than recruiting anyone with access to sensitive information.

"The major difference is the KGB, by nature of the control it exerts, is very persistent," a former CIA officer said. "They will say, 'That's the target, penetrate it.' They won't let go. Quite often, you look at something and say, 'There's no way I'm going to get anything on this, I'm going to do something else.' In that sense, they are probably better organized. They tell them step by step what to do."

The KGB also does its homework better.

"Americans," the former officer said, "will go to a cocktail party and start something. The Soviets will say, 'That guy is of interest, find out everything you can, and approach him.' They go about it differently. They do their homework before meeting him. When they decide to go after him, they know he's of interest.

"I think by nature, we are more impatient than other people," the former officer said. "The recruitment process, if done classically and well, should take a long time. If it's done in three sessions, he may not be worth a lot and he's probably not yours anyway. It should take a long time for assessment and vetting."

On the other hand, the CIA has the natural advantage of representing America. KGB officers are far more likely to want to work for the U.S. than the other way around. In the area of human spying, both the CIA and KGB have scored tremendous coups against each other.

"A lot of people recruit themselves," a former officer said. "A lot of people walk in."

"One of the problems you run into throughout the agency is quantity versus quality. Everyone preaches quality, but most of the time you get quantity," a former operations officer said. "Numbers have always been important. It's competition. They keep track, they count. 'What happened? You only got forty-six reports [from officers in one station] this month.'"

"That was how careers were measured and made—by the numbers," Tom Gilligan, another former CIA operations officer, said in his book *CIA Life*.[15]

To expand their own empires, some officers at headquarters constantly ask for more information about trivial subjects. The more information they obtain, the more they can justify requests for larger budgets.

"A lot of it is information for information's sake," a former officer said. "There are all sorts of little men sitting around, and their job is to keep track of iron ore production in Brazil."

In September, station chiefs write progress reports about the previous fiscal year and outline their budget needs for the next fiscal year. A shorter interim report is also prepared in March. The reports include a listing of each asset or agent by cryptonym. As the report is forwarded up the chain of command, the cryptonyms are deleted and are replaced by aggregate numbers to further conceal identities.

"What you want to do basically is to show that you did better in the last six months than the previous six," a former operations officer said. "If you are a new station chief or section chief, you want to show you did better than the last one. So you show you recruited x number of agents and got rid of x number of bad ones.

"In the end," he said, "quality is not taken into account as much as it should be. One good agent is not necessarily given more weight than a mediocre one."

One of the gravest problems confronting the CIA is the possibility that agents may in fact be double agents, meaning they work for the other side. This happened in Cuba, where nearly all the agents recruited by the CIA back to the early 1960s were found to be plants taking instructions from Cuban premier Fidel Castro. It was not until Juan Antonio Menier Rodriguez, who had worked for both Cuban intelligence and counterintelligence, defected in 1987 that the CIA began to learn of the deception. The real shock came a year later, when Maj. Florentino Aspillaga Lombard, who also had worked in Cuban intelligence, defected. He had far more detail than Rodriguez and identified as doubles thirty-eight Cuban agents working for the CIA—practically all of the agency's complement at the time. Nearly all of the agents had taken polygraph tests, and most had passed. The test results of many of the other agents were deemed inconclusive, meaning there was not sufficient evidence to show they were lying.

The revelation sent shock waves through the CIA and particularly the Latin American Division, which handles Cuba. Some could point to warnings they had previously made. For example, as early as 1976, the CIA's counterintelligence staff expressed concern that some Cubans on the CIA's payroll might be double agents. Their information was superficial and generally unhelpful. They also seemed to know too much about the operations of the CIA's Madrid station, the hub for operations against Cuba over the years. This was an indication that at least some operations had been compromised or were under Cuban control. The warnings were not heeded.

According to Rodriguez, the Cuban agents had all received extensive training in beating the polygraph. They were told that polygraph tests do not work and that if the agents failed the tests, they could always convince CIA operations officers that there was something wrong with the machine. As a result, most did not show any signs of increased tension—interpreted as deception—when they lied.

Rodriguez said the problem was that the American CIA officers who debriefed the Cubans were not themselves Cubans and did not understand their culture enough to interrogate them effectively.

"The polygraph is a big mistake," Rodriguez said. "We [in Cuban intelligence] get Chinese to recruit Chinese. We are not arrogant. They [the CIA] should use Cubans. If not, you will not detect [double agents]."[16]

Rodriguez compared the CIA's mistakes to its decision to mount the Bay of Pigs invasion.

"They didn't understand Cubans. Only a crazy would have thought in 1961 that the people would have gone against Fidel," Rodriguez said.

A former CIA operations officer familiar with what happened agreed.

"The relationship develops between the source and case officer," he explained. "There's a tendency to try to work out problems with the source. The Cubans knew this and told the agents that if they have a problem with a polygraph, appeal to the case agent. 'Don't get upset over this thing. Say you were harassed. After all, you gave them good information. There's something wrong with the polygraph.' "

The CIA's emphasis on quantity over quality also played a role.

"You want your agent to get through the polygraph successfully because you don't want the hassle of trying to establish by other means he is okay," a former operations officer said.

In general, "it's not uncommon for a case officer to fall in love with an agent," former CIA officer Saunders said. "Whenever a special bond develops, as it must between case officer and agent, there is some unique chemistry."

If the agent turns out to be bad—a double or a fabricator—the officer may not want to believe it.

"It's like a husband coming home at three A.M. and saying he was out selling encyclopedias," Saunders said. "[His wife] wants to believe him so badly that she does. A prudent case officer, however, is constantly vetting, checking, always cynical, often asking questions to which he already knows the answer. He doesn't trust easily, and if he doesn't pay attention, he may pay a price."

The result of the Cuban deception was that the CIA wasted a lot of time and money and was not able to get the information it really wanted. Much of the information given to the CIA by the double agents was true but not particularly damaging to Cuba.

"They [the Cubans] said, 'Tell them anything they want to know.' It wasn't that it was bad information. It was true and did not cause great policy errors to be made," according to a former operations officer familiar with the CIA's analysis of what happened.

After Aspillaga's defection was publicized, Cuban television aired a series that exposed many of the CIA's operations on the island over the years. The program showed CIA operations officers picking up documents left for them by double agents in a variety of out-of-the-way places, dropping off sophisticated communications equipment for their agents, and meeting with agents in foreign countries to give them instructions.

While some of the American diplomats the program claimed were CIA officers were not in the agency, most of them were. Some of the wilder schemes being discussed by CIA officers—such as substituting flimsy tanks to store ammonia so that the chemical would leak out and destroy crops—were presented as current plans but had actually been discarded by 1964.

Richard F. Stolz was the CIA's deputy director for operations when the double agents were exposed. A respected CIA veteran, Stolz had served in Rome, Moscow, Munich, Istanbul, Belgrade, and London and had been chief of the Soviet/East Europe Division. He told his officers that Cuba was able to fool the CIA with phony agents because of enormous pressure from the White House and from within the CIA to recruit. In addition, he blamed "ethnic egotism," saying that the ability of Latinos had been underestimated. Finally, he blamed overreliance on the polygraph, pointing out that polygraphy is an art, not a science.

During Stolz's tenure, the CIA began weeding out unproductive agents worldwide in an effort to improve quality and cut costs.

As the Cold War began to wind down, the CIA began concentrating even more than before on uncovering plans to develop nuclear, chemical, or biological weapons—one of the CIA's traditional and most important roles. Once evidence of these weapons is uncovered, the U.S. government can use diplomatic pressure, trade sanctions, or other economic weapons to halt the weapons programs. For example, in 1988, Taiwan had been working on a secret installation that could have been used to obtain plutonium, a main ingredient in the production of nuclear weapons. The effort to build an installation capable of extracting plutonium violated Taiwan's secret commitments to the United States that it would undertake no research for developing atomic weapons. Moreover, the Communist Chinese had warned that if Taiwan were to develop a nuclear weapon, they would invade the island.

As the work progressed, the CIA recruited Col. Chang Hsien-Yia, a scientist working on the project, and eventually he defected to the U.S. Based on his information, the State Department successfully applied pressure on the Taiwanese in 1988 to dismantle the operation.[17]

While there are five declared nuclear powers, a number of other countries have the atomic bomb and refuse to acknowledge it.

"Several countries either possess a nuclear device or can fabricate one on short notice," William Webster has said. "Others are developing key nuclear technology that could later be used for a nuclear explosive, should the decision be made to do so. And there are still other countries which are in the early stages of nuclear technology research and development."[18]

In addition, the CIA tracks development of ballistic missiles. According to Webster, at least fifteen developing nations could be producing their own ballistic missiles by the year 2000.

Even the possibility of life on other planets has been considered by the CIA to be within its purview. When he was CIA director, Walter Bedell Smith authorized a CIA study of unidentified flying objects, declaring that they have "possible implications for our national security."

Other intelligence gathered by the CIA helps the U.S. to foresee coming events or to gain an advantage in trade or arms talks. The CIA is perennially interested in the health of foreign leaders. When they visit the U.S., the CIA has arranged to obtain samples of their feces, hair, and other bodily fluids so they can be analyzed back at Langley for health problems. Kim Il Sung, the aging strongman in North Korea, has a growth on his neck that has never appeared in photographs. The CIA arranged to have an agent report firsthand on its appearance. It was benign.

The CIA has always tried to obtain the negotiating positions of other countries before arms talks or trade talks begin. Stations plant bugging devices in hotel rooms or tap telephones so that the State Department will know what it is facing before negotiations begin.

Like the problem of weapons proliferation, economic matters have been given higher priority by the CIA since the end of the Cold War. The CIA tries, for example, to find out overseas what kinds of computers the Japanese are developing. For years, the CIA had an official in the entourage of the prime minister of Japan on its payroll. Armed with inside information on what Japan's negotiating position will be on, say, imports, the State Department can make more informed counterproposals. It is something like being able to eavesdrop on a seller and his broker when negotiating to buy a house.

"When the Japanese prime minister is here to see the president or secretary of state, they'd like to know what he is going to talk about," a former operations officer said.

While the CIA cannot be in the position of handing over commercial secrets to selected American companies, it can pass the information along to the Commerce Department so that it can issue broad guidance to all companies. For example, the Commerce Department might issue an advisory on the direction of the Japanese computer industry.

But what happens when finding out what the other side is doing is not enough, when the U.S. government wants to take a more active role? That is when covert action is used, a term that covers any clandestine means to influence or overthrow a foreign power, leader, or political party.

5 | *Castro's Beard*

AS A RULE, COVERT ACTION IS CARRIED OUT BY THE SAME officers in each station who normally collect intelligence. It is coordinated by the Covert Action Staff within the Directorate of Operations. In addition, the directorate has a Special Activities Operations staff that conducts paramilitary activities, such as those in Afghanistan.

One officer estimates that overall, 75 percent of the time of operations officers in the field is devoted to gathering intelligence and the rest to covert action.

Today, covert action accounts for only 3 percent of the national foreign intelligence budget—roughly $500 million—or 15 percent of the CIA's budget. But covert action accounts for most of the black eyes the agency has received.

In the beginning, there were many successes—or what seemed to be successes. In 1948, the CIA funded the Christian Democrats in Italy, helping to prevent communists from taking over the Italian government. In 1950, Col. Edward G.

Lansdale, who was on loan to the CIA from the Air Force, helped the Philippine leader Ramon Magsaysay overcome the communist-backed Huk guerrillas. On August 21, 1953, the CIA, led by Kermit Roosevelt, overthrew the left-wing government of Prime Minister Mohamed Mossadeq in Iran after he nationalized the British-owned Anglo-Iranian Oil Co. Three days later the shah, who had fled the previous week, returned to the palace.

Buoyed by these triumphs, the U.S. became more aggressive. America interpreted the most innocuous developments as further evidence that the Soviet Union was about to encircle the world. In June 1954, the CIA supported the overthrow of Jacobo Arbenz of Guatemala after he nationalized 400,000 acres of idle banana-plantation land owned by United Fruit Co. Arbenz had offered $600,000, precisely what the company had declared as the land's value for tax purposes. Moreover, he had come to power in popular elections. But Arbenz's left-leaning politics and the fact that some of the people around him were communists were seen by Washington as reasons enough to overthrow him.

In most cases, the benefits of covert action were only temporary. Arbenz was replaced by even more objectionable and often ruthless leaders. Guatemala has been in turmoil ever since. In Iran, the shah lasted more than twenty-five years and was toppled and replaced by the Ayatollah Khomeini in 1979.

While twenty-five years of stability is a great feat, the CIA action in installing the shah "identified Iran and the shah more closely with the U.S. than was good for either of them," Gregory Treverton wrote in his book *Covert Action*. "It also set in motion a kind of psychological dependence by the shah on the United States that Americans no doubt liked initially but came to lament in 1977 and 1978."[19]

Meanwhile, the Soviets used the CIA's meddling in the affairs of other countries to great effect. The U.S. was seen as imperialistic and hypocritical. What more evidence was needed than the fact that it would overthrow a legally elected leader? David A. Phillips, a CIA officer who played a major role in the ouster of Arbenz, would later say that on balance, the CIA should not overthrow an elected leader.[20]

"Defenders of covert action would say we are fighting to preserve liberty and democracy and the American way," said Simmons, a former CIA officer who was later staff director of the Senate Select Committee on Intelligence. "But when you get into the details, you wonder if they are talking about the same thing. He may be an SOB and a dictator, but he is our SOB, whereas Arbenz, who was democratically elected, was not an SOB, but he wasn't ours."

On April 17, 1961, the CIA began the invasion of Cuba at the Bay of Pigs. It would be a dismal failure. The Directorate of Operations was so fixated on secrecy that it did not consult the CIA's Directorate of Intelligence for an assessment of whether the Cuban people would rise up against Castro once an invasion began. If it had, the judgment would have been that the Cubans would not support the invasion.*

Just before the invasion, CIA analysts had concluded that Castro "was likely to grow stronger rather than weaker as time goes by." One CIA memo warned that Castro "now has established a formidable structure of control over the daily lives of the Cuban people."[21]

Thanks in part to last-minute restrictions by President Kennedy, the CIA did not have enough firepower to pull off the invasion. While the Directorate of Operations kept the operation from other CIA components, the word quickly leaked out to the rest of the world. Even the *New York Times* knew about it but agreed not to publish the story. Finally, the CIA had the unrealistic notion that an invasion could be mounted by Cuban expatriates without Cuba's knowing that the U.S. government was backing them.

"My own personal view is that almost the worst mistake we made on that operation was clinging to the belief that this could be done in a way that was not attributable to the U.S. government," Richard M. Bissell, Jr., a former Yale University and MIT professor of economics who headed the in-

---

* The Directorate of Operations was previously known euphemistically as the Directorate for Plans.

vasion as the CIA's deputy director for operations, said. "Clinging to the idea that if our tradecraft was good, nobody could connect it to the U.S. government. That was just an utterly unattainable, and a very silly, hope. Anything of that magnitude would be blamed on the U.S. government, even if the U.S. had not had a role in it. But we paid a high price for disclaimability in terms of operational capability," Bissell said. "We weren't allowed to use volunteer U.S. air crews. We therefore didn't have enough air crews. We therefore didn't assemble enough B-26 bombers. We couldn't take off from any American-held territory such as Puerto Rico. There was a whole list of things. We weren't allowed to have any volunteer Americans go ashore with the brigade. That would have been a major benefit. So I think that from top to bottom, we made that mistake."[22]

Nonetheless, under pressure from President Kennedy, the CIA in December 1961 began a range of other covert actions aimed at toppling Castro, each more foolish than the last.

A CIA inspector general's report of August 25, 1967, recounts dozens of bungled attempts to assassinate Castro or embarrass him with his people. Under one such plan, the CIA would spray the air of a radio station where Castro broadcast his speeches with a chemical that would produce hallucinatory reactions similar to LSD. Another scheme was designed to contaminate cigars smoked by Castro with a chemical that would create "temporary personality disorientation." A third idea was to introduce thallium salts into Castro's shoes so his beard would fall out. This, according to CIA plotters, would destroy his public image. Finally, the CIA proposed setting off fireworks off the coast of Cuba that would portray an image of Christ in the sky—this to show that Castro was in disfavor with God.

The stupidest scheme was to enlist the aid of the Mafia in killing Castro. Bissell, the deputy director for operations, asked Sheffield Edwards, director of security, to contact Mafia leaders for the purpose.[23] Edwards enlisted Robert A. Maheu, a private investigator, who asked John Roselli, an associate of Mafia leaders, to offer up to $150,000 to remove Castro. Roselli agreed to contact Salvator (Sam) Giancana, a member of the Mafia, and Giancana asked for a lethal pill that could be given to Castro in his food. The CIA produced pills containing botulinum toxin for Castro.

The CIA passed the pills to the Mafia, but the gangsters reported they could not carry off the plot because their source had lost his position in the prime minister's office.

The CIA also developed plans that were never carried out to assassinate Patrice Lumumba, who headed what was then known as the Congo and is now called Zaire. Today, assassination plots are banned. The first presidential prohibition was contained in Executive Order 11905, signed by President Gerald Ford on February 18, 1976. It said no government employee could participate in attempts to kill foreign leaders. Executive Order 12333, signed by President Reagan on December 4, 1981, governs the CIA's activities today. It states, "No person employed by or acting on behalf of the U.S. government shall engage in, or conspire to engage in, assassination."

After fumbling in Cuba, the CIA went on to try to control elections in Chile. In 1964, the agency spent $2.6 million to support the election of the Christian Democratic candidate, Eduardo Frei, to prevent Salvador Allende's accession to the presidency. In 1970, the CIA tried to mount a military coup in Chile to prevent confirmation of Salvador Allende's victory in the Chilean presidential election. It also spent $8 million to prevent his confirmation—all in vain.

The CIA also became involved in covert action and paramilitary actions in Vietnam, Laos, Cambodia, Angola, Afghanistan, and Nicaragua. Only in Afghanistan was the CIA's intervention considered entirely successful.

It would be easy, as some CIA officers do, to blame the presidents at the time for urging the agency to undertake covert action that was ill-advised. Nearly every one was approved by presidents and policymakers who were looking for a quick fix for the problem of the day.

"We cannot overemphasize the extent to which responsible agency officers felt themselves subject to the Kennedy administration's severe pressures to do something about Castro and his regime," the CIA inspector general's report on the plots said. "The fruitless and, in retrospect, often unrealistic plotting should be viewed in that light."[24]

But that is not the whole story. The agency often encouraged the White House to think that covert action would work, then developed ill-advised schemes to carry it out. Too often, not enough thought was given to what was to be accomplished, whether it would work, and what would happen if the CIA's involvement became public, as it invariably did. In CIA lingo, such bad publicity is known as blowback or flap.

CIA officers often pursued covert action for the sake of doing something, without giving much thought to the possible consequences.

As a result of the Church Committee hearings in 1975 and 1976, strong congressional oversight put a stop to many of the ill-conceived schemes, but under CIA director William Casey, some bizarre or highly risky covert actions were again approved or at least considered. The prime example was the Iran-contra plan to exchange arms for hostages. While the CIA itself did not arrange it, Casey and National Security Council aide Lt. Col. Oliver L. North, Jr., used a few individuals in the agency to carry out the scheme.

In 1985, the CIA provided training and communications equipment to Lebanese intelligence officers who claimed they were antiterrorists and would help free William Buckley, the former CIA station chief in Beirut who had been kidnapped on March 16, 1984. President Reagan approved the plan in a written intelligence finding, the formal authorization required before covert action can be carried out.* But John McMahon, the deputy director of Central Intelligence, opposed it, saying the former intelligence officers were not to be trusted, and the CIA ran the risk of supporting people who might kill others.

According to McMahon, Casey then asked President Reagan to withdraw the finding, and the CIA never went ahead

---

* The document giving presidential approval to a covert action is referred to as a finding because it begins, "I hereby find that the following activities are important to the national security of the United States."

with the project. But the officers who were to get the aid hatched their own plan to kill Sheikh Mohammed Hussein Fadlallah, who headed a Shiite terrorist movement called Hezbollah, or Party of God. It was this group that was believed to be holding Buckley. Eighty people were killed on March 8, 1985, when a car filled with explosives was left near Fadlallah's apartment house in a Beirut suburb. Fadlallah escaped without any injury, and the CIA was unfairly blamed for having ordered the assassination attempt.[25]

"When that happened, I went to Bill [Casey] and said, 'See, goddamn it, that's exactly what I mean. That's what happens with these guys . . . we weren't associated with it but we got blamed for it," McMahon said.[26]

The same kind of problem occurred in Operation Phoenix, a program run by William Colby during the Vietnam War to identify Vietcong hidden within the South Vietnamese population. Both American and South Vietnamese intelligence agencies collected the intelligence, then turned the information over to the South Vietnamese. In most cases, the South Vietnamese incarcerated and questioned the Vietcong, but in some cases they killed them. As a result, the operation developed a reputation as an assassination squad, even though that was not its intent. Moreover, casualties that arose from military actions were often attributed to the program.

More recently, in Suriname, Casey decided the CIA should overthrow Désire D. Bouterse as the leader of the South American country because the government was killing opposition leaders and permitting the country to be used as a transshipment point for cocaine. This plan, too, never got off the ground after it hit opposition both in Congress and the administration.

"We were worried about what was going on there," McMahon said. "The question was, should we do it militarily or do it ourselves? We tried to round up enough people to go carry it out. It did fall by the wayside, and I don't think it was just because of the House or Senate. There were a lot in the administration who had some misgivings on it. But the agency gave it a college try and started drawing up plans on how to go about it."

Today, only a dozen covert action programs are carried out each year. Some of them are broad strategies that may be undertaken in a number of countries. Most of them are low-level propaganda efforts or innocuous aid to countries fighting terrorism or narcotics. For example, at the request of these countries, the CIA may provide weapons, vehicles, training, and data bases for checking on travelers going through customs. The only reason the funding is covert is that the countries themselves do not want their own people to know the United States is helping to combat narcotics or terrorism.

The CIA's propaganda efforts usually consist of printing books for distribution in the former Soviet Union or planting articles favorable to the United States or American ideals in countries where the media is anti-American.

During the Vietnam War, "we would present anything that made the Soviets or North Vietnamese look bad," a former CIA officer said. "It may not necessarily be untrue, or it might be facts that otherwise might not get into print. The Soviets do that all the time. Truth is generally thought to be a better weapon [in propaganda efforts]. In a lot of places, you can't get anything in the paper that is pro-American. Everything is pro-Soviet, so they only know that side."

In contrast to the days before the Church Committee hearings, the CIA today tends to be reluctant to undertake covert action.

"It has to be done on a case-by-case basis," a former National Security Council aide said. "There have been cases where it has been extremely effective. There are others where it didn't make any difference at all. In some cases, it probably was counterproductive. That depends on what is being implemented, how it is implemented, and what your goals and policies are."

Virtually every covert action eventually becomes public, often creating more harm than good because of the poor image it projects of the U.S.

"I would estimate that well over half of the covert action programs on the books have, at least in a general sense, been identified in the press in some fashion—not all the details and all the methods," according to Russell J. Bruemmer, a former

CIA general counsel under William Webster. "Probably almost all of the controversial ones have been identified."[27]

The cumulative effect of CIA covert action over the years has been that when anything negative happens, the CIA is blamed. Thus after the assassination of Rajiv Gandhi by a female South Asian suicide bomber in May 1991, leading Indian newspapers and government officials—perhaps unwilling to blame themselves—became firmly convinced that the CIA had ordered him killed.

"It is a difficult opinion to explain or refute since it seems to arise not from evidence or even coherent speculation, but from a deep-seated emotional conviction," according to a *Washington Post* news analysis from New Delhi.[28]

"Why do people find it easy to believe Dave Phillips killed Kennedy? I knew Dave well. There is not one chance that he ever would have been involved with such a thing. Yet he was a division chief, so he was an obvious target for that kind of accusation. People believe it because he was CIA," former CIA officer Simmons said.

At the same time, covert action, more than anything else, has tarnished the image of the CIA at home, making it more difficult to recruit the best personnel and to obtain the best consultants from the academic world.

"The negative attitude toward intelligence within academic circles I think has to do with tying the intelligence community to the failures of covert action," Russell J. Bowen, a retired CIA analyst who continues to consult for the agency, said. "We've had a tremendous amount of exposure to questionable covert action. That overshadows what is done positively by the analytical side of the house."[29]

"In principle, I think we ought to discourage the idea of fighting secret wars or even initiating most covert operations," George W. Ball, undersecretary of state in the Kennedy and Johnson administrations, has said. "When the United States violates those principles—when we mine harbors in Nicaragua—we fuzz the difference between ourselves and the Soviet Union."

In the last analysis, covert action has contributed very little to strengthening the national security of the U.S. If an action is worth taking, it should be done openly, as the U.S. did in driving Iraq from Kuwait during the Persian Gulf War. In pursuing covert action, the U.S. perpetuates the myth that its clandestine activities will remain secret, while avoiding asking itself the tough questions it would normally ask before taking action in the open. Those questions frequently lead to the conclusion that the action is not worth the risk. Like an elephant crapping during a circus, covert action is a sideshow to the CIA's main activities—one that grabs all the attention and in the long run, does more harm than good.

In contrast, intelligence gathering, the bread and butter of the CIA, is a relatively benign activity. While it entails breaking the espionage laws of other countries, it does not as a rule lead to violence or intervention in the affairs of other countries. By finding out more about each other, countries such as the U.S. and the former Soviet Union promote peace by preventing the kind of paranoia that might lead to a first strike. For that reason, no CIA activity has been so important to U.S. security as finding out what is going on inside the Soviet Union.

6 | *Weather Balloons*

FOR FORTY YEARS, THE CIA'S PRIMARY TARGET WAS THE Soviet Union, and with good reason. After World War II, Joseph Stalin, the Soviet leader, declared the Soviet Union a denied area and began building up the country's military. In speeches, he implied that war was inevitable between capitalist and communist countries. In 1944, the Soviets overran Hungary. By 1947, the Soviets had taken over in Poland and Romania. In 1948, a communist coup succeeded in Czechoslovakia, and Soviet harassment of Western traffic into Berlin had become a blockade. Finally, in 1950, North Korea, supported by Communist China, invaded the South. To suppress dissent at home, the Soviets established a secret police—the forerunner of the KGB—that brutally repressed the populace at home and became an effective and fearsome intelligence threat abroad. The U.S. government was convinced the Soviets would attack Western Europe next, and even America.

If it was a life-or-death struggle, it was also a frustrating one because it was so difficult to find out what was going on behind what Winston Churchill had dubbed the Iron Curtain. The Soviets declared their country closed. Without spy satellites or high-flying planes such as the U-2, the CIA knew virtually nothing about what was happening inside the Soviet Union. In the absence of knowledge, fear took over.

"Even the most elementary facts were unavailable—on roads and bridges, on the location and production of factories, on city plans and airfields," according to Harry Rositzke, a former CIA officer in charge of operations against the Soviet Union in the 1940s and 1950s. "Scores of Air Force researchers were compiling Soviet bombing target dossiers from out-of-date materials in the Library of Congress."[30]

"The first real big question we had which came out of the Korean War was how big is the Soviet Union," a former CIA Soviet analyst said. "We had identified our enemy as the Soviet Union. But we didn't know anything about it. They had stopped any information. There was a great experiment, a new system. We didn't know if it was working or not. How big were they relative to us in terms of their GNP? Were they growing rapidly or were they standing still?"

The CIA asked those few travelers who were allowed into the Soviet Union to look for missile sites. They never found any. The agency tried to piece together captured German aerial photographs of Soviet territory. It showed where construction had started on military installations but was out of date.

In desperation, the CIA began parachuting agents from airplanes behind Soviet lines. Because they had no diplomatic immunity, they could be executed if caught. Because of the rigid control the Soviets maintained over their society, it was virtually impossible to infiltrate foreigners into the country. As far as the CIA knows, all the "illegals" were caught.

Another CIA ploy was to send reconnaissance balloons equipped with cameras fifty thousand feet over the Soviet Union and Communist China, hoping that some would drift to the other side of the country and bring back photos of military installations or factories. To give them the appearance of weather balloons, the CIA outfitted them with signs in Russian asking for their return for meteorological research. Based on estimates of how long the balloons would take to cross Asia, a timer unfurled a parachute that would float the film to earth. Following a radio signal, Air Force planes could intercept the package and retrieve it. If they missed, a transmitter continued to signal the location of the package for twenty-four hours.

The Soviets shot down some of the balloons, while others fell inside Soviet territory or landed in Poland. In all, 516 balloons were launched. Of these, 40 returned 13,813 photos of Soviet and Communist Chinese territory, covering about 8 percent of their land mass. The U.S. stopped the program after the Soviets held a press conference and displayed 50 of the captured balloons.[31]

The CIA's most immediate concern was developing some system for detecting an imminent attack. In that event, steam locomotives would have to be fired up, and flat cars would be needed to ship tanks. So the CIA recruited people in railroad dispatchers' offices. The agency knew where the railroad cars were located and what their normal travel patterns were. The CIA also debriefed defectors and other émigrés. A former prostitute told the agency about the location of a missile site near Moscow. According to her, she could see the missiles while on the way to her assignations in military barracks.

The CIA's first major recruitment of a Soviet intelligence operative came in 1952 when Lt. Col. Peter Popov of the GRU, the Soviet military intelligence agency, offered in Vienna to spy for the agency. Besides giving away identities of Soviet intelligence officers, Popov delivered, according to William Hood, his case officer, one of the Pentagon's highest-priority targets—a copy of the 1947 Soviet army field regulations.[32]

The following year, the CIA built the Berlin Tunnel, which tapped into Soviet telephone calls in East Germany. The tunnel was six hundred yards long, six feet high, and fifteen feet underground. The lines—432 in all—connected the Soviet high command in East Berlin to the General Staff and foreign office in Moscow and all major Red Army units in East Germany, Soviet diplomatic installations, and Soviet intelligence headquarters in East Berlin. The interceptions provided the CIA with the complete order of battle of the Soviet Group of Forces in East Germany, as well as comments of Soviet officers about their troops in the field.[33]

In 1961, Col. Oleg Penkovskiy, a Soviet GRU officer, approached the British in Moscow. When he next visited London the following year, he began spying for the West. For sixteen months, he provided MI-6 and the CIA with running accounts of Soviet military strategies, the capabilities of the missiles that touched off the Cuban missile crisis in October 1962, and details of KGB and GRU operations targeted against the U.S.[34] In addition, he gave the CIA a series of articles from a "top secret" military magazine that had asked Soviet military leaders to express their views on policy. The articles provided insight into the Soviet military mind.

Penkovskiy had initially approached a CIA officer in Moscow, but the CIA, thinking he was a Soviet plant, rejected him.[35] After another unsuccessful attempt with a Canadian, he eventually approached Greville Wynne, a former British intelligence officer, who was visiting Moscow on business. Wynne introduced the GRU officer to the British MI-6. The CIA then agreed jointly to finance and run the operation with the British.

The CIA's initial rejection of Penkovskiy illustrates how effectively the Soviets protected their citizens from recruitment by the CIA. Almost any Soviet could be a potential KGB informer, and the CIA was constantly on the lookout for provocations that would result in expulsions of CIA officers assigned to Moscow. Today, the CIA recognizes that it is better to err on the side of accepting an agent, even if it means a CIA officer will occasionally be expelled because of a provocation.

In trying to penetrate the Soviets, the CIA's Directorate of Operations had to rely almost entirely on Soviets who volunteered to spy, either as recruitments-in-place or as defectors.

"With Soviets, they mostly fall into your hands. You don't recruit them," a former operations officer said.

Weather Balloons

At any given time, the CIA had no more than two dozen assets or agents in the Soviet Union. One of the most important was Adolf G. Tolkachev, a Soviet scientist whose information saved the U.S. Navy billions of dollars by providing the CIA with information that showed that the United States and its allies were moving in the wrong direction in developing systems for detecting and combating Soviet submarines. For many years, Tolkachev left photographs of Soviet military technical plans and specifications every two months in ever-changing CIA drop sites in Moscow. Typically, the film was concealed in fake rocks or dog droppings containing secret compartments ingeniously fashioned by the CIA's Office of Technical Service.

Other key recruitments were Victor I. Sheymov and Aleksandr D. Ogorodnik. Sheymov worked in the KGB's Eighth Chief Directorate, which handles communications intelligence. He defected in 1980 after working for several years as a CIA agent or recruitment-in-place. Ogorodnik, a Soviet diplomat, reported on internal Soviet deliberations. And Vladimir I. Vetrov—who had the cryptonym FAREWELL—reported to Western intelligence services that the Soviets had placed bugs on the printers used by the French intelligence service for communications. That led to closer examination of typewriters used to write sensitive memos at the American embassy in Moscow and the discovery of the same kinds of bugs.

Many other agents recruited by the CIA among Soviets either retired in place or defected without any publicity.

Because it is so difficult to move in Moscow without being detected, CIA officers assigned to Moscow station rarely recruit agents. Instead, they service dead drops for agents who were previously recruited when they traveled overseas or who volunteered while in Moscow. For example, Ogorodnik was enlisted to spy for the CIA when he was based in Venezuela. CIA officers who pick up film or leave money or equipment in dead drops in Moscow often are not the officers assigned to the case. Rather, they are the personnel who seem least subject to Soviet surveillance that day.

When the Cold War was at its peak, the Soviet/East Europe

Division may have seemed to be the most prestigious place to be assigned. But without agents to recruit, CIA officers in Moscow often came out looking second best.

While CIA officers there are merely picking up documents from agents recruited by others, "another guy is recruiting in Africa as if he's picking bananas off a tree. So all these guys are rated in competition with each other. You look and say you have to recruit agents," a former operations officer said.

"The press thinks SE [Soviet/East Europe] Division is more elite," a former officer assigned to the division said. "But there's usually no scramble to join it because of the drawbacks. Most of what [CIA officers do in Moscow] isn't spectacular. They'll service dead drops and walk miles to locate sites."

In most parts of the world, CIA officers use the State Department's political, consular, or economic sections as cover. But to make the KGB's surveillance job more difficult in Moscow, CIA officers are spread through more government agencies there. In Moscow, CIA officers may use as cover the military or the U.S. Information Agency, for example.

The State Department's laxity in maintaining security at the American embassy in Moscow has contributed to the problem. Because the State Department shipped typewriters to the old embassy on Soviet trains and allowed them to remain in Soviet warehouses, the KGB was able to implant bugging devices that transmitted the contents of classified memos to a nearby KGB listening post. The bugs in the typewriters were secreted in a horizontal aluminum bar in the typewriters' casings. The bar had been sliced in half and then resealed so the seam was barely visible. Because the devices were roughly the same density as the typewriters' casings, ordinary X-rays could not detect them.

Routine electronic sweeps of the embassy had not detected the bugs either. The bugs stored data and transmitted it only intermittently. The Soviets controlled when the bugs "dumped" or transmitted information, and they could turn them off when a sweep might be in progress. Moreover, the coded signals used the same frequency as a Moscow television station. When the bugs transmitted, viewers heard momentary static. Since the signals were on the same wavelength as the television station, sweeps of the embassy detected nothing. The Americans found the bugs only by using highly sophisticated scanning devices that bombard material with neutrons.

Meanwhile, the Soviets planted bugs in the new American embassy. They were so ingeniously designed that they were a part of the building structure and could not be removed. A primary purpose of the electronic penetrations was to find out what the CIA was doing so the Soviets could take action against the agency.

Over the years, dozens of CIA officers have been expelled from Moscow for spying. In March 1983, the Soviets declared Richard W. Osborne, a first secretary of the embassy, persona non grata. The Soviets said at the time that they caught him with spy equipment, including radio equipment for "transmitting espionage information via the U.S. Marisat communication satellites."[36] Marisat is the Maritime Communications Satellite system, which is used for commercial and Navy transmissions. The Soviets said they also seized Osborne's "own notes, which were written in a pad made of paper that quickly dissolved in water."

In June 1983, the Soviets expelled Lewis C. Thomas, an attaché and electronics expert, saying they caught him redhanded in a spying operation. In March 1985, they expelled Michael C. Sellers, a second secretary of the embassy. To buttress the case for the expulsion and to embarrass the CIA, *Izvestia* ran a photo of him disguised as a Ukrainian, wearing a false mustache and a wig.[37]

Paul M. Stombaugh, a second secretary, was expelled in June 1985. The Soviets said he had been caught taking documents from Adolf G. Tolkachev, who was later executed by a firing squad.[38] According to Tass, U.S. intelligence agencies had given Tolkachev miniature cameras for photographing secret documents, two-way radios, encoding devices, and special poisons.[39] Tolkachev had been compromised by Edward Lee Howard, a former CIA officer who defected to Moscow after the CIA fired him over drug and alcohol use.

The Soviets have few if any female KGB officers, and they

always seem surprised when the Americans use them. So the CIA has tended to use many women in Moscow. One, Martha Peterson, was expelled in 1977 after she was caught acting as the operations officer for Ogorodnik.

One CIA officer was expelled while testing the RT-804 transmitter, which sends ten thousand characters to satellites in coded bursts that last only a few seconds. The same model had been confiscated by Cuban intelligence several years earlier. The Soviets expelled another CIA officer after he paid off a man who had been sent to Moscow years earlier as a contract employee, then disappeared. The man resurfaced in the early 1980s. He claimed the Soviets had imprisoned him and had set him free after he had served time in prison. Now, he said, he wanted his back salary from the CIA. The CIA decided to make contact with the man, knowing it might be a provocation but feeling obligated to pay him since he had indeed been a CIA agent for many years. But the CIA's loyalties had been misplaced. The man had apparently been working for the Soviets all along. When a CIA officer approached the meeting site with money in hand, the KGB was waiting for him.

The CIA, with the help of NSA, intercepted a variety of civilian and military communications in Moscow. Besides equipment installed on the top floor of the American embassy in Moscow, the CIA used a device planted inside a tree stump outside of Moscow to pick up microwave transmissions and relay them to other receivers. Another device was installed in a sewer and tapped military telephone lines. The Soviets eventually discovered both devices.

While the CIA has always applauded officers who successfully recruit agents overseas, it has tended to treat those who handle defectors as baby-sitters. As a rule, defectors simply walk into an embassy and volunteer themselves. No cunning is required to elicit their cooperation, so no plaudits are handed out to the officers who bring them in and handle them. Yet defectors can provide information just as valuable as agents who remain in place. Because they can be debriefed more leisurely, their information is usually far more comprehensive.

It was these institutional attitudes that contributed to the redefection of Vitaly S. Yurchenko, who was easily the most important KGB officer to defect to the United States. After ninety-three days in the hands of the CIA, Yurchenko returned to the Soviet Union in 1985, claiming he had been kidnapped and drugged. In fact, the CIA had mishandled him, treating him coldly and assigning to him guards from the Office of Security who routinely treated him as a prisoner.[40]

Under William Webster, defector handling was upgraded. In 1990, he appointed a respected intelligence officer from the Soviet/East European Division to head the resettlement center and coordinate debriefing of defectors. With strong backing from Webster, the officer took charge of defector-handling and doubled the size of the defector handling staff to sixty employees, including clerical personnel. The staff now includes a full-time psychiatrist and a full-time psychologist to help defectors adjust. A financial adviser has been added to help defectors with the management of their funds. Each defector is now given two weeks of instruction in American life. A senior officer keeps in touch with chief executive officers of major corporations in order to place defectors in jobs.

Because of all the difficulties associated with recruiting agents in Moscow, some of the most fruitful operations directed against the Soviet Union have taken place in other countries. While these operations are carried out by local stations, they are coordinated by the Soviet/East Europe Division within the Directorate of Operations. SE Division is divided into four main groups: the CI Group, which is responsible for counterintelligence matters; the Internal Operations Group, which focuses on operations within the Soviet bloc; the External Operations Group, which focuses on Soviet-bloc activities elsewhere in the world; and the Reports Group, which processes intelligence reporting on the Soviet Union. In addition, a Support Branch oversees security, office furnishings, equipment, and personnel matters. A member of the staff of the chief of SE division is in charge of covert action—mainly publishing of books and other press material within the Soviet Union. The books are not traceable to the CIA.

A key goal of the Soviet/East Europe Division has been acquisition of Soviet military equipment, which may be uncovered in the most unlikely places. For example, when the Soviets left Ghana in 1966, they abandoned equipment that the CIA obtained. For a decade, the agency also procured some of the latest Soviet weaponry through the family of the late Romanian dictator Nicolae Ceausescu.[41]

The Defense Department publishes a classified list of Soviet equipment and parts it would like to obtain, including whole airplanes. Next to each listing is the price the department would be willing to pay. In tasking agents, the CIA can then quote the price tags for each item. Because of this program, the CIA was able to obtain Soviet missiles during the Vietnam War and design ways to beam false signals to disrupt their guidance systems.

By knowing what the other side was doing, the CIA was able to provide successive administrations with information that enabled the U.S. to initiate defensive measures and also dispelled fears that might have led to preemptive strikes.

"The success was there was no war. That was the biggest success, that deterrence actually worked," Edward W. Proctor, who was deputy director for intelligence from 1971 to 1976, said.[42]

As the Cold War ended and the Soviet Union and the U.S. inched toward being friends rather than foes, the CIA began to shift its resources from the Soviet/East Europe Division into other areas. To coordinate these new priorities, the CIA established special centers to focus the efforts of all the directorates on the latest international problems—terrorism and narcotics.

7 | *New Targets*

WHEN FBI AGENTS ARRESTED FAWAZ YOUNIS, A LEBANESE terrorist who had hijacked a plane at Beirut International Airport, it looked like another coup for the bureau. Younis, a used-car dealer who reported directly to the leadership of the Shiite Amal militia, had commandeered a Royal Jordanian jet on June 11, 1985. He brutalized its armed guards and demanded that the plane fly him and his henchmen to Tunis so he could deliver a message to a meeting of the Arab League. When the plane was denied landing privileges, Younis had the pilots fly him back to Beirut. After allowing the passengers to leave, Younis had his fellow terrorists blow the plane up as he read a ringing statement on the need to expel Palestinians from Lebanon, his embattled homeland. Three Americans were among the passengers who were released unharmed.

Two years later, the FBI arrested Younis after he had been lured to an eighty-one-foot yacht off the coast of Cyprus. Not revealed at the time was the fact that the CIA had enticed Younis onto the boat in the first place.

The CIA's involvement was made possible by a classified intelligence directive, known as a "finding," signed by President Reagan in January 1986. It authorized the CIA to identify terrorists who had committed crimes against Americans abroad and help bring them to the U.S. for trial. The action resulted from a recommendation by a task force under the direction of then vice president George Bush. A few months later, Congress passed legislation giving the FBI authority to investigate all terrorist acts against Americans and to go after those responsible, no matter where.

That same year, CIA Director William Casey established a counterterrorism center. Its purpose was to bring together each of the agency's directorates to deal with terrorism and to coordinate the CIA's efforts with other federal agencies. Since then, three other centers have been established: one to combat narcotics, one to direct counterintelligence, and a third nonproliferation center to coordinate intelligence on the spread of nuclear weapons and delivery systems. While the centers are housed within the CIA's Directorate of Intelligence or, in the case of the counterintelligence center, in the Directorate of Operations, they are considered to be intelligence community activities that coordinate with the dozen other intelligence agencies in the government. Under the U.S. intelligence system, the director of Central Intelligence coordinates the work and submits the budgets of each agency within the intelligence community.

The first director of the counterterrorism center was Dewey Clarridge, a flamboyant CIA operations officer given to smoking large cigars and working sixteen-hour days. It was the Counterterrorism Center, under Clarridge's direction, that lured Younis into the trap. The instrument for that scheme was Jamal Hamdan. Originally a Drug Enforcement Administration informant, Hamdan knew Younis, and in March 1987, the CIA began paying him to renew their friendship.

Over the next seven months, the two men had nearly sixty phone conversations and meetings—most of them recorded by the CIA. Obligingly, Younis detailed his complicity in the hijacking for his friend. In one such encounter in Hamdan's high-rise apartment in Cyprus, Younis confided, "I got inside, and I locked the plane's captain in the cockpit. The people were on the floor, their hands on their heads—everyone, no exceptions. I got a stewardess and asked her about the security men. There were eight. I took their neckties and tied their hands behind their backs. . . . We started beating them. We took four machine guns and eight pistols from [them]. We kept them tied up forty-eight hours."[43]

Under CIA direction, Hamdan conned Younis into thinking he could make him rich. At one point, he lent him $4,000. Finally, he told him he would introduce him to a drug dealer named "Joseph." Younis, who was then unemployed, had two young sons to support. He could not wait.

Hamdan arranged for Younis to meet him in Cyprus on September 11 at the Sheraton Hotel in Limassol, Cyprus. On the morning of September 13, they took a speedboat from the hotel marina. After ninety minutes, they were in international waters. It was then that they boarded a yacht called *Skunk Kilo,* supplied by the Pentagon. Two attractive women—both FBI agents—were lounging on the deck. But instead of introducing Younis to "Joseph," two other FBI agents kicked Younis's feet from under him and slammed him to the deck. Younis landed on both his wrists, breaking them. FBI special agent Dimitry Droujinsky, who spoke Arabic fluently, informed Younis that he was being arrested for a terrorist act against American citizens and would be taken to the United States for trial.

Younis was convicted of conspiracy, hostage taking, and air piracy. He is serving a term of thirty years at Leavenworth federal penitentiary in Kansas.[44]

Well before the CIA established a counterterrorism center in 1986, the agency had been involved in combating the problem. For example, seven South Moluccan terrorists, armed with explosives, a carbine, pistol, and knives, took over the Indonesian consulate in Amsterdam on December 4, 1976. Demanding that the Dutch government recognize the nonexistent Republic of South Molucca in Indonesia, they took hostage twenty-one children who were attending school that day in the building, along with fifteen others. The terrorists lined a room with explosives. They threatened to blow up the hostages. The Amsterdam police decided they would only storm the embassy if any hostages were shot.

Meanwhile, with the consent of the Dutch government, the CIA dispatched a technician who crawled through a sewer pipe and into the embassy's basement. There, he planted a listening device in a wall so the CIA could eavesdrop on the terrorists. Several days later, a gun went off inside the embassy. The police were about to storm the building, which would have meant many of the hostages would have been killed. But the listening device picked up the fact that one of the terrorists had accidentally dropped his gun, and it had gone off. The police waited out the terrorists. After fifteen days, they finally gave up. Each was sentenced to six years in jail. Because the CIA had known what was going on inside the embassy, no lives were lost.

Operating from the sixth floor of the old CIA building in McLean, the counterterrorism center today has some two hundred CIA employees. In addition, ten people are detailed from other agencies, including the FBI, NSA, the Federal Aviation Administration, and the Defense Department. Among other things, the center lists terrorist organizations and threats on a computer system available to other government agencies. Known as Desist, the system is manned twenty-four hours a day.

The counterterrorism center coordinated the government's investigation of the destruction of Pan Am 103, the plane that exploded four days before Christmas, 1988, over Lockerbie, Scotland, killing all 259 passengers and crew members on board. With the help of other agencies and countries, the CIA determined that high-ranking Libyan officials, including the brother-in-law of Libyan leader Muammar Qaddafi, ordered the bombing of that plane and a French jumbo jet that exploded in midair in 1989. The bombings were believed to be in retaliation for the 1986 bombing of Tripoli by U.S. warplanes.[45]

In preventing terrorism, the counterterrorism center operates behind the scenes. If a known terrorist is traveling, the

CIA passes the word to each country on his itinerary. The countries either refuse to allow the terrorist to enter or if he is a fugitive, have him arrested. The CIA's role rarely comes out.

Several years ago, the CIA proposed to the State Department that it threaten to expose the fact that countries such as Hungary were helping to subsidize the operations of Abu Nidal's terrorist organization by allowing it to set up companies that traded with Hungary. It later turned out that Hungary had also given refuge to an international terrorist known as Carlos in 1979. The State Department agreed to the plan, which entailed drawing up a "white paper" detailing Hungary's complicity. The plan worked.

"We discovered we had a new weapon—the threat of publicity," a former State Department official said. "In every case, it worked. . . . We got cooperation."

"We've taken terrorism from the late 1970s, when there were more than one hundred incidents a year, with several casualties and deaths, to the point where it is *de minimis* domestically, including foreign groups operating in the U.S.," Oliver (Buck) Revell, a former associate deputy director of the FBI, said.[46] This is due, in part, to the counterterrorism center.

The coordinated approach has been so successful that William Webster set up two additional centers, one to combat narcotics and one to coordinate counterintelligence. A third center to combat proliferation began in September 1991, under Acting CIA Director Richard J. Kerr. Headed originally by Howard Hart, a ruddy-faced former operations officer, the counternarcotics center consists of several hundred CIA employees who work in windowless offices in the basement of the new CIA headquarters building. The staff includes photo interpreters, political analysts, operations officers, and technicians. In addition, representatives of each intelligence organization and federal law enforcement agency in the government are detailed to the center for two-year terms.

The center collects information about narcotics trafficking so it can be used by law enforcement agencies to help obtain arrests and convictions. With the aid of satellites, the center tracks drug shipments on the high seas and pinpoints laboratories and fields where the coca and other drug-related plants are grown. It then passes the information to local law enforcement agencies so they can take action. Until the Gulf War, the counternarcotics center was one of the largest users of satellite time in the CIA.

Like the other two centers, the CIA's counterintelligence center is a community-wide function. Originally headed by Gardner R. (Gus) Hathaway, a former chief of the Soviet/ East Europe Division and a former Moscow station chief, it concentrates on countering efforts by hostile intelligence services to thwart and penetrate the CIA within the U.S. and particularly overseas. Its function overlaps to some degree with the Office of Security, which is charged with protecting the agency and its secrets.

Within the modern CIA, the approach that James Angleton brought to counterintelligence is a bad memory. There is a misconception that counterintelligence officers need to be a different breed—suspicious to the point of being paranoid. Often, this outlook is referred to as a "counterintelligence mentality." This is pure malarkey. People who catch spies need to be no more and no less suspicious than people who catch murderers, bank robbers, or white-collar criminals. To be effective, any professional investigator must bring a balanced approach to his job.

Angleton's paranoiac mind-set cast a pall on efforts to use information from defectors. At the same time, he created suspicions about anyone who had anything to do with Soviets, damaging the CIA's efforts to recruit agents. Angleton refused to believe that there was a split between the Chinese Communists and the Soviets even after soldiers from both sides had killed each other. He insisted on believing Anatoliy M. Golytsin, a KGB officer who defected in 1961, when all the evidence showed that Golytsin tailored his stories to suit Angleton's preconceptions.

Angleton was convinced that debriefing defectors would somehow contaminate the CIA by revealing the agency's secrets. In fact, the questions asked of defectors are what anyone would expect to be asked, based on the defector's status and access. They give away no secrets at all. The fact that the CIA asks a defector if there are any moles in the agency, for example, does not necessarily mean the CIA has a clue that one actually exists.*

According to Tom Mangold's *Cold Warrior,* Angleton sat on tips about major spies in foreign countries because they came from an FBI source code-named NICK NACK rather than from his favorite defector, Golytsin. NICK NACK was an officer with the GRU, Soviet military intelligence, who had temporarily been posted to New York and other locations in the early 1960s and again in the early 1970s.

When Angleton's successors uncovered the files years later, NICK NACK's tips led to the arrests of former Swiss air defense chief Jean-Louis Jeanmaire in 1976, and in 1978 of members of a spy ring in France led by Serge Fabiew. Because the FBI immediately passed some of NICK NACK's information directly to the British, his leads had already led to the conviction of Frank Bossard, a former British Royal Air Force officer working as an engineer in guided-missile research in the Air Ministry of the War Department.[47]

If any other CIA officer or FBI agent had suppressed such information, he would almost certainly have been fired and would probably have faced a criminal investigation as well.

Beyond his ineptitude, Angleton presided over some of the worst abuses later exposed by the Church Committee, including the CIA's programs for opening mail between the U.S. and Soviet-bloc countries and for compiling files on dissident Americans. Besides exceeding the CIA's charter, neither of these programs ever developed any information of any value: no Soviet spies were ever uncovered as a result. Nor did the CIA find any foreign involvement in the antiwar movement during the 1960s. Much of what Angleton did was not only a waste of time, it was foolish. For example, after *Ramparts* exposed in 1967 that the CIA was funding the National

---

* *Mole* is a popular term that refers to an intelligence officer who penetrates an opposing intelligence service, usually having already worked there.

Student Association, Angleton prepared lengthy analyses of the themes in *Ramparts* articles.

In an attachment to a memo he sent to the FBI, Angleton wrote that the magazine had hardened "from a New Left organ to an outlet for standard Soviet propaganda." He based this on the percentage of times certain themes appeared in the magazine's articles—how many times they said the United States was "sick," for example; how many times they said the present U.S. government was fascistic; how many times the magazine said the Catholic Church was reactionary and hierarchical; and how many times the publication said the FBI and CIA were "evil."[48]

The fact is, for all the harm Angleton did by closing off potential sources of information, ignoring tips, abusing the rights of Americans, and unfairly accusing CIA employees of consorting with the enemy, Angleton never did catch a spy. During Angleton's tenure, Karl Koecher, a Czech intelligence service officer, became a CIA employee and was given sensitive translating tasks. It was Koecher who compromised Aleksandr D. Ogorodnik, a high-ranking Soviet diplomat then working for the CIA. Yet Angleton never had a clue about this major spy case within his own agency.

The author interviewed Angleton in April 1987, a month before he died, and brought up the subject of Koecher. All along, there really *had* been a mole in the CIA, one who had been hired a year before Angleton was forced to retire and who had later done great damage to the agency. While totally lucid, Angleton showed no interest in the case. For Angleton, it seemed, it had all been a game: Koecher was not the mole he was seeking. Since he was not *his* mole, Koecher was of little interest to him.[49]

Before the Church Committee hearings, the CIA underwent little outside scrutiny and could easily lose sight of its mission. Operations took on a life of their own, and art was pursued for art's sake. Angleton was a prime example of that danger—an amateur who was allowed by a string of CIA directors to wreak havoc within the agency. In contrast, the FBI is held accountable by the courts when it develops an espionage case against a suspect. That means it must deal in the real world of evidence and facts, and the goal is always clear—to put spies in jail. Before a case ever gets to court, it is reviewed by the Justice Department. In the face of outside scrutiny, an amateur is quickly detected.

When he became CIA director, William Colby realized Angleton was doing far more harm than good.

"You will now leave, period," Colby told Angleton in December 1974.[50] Angleton died on May 11, 1987.

For all his faults, Angleton was a brilliant, gracious man, a poet and a grower of orchids, who still has a following among some retired CIA officers of his era. His greatest contribution was obtaining through Shin Bet, Israel's domestic security agency, Nikita Khrushchev's secret speech in 1956 denouncing Joseph Stalin for his criminal cruelty and misgovernment.[51] But within the modern CIA, Angleton has virtually no defenders.

"I think there were a number of things done under Angleton that should not have been done," a recently retired operations officer said. "Watching students, keeping lists of names, opening mail. He ran his own little world and got away with it somehow."

Counterintelligence under Angleton was "more of a suspicion-building program rather than a shield, which it should be and which it certainly is today," William Webster said at a final breakfast meeting with reporters who cover intelligence, just after he announced his retirement from the CIA in 1991.[52]

But it would be unfair to single out Angleton for blame. Most of the abuses he engaged in had been approved by CIA directors at the time and even attorneys general of the U.S. Nor was counterintelligence the only area where those abuses occurred.

8 | The Rogue Elephant

On June 17, 1972, burglars broke into Democratic National Committee headquarters at the Watergate office building in Washington. A security guard called the District police, who promptly arrested the burglars. As their story unraveled, it turned out most of the participants in the break-in had some sort of CIA connection. James McCord had retired from the CIA's Office of Security in 1970. E. Howard Hunt had retired the same year from the CIA's Directorate of Operations. Bernard Barker had been recruited by the CIA when he was in the Cuban police, and he later worked for Hunt when Hunt was in the CIA. He stopped working for the agency in 1966. Eugenio R. Martinez had been a CIA contract employee and was still on the CIA's payroll when the break-in occurred.[53]

As it turned out, the CIA knew nothing about the break-in. But the connections to the agency fueled suspicions that the agency was out of control. Because of the growing mistrust of the government because of its handling of the Vietnam

War, these suspicions received more credence than they might otherwise have. The suspicions had begun in 1967, when *Ramparts* magazine revealed that the CIA had been providing funds to the National Student Association. The money was to be used to help the student group prevent takeovers of international youth organizations by communists. Unlike opening mail and infiltrating dissident groups, supplying money to domestic organizations was not a direct violation of the CIA's charter. Supporting an American organization did not mean the CIA was engaging in "internal security functions." But the funding did raise the specter of the agency trying to influence America rather than the overseas targets it was supposed to sway. Moreover, it raised suspicions both in the eyes of foreigners and of Americans that U.S. institutions might have dual allegiances—one to their directors or trustees and one to the CIA.

In the long run, the broader corruption of American institutions posed a greater threat to American freedoms than whether communists gained a foothold in an international youth organization. Ultimately, it was America's image as a land of freedom that was most effective in influencing nations torn between communist and democratic factions.

In response to the *Ramparts* exposé, President Johnson appointed a three-man committee headed by former attorney general Nicholas de B. Katzenbach to look into the problem. It recommended that such funding be cut off. Presidents have since specifically reaffirmed the policy.

Later Watergate investigations revealed even more troubling links to the CIA. The CIA had supplied Howard Hunt with a wig, a camera, a speech-altering device, and false identification papers, including a driver's license, to be used during Hunt's break-in at the offices of Dr. Lewis J. Fielding, Daniel Ellsberg's former psychiatrist, in September 1971. The Nixon White House had ordered the illegal break-in to learn more about Ellsberg's involvement in leaking the Pentagon Papers to the *New York Times*.

Then President Nixon tried to use the CIA to cover up White House connections with the Watergate break-in. His aides summoned Richard Helms, then the CIA director, to the White House. They told him that Nixon wanted him to call L. Patrick Gray, the acting director of the FBI, and tell him not to pursue some of the leads arising out of the Watergate break-in because they might reveal CIA operations or sources. Helms told the aides the story was not true, and he refused. Nixon then eased him out of the CIA, sending him to Iran to be ambassador.[54]

In his inept fashion, Nixon replaced Helms with James R. Schlesinger, who was not about to participate in any cover-ups. The revelation of the CIA's peripheral involvement in the break-in at the office of Ellsberg's psychiatrist infuriated Schlesinger. To make sure no other improper activities were going on, he issued an order in May 1973, drafted by Colby, then the CIA's deputy director for operations, ordering employees of the CIA to report any suspicions they had that laws or the agency's charter had been violated. The result was what came to be referred to as the "family jewels"—693 single-spaced typewritten pages, with each page or two devoted to a possible infraction.

After he had been nominated to replace Schlesinger as CIA director, Colby turned the list over to Congress, convinced that this was the proper way to handle the matter. Consistent with their hear-no-evil, see-no-evil approach, the committee chairmen with whom he discussed the "jewels" decided to keep it all quiet.

"There was a general consensus that these matters of the past should be left in the past in order that the agency could continue to do its positive work in the present and future," Colby wrote in his autobiography, *Honorable Men*.[55]

But a year and a half later, Seymour Hersh of the *New York Times* got wind of the story. In an effort to put it in perspective, Colby met with Hersh and wound up confirming the gist of what Hersh had developed independently about the abuses. Hersh's front-page December 22, 1974, story, headlined, "Huge CIA Operation Reported in U.S. Against Anti-War Forces, Other Dissidents in Nixon Years," opened up the CIA to two years of investigations and turmoil. While many of the items turned out not to be violations or to be insignificant, the "jewels" contained enough dynamite to forever change the CIA and the way it does business.

According to the documents and the later investigations, the CIA had begun a program in 1952 of surveying mail to and from the Soviet Union. In 1953, it began opening some of this mail in violation of federal statutes. By 1973, the CIA was examining 2.3 million pieces of mail a year, photographing 33,000 envelopes, and opening 8,700 of them.

In 1967, the CIA established a Special Operations Group within the agency to report on domestic dissidents. The program, aptly called Operation CHAOS, resulted in the accumulation of 13,000 files, including ones on 7,200 American citizens. The documents in the files included the names of 300,000 American citizens and organizations. They had all been gathered as part of an internal security function, exactly what the 1947 act establishing the CIA had forbidden.

A third major area of abuse was the CIA's program for testing drugs to control behavior on unwitting victims, a violation of criminal laws. Frank E. Olson, an Army civilian scientist, committed suicide on September 28, 1953, after the CIA had given him LSD without his knowledge.[56] The CIA officer in charge of the experiment had not checked medical records and was not aware that Olson had had suicidal tendencies over the previous five years.[57]

Finally, the CIA imprisoned Yuri I. Nosenko, the KGB major who defected to the U.S. in 1964, for three and a half years simply because the agency did not believe his story that the KGB had nothing to do with the assassination of John F. Kennedy.

"That frightened me more than anything else, the idea that an intelligence agency could secretly hold a man in prison. Habeas corpus stopped that several centuries ago," Colby said.[58]

As if the illegalities were not bad enough, the ineptitude of many of the operations was astonishing. The agency's many failed assassination attempts against Castro, its mad effort to enlist the aid of the Mafia, and its foolish attempts to embarrass Castro were prime examples.

The exposure of the agency's activities became a watershed,

one that led to a rigorous system of oversight by Congress and generally tightened procedures within the agency to insure that it stayed within the law. Until then, subcommittees of the Senate and House armed services and appropriations committees had passed on CIA legislation. In practice, during much of the CIA's early existence, the chairmen and a few other senior members of the two committees formed an ad hoc oversight committee that made all the key decisions. They took the position that the less they knew about the CIA's operations, the better.[59]

Hersh's exposé led to appointment of a president's commission chaired by Vice President Nelson A. Rockefeller to look into the abuses, an investigation in the Senate led by Sen. Frank Church, and a third, more partisan probe in the House led by Rep. Otis Pike, a New York Democrat. At the height of the probes, the Church Committee had 155 staff members looking into the CIA and other intelligence agencies.

"Before that [the Church investigation], supervision was virtually nonexistent," Robert R. Simmons, a former staff director of the Senate Select Committee on Intelligence, said. "They didn't want to be responsible for it. I consider that a failure of the Congress. If the Congress had acted sooner to extend its authority over this, some of those problems may never have occurred."[60]

"Part of the problem in the early days was the oversight committees, particularly the chairmen, who were interested in the agency being as anonymous as possible, and they made this very clear," Helms agreed. "As a matter of fact, on one occasion after he became chairman of the Armed Services Committee . . . Senator Stennis said, 'You're doing a great job at the agency. I haven't seen your name in the paper in six months.' That was his idea that you should be quiet about it."[61]

Yet the CIA nearly always had partners in these bizarre activities—a president or a cabinet officer. The program to collect files on dissidents had been undertaken under pressure from President Johnson. Attorney General John Mitchell and three postmasters general had been informed of the program to open mail. President Kennedy or then attorney general Robert F. Kennedy had either authorized or been informed of the efforts against Castro.

"All I know is Jack Kennedy and his brother were bound and determined to have us take on this effort [to get rid of Castro]," Helms said. "If you want me to take off my jacket and show you the beatings I got over that, I'd be glad to. In retrospect, it was undoubtedly a mistake; it was feckless. But they insisted that this go on."[62]

Likewise, both Johnson and Nixon ordered the CIA to become involved in investigating dissidents.

"Johnson was absolutely convinced that there was foreign money and influence that caused all this student unrest," Helms said. "No matter how you talked to him about this, he was convinced. Nixon was convinced in much the same way. They couldn't understand that there wasn't foreign involvement. That was how this whole thing started, to find out if this was true."

Many of those involved in the questionable activities still defend them.

"Supporting NSA [the National Student Association] was the right thing to do overall," Cord Meyer, a former CIA officer who directed the operation, said. "If it breeds mistrust, you have to make a choice between them. Either you are going to try to compete abroad or just hope for the best."[63]

Richard Bissell, who oversaw the student operation as deputy director for operations, said, "That was a highly successful operation to combat communist-funded groups. It was not only justified but quite effective. Today I would approve of it, although it is much less necessary. It would have to be done in a different way, but I would like to see that capability reconstructed."[64]

Perhaps the best case for the present system of oversight was made unknowingly by Bissell, who directed the abortive 1961 Bay of Pigs invasion of Cuba as deputy director for operations. Arguing against congressional approval of covert action such as the Bay of Pigs, Bissell said that "the need for congressional notification has a suffocating effect. You have to tailor the mission to them and their staffs."

If that is true, would not the devastating failure and loss of lives at the Bay of Pigs have been avoided if congressional approval had been required?

"If we had had to do that in the Bay of Pigs, I suspect the operation would have been called off," Bissell acknowledged. "You could say we would be ahead, but you would do better to cancel every third operation on the principle that that way you will save some grief. You can't run an organization on that assumption."[65]

Bissell's response is telling. It illuminates the real reason for the failure at the Bay of Pigs—arrogance. By Bissell's reasoning, only CIA officers know what is good for the country. Elected officials may be the representatives of the people, but they have no business questioning the judgment of the CIA.

"Dickie Bissell was confident the agency could do anything," John A. Bross, a longtime CIA hand, said.[66]

"In the old days, if something was doable, it often was tried. Short-term success was all they looked for," Russell J. Bowen, a retired CIA analyst who continues to consult for the agency, said. "The fact short-term success could be long-term failure was not important to them. Guatemala was touted as a success. But Guatemala has had an unstable government ever since."[67]

As might be expected, CIA officers were stung by the investigations and resented them. To many CIA officers involved in the abuses, William Colby was a traitor for helping to make the "jewels" public.

"It had always been our understanding," Helms said, "that as long as we were testifying properly and in detail to the oversight committees, that this stuff would remain secret. So when the Church Committee hearings came along, it seemed to many of us that this was a betrayal of the understanding we had."

"Some people disagreed with my handling of it," Colby later recalled. "Some think it was the only way. A lot of people wish it hadn't happened. So do I," Colby said, meaning he wished the CIA had never engaged in the activities he felt he had to bring to light.[68]

"The CIA's activities ten or twenty years earlier were being judged by the Church Committee based on criteria established ten or twenty years later in a political atmosphere," Edward W. Proctor, a former CIA deputy director for intelligence, said. "Church was running for president, the House committee staff was a bunch of clowns. The Senate staff had some good people who were looking for the truth, while others were looking to make a name for themselves."[69]

"It [the CIA] becomes a very tight, small family," Robert Simmons, a former CIA officer who later became staff director of the Senate Select Committee on Intelligence, said. "When you go overseas, you're in a hardship post at risk. You value the support you get from your own people. So you develop an 'us against them' mentality. When you see Church holding up a pistol and saying, 'Look at what the CIA is doing,' you say, 'Screw him.' "[70]

What most infuriated CIA officers was Church's assertion —later retracted—that the agency was a "rogue elephant." They pointed to the fact that nearly all the abuses had been approved by presidents or cabinet officers at the time. Moreover, most of the abuses had been stopped by the time of the committee hearings. The picture that most sticks in people's minds is a photo of Church grimly holding up a poison-dart gun found at the CIA. The fact that it had never been used and had been brought to the attention of the committee by the CIA after it had been found never caught up with the picture. And because it appeared in CIA files, a description of an Army experiment to see how fast poison would spread in the New York City subway system created the impression the CIA had been running through the subways spreading poison.[71]

"I never believed it was a rogue elephant," William G. Miller, who was staff director of the Church Committee and later of the Senate Select Committee on Intelligence, said. "We had a dispute about that. Church was convinced it was. I did not. I felt White Houses knew this [the abuses] all the way through.

"He came to a judgment before all the evidence was in," Miller said. "He made that comment after looking at several crazy cases, in which there were runaway characters. But that wasn't the general pattern. In a sense he is right, because there were cases where cowboys ran things and were out of control. But there were very few."

As for the fact that most of the abuses had stopped, "that was not the issue, at least not for me or for most of the senators," Miller said. "The question was how to prevent it. What were the results, what should we do for the future?"[72]

In contrast to the attitudes of those involved in the abuses, CIA officers in today's agency for the most part condemn the abuses of the past as being both unnecessary and foolish. Even when they were going on, most CIA officers were not involved in them and knew nothing about them.

Citing the plan to portray an image of Christ over Cuba, Herbert Saunders, a former CIA officer, said, "I suppose there have always been crackpots around who think good intelligence work consists of some puerile attempts to embarrass Castro. However, I don't think that anybody would give you two cents for that approach now. In the modern world of intelligence, there is less interest in gimmicks and more in painstaking intelligence work by the traditional methods. It's a matter of being confident in your ability."

"The agency became very depressed because the information within the agency became public," John McMahon, a former CIA deputy director of operations under Casey, said. "It was the first time a lot of the employees knew some of the things that the agency did. This . . . screwing around with the drugs just everybody abhorred.

"The agency deserved to be chastised over that crap," McMahon said. "Even though it was just a handful of people in the agency who did it, and they're a bunch of jerks, the fact is that the atmosphere permitted it. That's why I'm a great proponent of oversight. Oversight is the greatest protection for the agency because it precludes these things from happening."

As one might expect, most of the abuses had occurred in the Directorate of Operations, the clandestine service devoted to breaking the laws of other countries. This raised the question of whether people who choose to be spies could ever be trusted to obey the law in this country.

"Evangelists do not necessarily do well in the CIA," Saunders said. "The nature of the work may require that you go overseas and break the law—foreign law, not American law. You may have to cheat and steal and tell some lies about working for some funky organization other than the CIA. It can be a pretty schizophrenic existence, and not everyone can keep their marbles rolling right."

But the best officers keep it all in perspective.

"They may spend the good part of the day trying to figure out how to spirit the code cards out of the local Soviet embassy, but when the sun goes down, they punch out and take the wife and kids to the movies," Saunders said. "Those who don't punch out sometimes find it is more than they can handle.[73]

"I don't think anybody in the CIA ever had a problem with responsible scrutiny and regulation," Saunders said. "The problem is irresponsible scrutiny. The winks and nods and tacit approvals: 'I don't want to hear these things. Don't tell me this. I need to deny any knowledge.' Yet when an operation goes awry, these very same people turn on you."

Despite all the abuses, "probably the CIA as an organization has fewer criminal indictments than any other branch of the government, certainly fewer than Congress," Thomas Polgar, a former CIA officer, said. "Day in and day out, the level of morality in the agency, particularly in the clandestine service where there are opportunities to do otherwise, has been quite high."[74]

Simmons, the former staff director of the Senate Select Committee on Intelligence and a former CIA officer himself, said the CIA never was a rogue elephant.

"What you had was an elephant taking orders from the White House," he said. "The president and his men were instructing the elephant. The CIA also generated ideas. If a clandestine organization is tasked by the president to come up with a solution to a problem, there is a tendency to say, 'Let's do something.' "

For most Americans who lived through the hearings in 1975

and 1976, the revelations of assassination plots and attempts to remove Castro's beard are their only picture of the CIA and what it is all about. Because the agency operates in secret, they have no way of knowing of the changes that have taken place.

"I think the first thing that's important to recognize is the generational change in the agency," said Robert M. Gates, deputy director of Central Intelligence under Webster and Casey and later director of Central Intelligence. "The bulk of the people that founded the agency and were around for its so-called halcyon days for the most part had retired by the mid to late 1970s.

"The result is that today only a quarter of the agency worked there before the Church Committee. So what you have is a whole new generation of employees and managers who have grown up in the agency in an atmosphere of both intense public scrutiny of the agency and an environment of congressional oversight. I think this group of people has grown up very much accepting of congressional oversight," Gates said.[75]

Today, as a result of the Church Committee hearings, the CIA and other intelligence organizations come under the jurisdiction of House and Senate select committees on intelligence. The Senate committee has fifteen members and forty staff members, including twenty-five professionals, who concentrate on particular subjects or geographic areas. The majority and minority members have access to the same information and the same staff members.

Staff members receive briefings from CIA officers in room SH 219 of the Hart Office Building, around the corner from the committee. An unmarked door opens into a foyer guarded by a member of the Capitol Hill police. Only members or staff of the committee are allowed any farther. If they bring visitors, the visitors must sign in.

. Inside is one of the most secure installations in the U.S. government—a bugproof, soundproof chamber that would give the wiliest KGB bugging expert a run for his money. Protected by vaulted doors, it is a room within a room, raised so that all sides can be inspected for bugs. Made of steel, the room prevents any electromagnetic waves from entering or leaving. Even the electrical supply is filtered electronically to prevent any signal emanations.

The inner room is divided into smaller rooms where CIA and National Security Agency briefers drop the biggest secrets in Washington. There is also a hearing room where the senators take closed testimony. It has mauve chairs and a map of the world over the horseshoe-shaped desk where the senators sit.

The witness desk is outfitted with a public address system, but it was not loud enough to make former CIA director William J. Casey's muttering audible, so the committee installed a separate system just for Casey. It allowed senators to plug in earphones and turn up the volume. But it did no good—those who knew him say Casey was perfectly understandable, but only when he wanted to be heard—and the system is not now used.

The House committee is largely a mirror image of the Senate committee, except that it has a staff for the minority party and one for the majority party. The House committee has nineteen members and twenty-two staff members, including fourteen professionals. In addition to passing on everything the Senate committee approves, the House committee approves the budget for tactical intelligence and related activities by the military. Known as TIARA, this amounts to $11 billion a year.

The committees receive all of the CIA's finished products such as the National Intelligence Estimates and the National Intelligence Daily. Occasionally, staff members visit Langley to look at raw files, as the Senate committee did during an investigation of the CIA's activities in El Salvador. The Senate committee has three certified public accountants who examine the books of the agencies.

Generally, the Senate committee holds as many as eighteen budget hearings each year on what is known as the national foreign intelligence budget—some $18.3 billion a year. Of that sum, the CIA receives $3.2 billion. The greatest allocation—$6.2 billion—goes to the National Reconnaissance Office, which is in charge of developing satellites. The next highest sum of $3.9 billion goes to NSA. Together with tactical collection, the total spent for intelligence by the U.S. government is $29.3 billion a year.[76]

In addition to budget hearings, the committees hold hearings on subjects like the Soviet Union or particular problems, such as the poor security at the old American embassy in Moscow. Sometimes, the committees' best information comes from the press, as happened when *Al Shiraa,* a Lebanese magazine, reported on November 3, 1986, that then national security adviser Robert McFarlane had accompanied a shipment of U.S. arms to Iran, opening up the Iran-contra scandal.

Under the 1974 Hughes-Ryan Amendment, a presidential finding declaring it is in the national interest had to precede any covert action. Each covert action had to be reported in "timely fashion" to the Senate and House committees. In 1980, Congress amended the National Security Act of 1947 to add a new section on oversight of intelligence activities. Under that section, the CIA had to keep the two intelligence committees informed of "significant anticipated intelligence activity," which would include any unusual and especially sensitive intelligence gathering in friendly countries. In 1991, Congress passed new legislation that added more precise definitions and safeguards to the reporting requirements. It also broadened the requirements to cover any U.S. government entity, including the National Security Council.

In practice, the CIA informs the committees of any important events—covert action and unusual intelligence operations—within forty-eight hours. Most spying in friendly countries is not considered unusual and therefore is not reported. Only rarely do congressional committees learn identities of assets or agents, and then it is usually when one has gone bad and created problems.

Until William Webster became director of Central Intelligence, the committees rejected a covert action at least once a year, usually when it had something to do with supporting candidates in elections in foreign countries. One or both of the committees then wrote a letter to the president. If the president insists on going ahead with a plan, either of the committees can stop the funding for the project. More recently, the committees—while never enthusiastic about covert action—have almost never rejected a proposal.

Looking into requests for covert action takes up 30 percent to 40 percent of the time of the Senate Select Committee on Intelligence, according to former staff director Robert R. Simmons.

"Covert action is a high-profile item for congressional oversight," he said. "Does that mean mistakes can't be made? No. But it is politically charged. It is budgeted on a line-item basis."

When Casey was director of Central Intelligence, the CIA engaged in covert action without obtaining a presidential finding in order to carry out the Iran-contra scheme. A year after arms had been shipped to Iran, Casey, at the insistence of his deputy, John McMahon, asked President Reagan to issue a finding. That finding authorized the sales retroactively. The finding specified that Congress was not to be told about it. John Poindexter, the national security adviser at the time, testified that he destroyed the only copy of the December 1985 finding, to save the president political embarrassment.[77]

The CIA had come full circle from the days of the Church Committee hearings. Again it had violated the law by acceding to pressure from the White House. Again it had gotten itself into trouble by not informing Congress of its activities.

"In intelligence, you have to lie, cheat, and steal to get the truth," Simmons, the former staff director of the Senate Select Committee on Intelligence, said. "The reason is it is for your national security. But it must stop when you are dealing with your own government. Sometimes it didn't. Some of them treated Congress as they would a foreign country.[78]

"If you read the Constitution, which many of those people have never done, they would find the founding fathers described the powers of the legislature first," Simmons said.

But this time, there was a difference. In the Iran-contra affair, Congress was not at fault for not wanting to hear about it. And this time the CIA's role in the arms sales and the diversion of profits to the contra rebels was that of expediter. Both Casey and Oliver North knew that they could not get the CIA itself to arrange and carry out the operations. The CIA could be pushed only so far, and setting up proprietaries—companies owned by the CIA as a cover—and arranging the details of arms shipments was the most it would do. That was why Oliver North had to arrange for the operation to be carried out by a self-financed arm of the National Security Council.

"It shows Casey could not use the agency, even though he was an aggressive director," Miller, the former staff director of the Church Committee, said.

But there is another side to the story, one that rarely comes out. That is the pressure that members of Congress sometimes bring to bear on the agency to violate its own rules. Sometimes the pressure is to buy from constituents, to reinstate security clearances for employees whose clearances have been revoked, or to locate buildings in home districts of members of Congress—a rather routine occurrence in government. But at times the pressure takes a more unusual turn.

In May 1990, the CIA invited Rep. Bud Shuster, a Pennsylvania Republican and a member of the House Select Committee on Intelligence, to speak at the agency's training center at Camp Peary in Virginia. The CIA said the agency would fly him down for the talk on a Thursday and fly him back the same day. Shuster agreed to do it, but asked to be flown back instead to Hagerstown, Maryland, not far from Chambersburg, Pennsylvania, at the center of his district.

Since Hagerstown is 60 miles beyond Washington, the CIA's plane would have had to travel an extra 120 miles to accommodate Shuster. The agency told him it would be against government regulations to fly him the extra distance.

Shuster said he was going to his home state for legitimate business. But that made no difference to the CIA. As a member of Congress, Shuster had an official allowance to cover trips. If he went beyond that allowance, he was personally liable for them. Under the complex rules that bind government agencies, the CIA could only pick up and return Shuster to his office in Washington.

Infuriated, Shuster refused to give the talk, and on May 8, 1990, he wrote an angry letter to William Webster. Likening the CIA's decision to "risk aversion" in the intelligence business, Shuster said the symbol of the intelligence community had become a turtle with its head pulled in. He called the agency's officials "Lilliputians"—small-minded, petty people.

"Judge, you've got a problem. We've got a problem. I fear for the security of my country," he wrote.[79]

Instead of Congress's berating the CIA for breaking the law, a member of Congress was now berating the agency for refusing to go against government regulations. Like the agency when it broke the law, Shuster was using the rubric of national security to justify his own ill-advised actions.

When measured against the importance of the CIA and its effectiveness at carrying out its mission, the abuses—outrageous though each one may have been—seem relatively small. More than anything, the mission of the agency has been to uncover military developments in foreign countries so the U.S. can defend itself. To that end, no component of the CIA has been more effective than the Directorate of Science and Technology.

PART II

The Directorate of Science and Technology

9 Seeing Through Clouds

THE MOST CRITICAL QUESTION FOR THE UNITED STATES since the beginning of the Cold War has been the size and nature of Soviet weapons and military force. Only aerial reconnaissance can answer the question consistently with accuracy and precision. In many ways the most important task of the CIA, this job is carried out by the Directorate of Science and Technology, which has five thousand employees.

Besides watching from space, the Directorate of Science and Technology, through the Office of SIGINT Operations, monitors the Soviet military with radar and sensors that pick up radio transmissions, called telemetry, from missiles being tested. The office also intercepts communications within countries and inside foreign embassies and messages sent by terrorists and drug cartels. While the office often works with the National Security Agency (NSA), it specializes in tactical interceptions to supplement operations within the CIA. More generalized interception and analysis of communications is performed by NSA.*

The directorate's Office of Special Projects uses sensors to determine locations of nuclear devices and facilities and does other special collection projects.

Through the Office of Technical Service, the directorate supplies the James Bond equipment of the spy trade—the clandestine recording devices, the transmitters that bounce encrypted messages in bursts off satellites, secret-writing papers, and disguises that are essential to the job of the human spy. The directorate's Office of Research and Development conducts research for all the directorates, attempting to develop prototypes and go beyond the state of the art in such areas as communications, sensors, artificial intelligence, management of data bases, and high-speed computing. Through the Foreign Broadcast Information Service (FBIS), the directorate monitors and translates foreign media so that the government and the public will have accurate translations and transcripts of foreign newspaper articles and radio and television news programs. The FBIS also picks up and translates broadcasts of clandestine radio stations. Finally, the National Photographic Interpretation Center (NPIC), also housed within the Directorate of Science and Technology, analyzes the take from aerial reconnaissance and helps determine the meaning of the images.

None of the offices is more important than the Office of Development and Engineering, which develops the major satellite systems. Its predecessor in 1954 developed the U-2 reconnaissance aircraft, a desperate attempt to find out what the Soviet Union was up to when practically every other effort had failed. Meanwhile, clandestine Soviet agents could walk into any airport, rent a plane, and fly all over the U.S.—but not over military installations or the White House.

The idea for the U-2 originated with the Technological

---

* Signals intelligence (SIGINT) is intelligence obtained by monitoring electromagnetic waves or signals from any source, including foreign radio transmitters, radar, missiles, satellites, and spacecraft. Human intelligence (HUMINT) is intelligence collected by humans.

Capabilities Panel, a committee headed by MIT president James R. Killian, Jr., one of President Eisenhower's science advisers, to improve U.S. safeguards against surprise attack. The panel's intelligence committee, headed by Polaroid founder Edwin H. Land, reviewed a number of proposals, including several submitted by the Air Force, to peek at denied Soviet territory.

Over the short term, the panel recommended a high-flying plane that would come to be called the U-2. Killian and Land met with President Eisenhower to push the idea. The project was approved, and the CIA had the job of carrying it out. If a pilot was shot down, the government wanted him to be a civilian who could claim to be conducting meteorological research. Over the long term, the panel recommended lofting satellites into space.[80]

Allen W. Dulles, then director of Central Intelligence, asked Richard Bissell, who would later go on to oversee the Bay of Pigs invasion, to direct the U-2 project. Bissell got in touch with Kelly Johnson, who ran Lockheed's Advanced Development Projects office, and he came up with the design for a plane that would fly as high as seventy thousand feet.

"Before that, we didn't have many successful spy operations into Soviet territory," Bissell recalled. "They were too tough and too good. When a society is that regimented, it is very hard for an outsider to move in and move around."

What never came out at the time was that midway through the program, the British began participating in the flights, often alternating their pilots with American pilots. Eisenhower approved American flights only reluctantly, and Bissell said he approached the British as a way of getting more flights.

"There wasn't a fixed arrangement, but there were some British pilots," Bissell said.[81] "I arranged it. I thought it would improve our chances of being allowed to fly reconnaissance missions."

Aware of the flights almost from the beginning, Nikita Khrushchev, the Soviet leader, protested secretly through diplomatic channels. At times, the Soviet military tried to knock the planes out of the sky, but its MiGs and surface-to-air missiles could not reach the altitude of the U-2.

The flights continued for four years. Near the end, their goal was to determine if the Soviets were ahead of the U.S. in producing the intercontinental ballistic missile (ICBM).

"The question was, 'Do they have them and where are they?' " a former CIA officer who worked on targeting the U-2 said. "We watched them test them on radar. . . . We were hoping to get the capability sooner or later. But it was terrifying to Americans. The thought of coming under the bomb was terrifying."

Khrushchev had boasted that the Soviets had ICBMs that could hit U.S. targets. The claim was given added credibility by the Soviet launch on October 4, 1957, of *Sputnik I,* earth's first artificial satellite. Then came the "missile gap," a perception that the Soviets were ahead of the U.S. in missile production. During the 1960 presidential campaign, John F. Kennedy had claimed a great gap existed in the numbers of operational ICBMs each country had. Previously, a controversy had erupted over a "bomber gap." This misperception was a new twist on an old military ploy—fooling the enemy by marching the same regiment through a clearing over and over. Only in this case, the Soviets ordered the same plane squadrons to fly repeatedly overhead during parades.

At the time, neither the U.S. nor the U.S.S.R. had any missiles in production. The U.S. Air Force estimated the Soviets would soon have many more than the U.S., while a more conservative view of the Army, Navy, and CIA proved to be far more accurate. By 1963, the Air Force was estimating that the Soviets had 1,500 ICBMs, while the CIA said they had 400 to 500. In fact, the Soviets had 150 ICBMs in 1963, while the U.S. had 400.[82]

This illustrates a common problem when the military assesses the strength of opposing forces. Each service wants to use intelligence to support its own budget requests.

"The Air Force came in with an estimated number [of missiles] several times higher than ours, standard practice in the 1950s that became traditional over the next two decades," according to R. Jack Smith, the CIA's deputy director for intelligence from 1966 to 1971. "Theirs, as usual, was the worst-case stance, quite defensible in military tradition in determining what is the worst threat the enemy can pose. The CIA approach was to search out the *most likely,* not the worst possible, and then leave it to the president and his advisers to decide whether it was better to prepare defenses for the conceivable worst, the most likely, or something in between."[83]

On May 1, 1960, on the eve of summit talks with Khrushchev, the Soviets shot down a U-2 piloted by Francis Gary Powers, who had been an Air Force pilot. One of the targets of the flight was a suspected ICBM site at Plesetsk in northwest Russia.

The CIA had assured Eisenhower that evidence that the plane was on a spy mission would never be recovered. Based on that assurance, he issued a public denial that the U-2 had been spying. Khrushchev promptly displayed reconnaissance photographs taken by the U-2, and the Soviet leader canceled the summit. After being captured, Powers was imprisoned and later traded for KGB officer Rudolph Abel. Powers died on August 1, 1977, when the Cessna he was piloting as a traffic reporter for WGIL radio in Los Angeles crashed.[84]

Eisenhower ordered a halt to the U-2 program, but by then the CIA had already begun development of its first satellite program, code-named CORONA. The first satellites could see for two hundred miles in any direction, whereas the U-2 could see only for twenty-five miles. Resolution was inferior to that of photos taken from the U-2, so the CIA employed analysts to decipher the images. A satellite indeed located a Soviet missile site in Plesetsk, the area where the U-2 was headed when it was shot down.

From then on, the CIA successfully tracked the development of every Soviet weapon. The agency could see Soviet military hardware while it was being made and could predict how long it would take before it was deployed.

"The first satellite increased our knowledge fifty percent," a former CIA officer involved in the project said. "We were seeing things we had never seen before, the military and scientific installations. It was virginal information on their shipyards. We watched submarines, ships come on."

While the U.S. agreed not to fly the U-2 over the Soviet

Union, it did not agree to ground it. It was the U-2 that spotted Soviet missiles being installed by the Soviets in Cuba, leading to the Cuban missile crisis in 1962.

The first satellites catapulted the film toward earth by parachute. Planes scooped up the exposed film in midair with buckets. Each successive satellite system improved resolution and range. The latest satellites, called KH-11s, transmit images electronically to earth. At any given time, the U.S. has at least two KH-11s working. More recently, the U.S. has begun launching KH-12s, a more advanced satellite that takes in a wider swath of the electromagnetic spectrum. While they can read numbers on license plates, the satellites are usually set to spy on a wider area with resolution that is not as great.

The Soviets have never come close to American ingenuity in developing satellites. The U.S. compensated for motion by rotating the cameras within the satellites. The CIA generally takes thirty to forty shots for every three taken by the Soviets, making better use of satellite time.

Meanwhile, the Directorate of Science and Technology developed methods for snooping on the Soviets underwater. One of the more ingenious projects was the *Glomar Explorer,* a ship built by the CIA to raise a Soviet submarine that had sunk in 1968 in 17,500 feet of water off the coast of California.

As a cover, the *Glomar* was outfitted to gather manganese nodules from the ocean floor. In fact, it contained elaborate machinery for raising the Soviet submarine.

In 1974, the *Glomar* set out for the site where the Soviet submarine had gone down. Because of undersea listening devices, the CIA had heard the ship go down and knew exactly where it was on the ocean floor. The *Glomar* lowered a recovery vehicle with several sets of claws to grab hold of the submarine. The recovery vehicle was lowered by extending twelve-inch-diameter pipes that were screwed together by the crew end to end and attached to the vehicle. When the submarine had been raised to the mother ship, a chamber in the hull of the *Glomar* opened up and allowed the vehicle carrying the submarine to enter the ship. Meanwhile, television cameras monitored the project. After the sub was inside the hull, the water was pumped out.

When Jack Anderson publicized the story, the CIA put out the word that the mission had been largely unsuccessful and that most of the important parts of the submarine had been lost when the sub broke in two. The submarine had broken in two, and half of it sunk once again to the bottom of the sea. But from the portion retained, the CIA recovered a number of key components, including two nuclear-tipped torpedoes, cryptographic machines, and parts of missiles.

"You got the sense of the state of the art of the Soviets—electronics, code books, nuclear devices. What wasn't pulled up was more of the same," said a former CIA officer with knowledge of the take. "The stories saying it was unsuccessful were part of the cover. Were you going to say, 'We did a great job'?"

In 1976, the Navy took possession of the *Glomar Explorer,* and now it is in mothballs in Suisun Bay, near San Francisco, as part of the National Defense Reserve Fleet.

Today, the Directorate of Science and Technology controls billion-dollar satellites that see through clouds and even buildings with radar and infrared imaging that senses heat. Other satellites can intercept conversations of terrorists, trace narcotics dealers' electronic transfers of money between bank accounts, and see mobs in places such as Iraq, a machine gun under a tent, and water or oil under the desert. The satellites pick up virtually every part of the electromagnetic spectrum. Most important, they can see and transmit in real time any hostile moves by the Soviets or other countries.

The National Reconnaissance Office (NRO), started in 1960, determines what types of satellites to develop and how they will be used. The NRO is, in fact, a committee that consists of representatives of the dozen agencies that make up the intelligence community. It has staff offices behind a locked door in Room 4C-1000 of the Pentagon, and in other locations. Its members often meet in the office of the deputy secretary of defense. Despite repeated references to the NRO in the press, it is still considered a "black" program, meaning that from the standpoint of the U.S. government, it does not exist.[85]

The critical decisions are made by the NRO's executive

committee, which consists of the deputy secretary of defense, who is the chairman; the science adviser to the president; and the director of Central Intelligence. It is the DCI, in his role as director of the intelligence community, who is in charge of requirements. This gives him the authority to control the satellites, assigning them to different areas of the world and making the decision to turn them on and off. The NRO receives proposals for new systems from each of the intelligence agencies. Larger projects must be approved by the president. Once the NRO approves a project, it is carried out either by the CIA's Directorate of Science and Technology or by the Air Force Space Command.

Some 70 percent of the funding for the projects comes from the Defense Department, while the rest comes from the CIA funneled through Defense Department accounts.

Day-to-day tasking of the imagery satellites is done by the director of Central Intelligence through the Committee on Imagery Requirements and Exploitation (COMIREX), which is headed by a CIA officer. Usually, the committee meets at the office of the intelligence community staff at 1724 F Street NW in downtown Washington. The staff of 240 helps the director of Central Intelligence coordinate the dozen agencies that make up the intelligence community.

In effect, while the NRO operates the satellites, it is the director of Central Intelligence who clicks the shutter. It is also the CIA, along with the military, that analyzes the results through the National Photographic Interpretation Center.

10 ‖ *Crateology*

BUILDING 213 NEXT TO THE WASHINGTON NAVY YARD IS a seven-story, concrete complex that consists of three cubelike buildings covering two city blocks. Surrounded by a Cyclone fence topped with triple rows of barbed wire, the complex, at First and M Streets SE in Washington, is manned around the clock. What few windows the buildings have are tinted brown so outsiders cannot see in. Nearly two thousand people go in and out every twenty-four hours.

This is the National Photographic Interpretation Center (NPIC), a component of the CIA's Directorate of Science and Technology that analyzes and interprets images. The center was started by Arthur C. Lundahl, a brilliant former Navy man and University of Chicago graduate who went to work for the CIA in 1953 when the agency was located in dusty temporary buildings at Twenty-third Street and Constitution Avenue NW. Lundahl became chief of the Photographic Interpretation Center. In 1961, the division became NPIC.

The CIA runs the center, but all the military intelligence services participate in it. For many years, it was located on the four top floors of the Steuart Motor Co., a huge, factorylike brick building at Fifth and K Streets NW in Washington.

At first, the photo interpreters used nothing more than magnifying glasses and measuring devices to help them analyze aerial photographs. Slowly, they built up a library so they could compare one frame with a similar frame taken a year or two earlier, allowing them to pinpoint changes.

"You look at a place and then what was it like last year or yesterday," Lundahl said. "It's like looking at a movie. The frames are further apart, but you can infer much more of the intentions by seeing the changes on the ground than by doing it one frame at a time."[86]

To bring out small differences in elevation, NPIC had CIA reconnaissance pilots take pictures separated by dozens of yards of the same area. By using stereo techniques, NPIC could use the exaggerated dimensionality of the pictures. For example, depressions in the grass from tires or people walking would leap out of a photograph when viewed in this way.

For the most part, NPIC concentrated on strategic intelligence and research that could be used to predict long-range trends. Tactical intelligence, which could be used to pinpoint targets for bombing missions, was left to the military.

Whether it happened on earth, in the air, or in the sea, NPIC learned to interpret and make sense of it. For example, photo interpreters looking at Virginia could tell that the people were meat eaters because they could see hog pens and cattle. They could pick out the industrial plants where rail lines enter. They could draw a floor plan of each house based on outside clues: the kitchen is under the exhaust vent on the roof. There is a sewer vent over the bathroom. The living room has a chimney. Everything else in the house is bedrooms. Based on the growth of the cemeteries, photo interpreters could tell how many people died each year. From that, they could estimate the area's population.

Computers added another tool to the photo interpreters' bag of tricks. As William E. Burrows described them in his book *Deep Black,* the computers inside Building 213 were "routinely being used to correct for distortions made by the satellites' imaging sensors and by atmospheric effects, sharpen out-of-focus images, build multicolored single images out of several pictures taken in different spectral bands to make certain patterns more obvious, change the amount of contrast between the objects under scrutiny and their backgrounds, extract particular features while diminishing or eliminating their backgrounds altogether, enhance shadows, suppress glint from reflections of the sun, and a great deal more."[87]

The computers could even analyze the smoke coming from smokestacks and determine, through spectral analysis, what was being burned. With infrared, which senses heat, analysts could not only see inside buildings, they could tell that a plane, for example, had been on a runway hours after it had left.

The most critical need when NPIC was started in 1961 was to determine what missiles the Soviets had. It was NPIC that counted Soviet missiles during the missile gap debate, demonstrating that there was no gap at all. NPIC went on to use the same techniques to uncover the Soviet missiles being sent to Cuba. By then, NPIC knew what the erectors and transporters for the missiles looked like and what kinds of crates they were shipped in. Even though the missiles were covered with canvas before being deployed, their length, shape, and width gave them away. NPIC analysts developed expertise in interpreting missile packaging.[88]

"There was a science of crateology," Lundahl said. "Also they had shelters for steamrollers and other heavy equipment, so we had shelterology. Cuban troops slept in one kind of tent, Soviet troops in another kind."[89]

"The Soviets used a standard deployment pattern. The cable lines ran in a certain way. There had to be a place for fuel storage. The minute we saw that we knew what it was," R. Jack Smith, who was assigned to the Directorate of Intelligence at the time, said.[90]

Based on its previous experience in analyzing missile deployment in the Soviet Union, NPIC was able to tell President Kennedy how long it would take for the missiles in Cuba to become operational. This was supplemented with information from the manuals to the missiles provided by Col. Oleg Penkovskiy, the Soviet intelligence officer who began spying for the British in early 1962. Finally, on October 16, 1962, Lundahl presented Kennedy with photographs that convinced him that the missiles really were there. On that basis, Kennedy confronted Khrushchev and by threatening retaliatory strikes, got him to remove them.

"Politically, the Cuban missile crisis had demonstrated that overhead reconnaissance, and satellite reconnaissance in particular, was a stabilizing factor because it greatly reduced the element of surprise and, in the process, lessened the chance of a dangerous, all-out preemptive attack for fear that the enemy was getting ready to do the same thing," Burrows wrote in *Deep Black*. "The satellites substituted imagery for imagination and provided a realistic look at what the opposition had and did not have."[91]

"We gave our leaders answers, gave real substance to our national estimate, gave enlightenment when there had been darkness," Lundahl said. "I think we avoided nuclear war a couple of times, particularly in Cuba when people knew exactly what the facts were. We provided a basis for the strategic arms limitations treaty, which for years they referred to as confirmation by National Technical Means of Collection. Generally, the whole litany of our national intelligence was moved steadily into a technical arena, where the scope and speed and detail of information kept track of world events. People from the president on down became accustomed to this kind of service."[92]

NPIC helped to predict that the Soviets would launch an earth satellite before the U.S. and that the Chinese Communists would detonate an atomic bomb. With its help, the CIA also predicted the 1967 Arab-Israeli war, the India-Pakistan war, and the Soviet invasion of Afghanistan. NPIC ensured that the Soviets were complying with arms limitation agreements. In 1990, it was NPIC that first pinpointed the movement of Iraqi troops toward Kuwait three weeks before the invasion. The center's photo interpreters pointed out that

Iraqi troops had months of supplies of fuel—far more than would be taken on a training exercise. Once the war started, NPIC pinpointed biological and nuclear facilities.

NPIC routinely forecasts harvests, predicts natural disasters, pinpoints marijuana fields, and estimates the size of oil spills and forest fires. Some of the information is provided to other government agencies, such as the Commerce Department, to help them plan relief programs. By tracking the size of wheat and other critical harvests, the Agriculture Department can better estimate what prices will be like on the world market.

"A camera can take a picture of anything, and ipso facto you are involved in everything, whether it be economics or crops or biological warfare or missiles or submarines or missile testing," Lundahl said. "Anything at all that man does on the face of the earth that is exposed to the sky, you get images that, if interpreted correctly, can tell you a tremendous amount of information."

Today, nearly all the CIA's satellites provide data in real time, meaning that a battlefield commander can see enemy movements while they are happening. By combining images from magnetic, heat, radar, and visual-based images, NPIC can zero in on particular questions. This is particularly helpful when the Soviet Union or other countries try to camouflage their facilities.

"It's a game between hiders and seekers," Lundahl said. "The art of camouflage, decoys, deception, is very well developed."

Yet for all the wonders of science, no technology can divine an adversary's intentions.

"Photo interpretation when well done can give you an excellent view of an enemy's capability," Lundahl said. "You can't get his intentions. You can get some intentions. If you see a furnace is being moved or a railroad track is being torn up, you can tell it is being moved. Or cement is being poured."

These developments, in turn, may mean the enemy is planning to build a missile silo, for example. But the facility could initially be made to look like a factory. Nor can photos convey long-range plans and intentions.

"Nothing will replace a good human spy," Roland Inlow, a former chairman of COMIREX, said.

In the area of human spying, too, the Directorate of Science and Technology plays a major role through its supersecret Office of Technical Service.

11 ‖ *James Bond*

IN WINDOWLESS OFFICES WITHIN CIA HEADQUARTERS, THE Office of Technical Service (OTS) within the Directorate of Science and Technology devises state-of-the-art devices for bugging rooms, tapping phones, sending covert messages, and photographing documents. Several hundred CIA employees —including engineers, cabinetmakers, woodworkers, leatherworkers, and physicists—plant bugs or create secret compartments in everything from kitchen cutting boards to felt-tip pens. Over the years, to conceal its devices, the office has used car oil filters, videotape cassettes, false bottoms of toolboxes, toy trains, batteries, cigarette lighters, basket covers, teddy bears, chess sets, paintings, wallets, statues, hot plates, and toilet kits.

For an agent of the CIA in such areas as Cuba or the Soviet Union, these tools of the spy trade are critical for maintaining security and carrying out his mission. An agent must photograph documents, deliver messages to his case officer, receive cash, and arrange meetings. Of greatest importance, he must have a way to signal in an emergency that he needs to leave—or "exfiltrate"—the country. The CIA usually provides agents with several alternative escape plans. One plan requires the use of a signaling device that sends a coded message to an embassy or other listening post.

Sometimes the simplest methods are best. In Moscow or Havana, a window left open at night or a shade drawn halfway may signal a meeting or a drop at a prearranged site. In such cases, no high-tech methods are necessary. Instead of a custom-fitted wig, an operations officer may slick down his hair and wear glasses.

"I might walk out of the embassy at the end of the day with a suit and tie and long hair and my briefcase," a former operations officer said. "I might go into the bathroom of a hotel and take off my coat and tie, put them in a briefcase, put on a sport shirt, wet my hair and slick it back, and walk out with maybe my raincoat draped over my briefcase. If I am arrested, I don't have any spy gear. If you use spy gear, you are in trouble. If you are arrested and they peel your face off, you have a lot of explaining to do."

Bugging and wiretaps also have their limits.

"You can get too much data," a former officer assigned to the Office of Technical Service said. "The case officer thinks, 'I'll just put a bug in the room, and then I'll know everything.' It's not that easy. Number one, you've got to be able to make sure one can do that. Number two, you've got to make an installation, and you've got to worry about the other side finding it. Then you have to have a listening post where it comes in. You have to have someone changing the tapes. Then you have to translate and transcribe the tapes. Once a month, something worthwhile comes out. But often you are inundated with a lot of marginal data that requires a lot of sifting. Is it worth it? The answer is frequently no. One guy in a key location can often tell you more in five minutes than all of the taping."

But for most jobs, the Office of Technical Service provides invaluable aids—the most advanced spy equipment in the world. Many of the items have cost millions of dollars to develop. Sometimes the devices are developed within OTS and sometimes by outside contractors cleared for security.

"There's merit in both approaches," a former OTS officer said. "The practical way would be to do both. If it's way beyond the state of the art, for security reasons it might be done in-house. The problem is you don't have the production capability in-house. If you want a hundred and thirty-five of them, you don't want to tie down people soldering. If you want one, you can put two guys in a room for two years. But if you want a big order, you might do them outside."

One of the most commonly used items supplied by OTS is disguises. Before going overseas, some operations officers are fitted with several. In rare cases when CIA officers have to break into a house or embassy, why take a chance that a witness might identify them? Or if a case officer is about to try to recruit an agent, he might wear a "light disguise"—a wig and glasses—so that if a potential recruit turns down the offer, he cannot readily identify the case officer who made it. A disguise is more likely to be used in a denied area such as the Soviet Union or if the potential recruit is a terrorist or drug dealer.

The material used for masks is of high-tech design that permits the skin to breathe.

"The agency has a disguise capability that no one can touch," a former OTS officer said.

Because of electronic listening devices designed by the OTS, a number of Soviet-bloc embassies in foreign countries have been penetrated. The OTS supplies the installers—called audio-operations officers—who are often assisted by officers from the local stations. One installer was an extremely supple Japanese American who stood four feet nine inches tall and weighed just eighty pounds. He wormed his way into air ducts in order to plant bugging devices.

"The installers are guys willing to climb a fence in the middle of the night. If they're caught, they're in deep shit. They might spend fifteen hours on a job," a former OTS officer said. "It is not a simple thing to do. They may need to drill a hole in a wall and put in something that will transmit for years. If the target sees a hole, he tends to get suspicious.

They may have to replaster the wall and match foreign paint that is six years old.

"It's risky business," the former officer said. "It's hard to explain why you're in the building in the middle of the night with a bag. 'I'm a plumber.' 'You're in the wrong room. The toilet is over there.' "

To make listening devices difficult to detect, OTS will sometimes transmit on the same wavelength as a local radio or television station.

"You mask the signal," a former officer said. "There are ways to snuggle up to a standard radio signal: 101.4 plays oldies. You might snuggle up to that. So my signal is hidden by that. That would be a typical way. You hide it or burst it so it's on the air a short period."

"Today you have low probability of intercept [LPI]," the former officer said. "The name of the game today is spread spectrum, which operates on a variety of frequencies, so the signal is difficult to find."

OTS operates its own secret printing plant at CIA headquarters with type for most foreign languages. It can produce old or foreign paper and foreign driver's licenses and birth certificates.

"If you have a printing press, you can make anything you want," a former OTS officer said, "but there are rules on what can be done."

CIA regulations prohibit the agency from producing false U.S. documents such as passports, birth certificates, driver's licenses, or college degrees. However, the agency can print less important, nonofficial documents such as library cards or membership cards. It also can request a blank driver's license or college certificate from the issuing authority and if approved, imprint its own data on it.

"You go to a high authority and say, 'I'm from the CIA,' " a former officer said. "You show credentials, and you tell him what you want. Perhaps you deal with the director of motor vehicles, appealing to his patriotic spirit to provide an authentic blank license to help establish the identity of an agent or officer in an operation. Or you go to a university [for a college degree]. 'Any chance of a blank? If you want, I'll tell you generally how we'll use it and who it is issued to. It may not be his real name, but you can be assured it's for a good cause in the service of your country.'

"One college administrator will say, 'Take a hike.' Another will give three, with tight controls. Another will say, 'Three dozen, it's my country, good luck to you.' "

The military freely provides identification cards to the CIA, but the State Department rarely does. Obtaining a U.S. passport in an alias requires high-level approvals and is only infrequently done.

If the documents are needed to establish "a light legend," meaning a superficial cover story, no steps are taken to make sure that if someone calls the college or motor vehicle department, the name on the document will be registered. But if a more sensitive operation is involved, the CIA will try to elicit the cooperation of the issuing authority in "backstopping" the document. In those cases, if someone calls the motor vehicle department, he will be told that a license has been issued to the individual whose name the CIA has imprinted on the blank driver's license. Similarly, a college president may agree to make sure someone is listed as having graduated from the college, usually for only a month or two while the operation is going on.

"If your agent is going to be subjected to any kind of scrutiny, you want a real address. In the old days we would say 32 Prince Avenue. There wasn't any. Today, you better make sure it's real. Pick a large apartment building, but don't put down the apartment number," a former OTS officer said.

CIA assets or agents are often used to backstop an identity. An inquirer calls the asset to verify alleged employment. The asset says, "He's been here twelve years, and he's one of our best employees." In fact, the asset wouldn't know him if he walked in the door.

Because of the change in attitudes since the Church Committee hearings and the generally tighter approach to corporate responsibilities, companies are less willing than before to help the CIA establish cover for agents.

"What you want to do most is to handle your documents and your agreements carefully," a former OTS officer said.

In obtaining cooperation from companies, the CIA today tries to warn of every conceivable consequence, including possible loss of business if the word gets out that the company has helped the agency, becoming known as an agency "front."

CIA director William Casey tried to enlist the support of more U.S. companies in helping the CIA to establish at least temporary cover. He was largely successful. But even before the Church Committee hearings, few companies wanted to commit themselves to the kind of complex relationships required to establish long-term cover for CIA officers.

In forging foreign documents, anything goes. OTS may produce fake passports of other countries, fake foreign birth certificates, and fake foreign driver's licenses. Since CIA officers generally do not want to be identified as Americans, these are the documents most commonly used.

Early in CIA history, OTS made such items as Dog in Heat, the essence of a chemical that sexually attracts male dogs. As conceived, the chemical would be sprayed on the doorsteps of the homes of Communist Party members overseas so they would be besieged all night by yelping dogs. It was never used, but a stink bomb known as Who Me? meant to be thrown into Communist Party meetings was.

"Every five or six years at someone's retirement party, someone brings it in a vial. 'I just happened to find it. It's the last one in existence.' Great guffaws and laughter. That kind of crap hasn't been used in thirty years," a former OTS officer said. "I don't think any serious officer feels, by and large, that that sort of thing is worth the effort."

The OTS has tried everything, from extrasensory perception to psychics, to try to penetrate KGB tradecraft, such as where the KGB locates dead drops.

"What we wanted to know was, where do the Soviets leave their dead drops in Washington?" a former OTS officer said. "The answer was a very large oak tree at a busy intersection in northwest Washington," meaning the answers were too general. "Anytime you got to specifics, that happened. We lost interest in it."

Not the least of OTS's duties is fashioning mementos or gags for CIA officers who are retiring. When William Baker left the CIA as director of the Office of Public Affairs to become an FBI assistant director over the criminal division, OTS supplied a Sherlock Holmes outfit that William Webster gave him at his going-away party.

For all the James Bond devices and the billion-dollar satellites, the CIA would be helpless if it did not have a way of bringing all the information together and making sense of it. That is the job of the Directorate of Intelligence.

PART III

The Directorate of Intelligence

12 | Mirror-Imaging

Special National Intelligence Estimate
Dec. 4, 1941

For the past two weeks, Japan has been warning its diplomats that war may be imminent.

Interception of Japanese diplomatic traffic indicates the message "East wind rain" has been repeated on a regular basis. Intelligence officials believe this code means Japan has made a decision to go to war in the near future.

In addition, there have been these other signs that Japan may be preparing to go to war:

• On Nov. 22, Foreign Minister Togo informed Ambassador Nomura that negotiations between Japan and the United States must be settled by November 29 because after that "things are going automatically to happen. . . ."

• For the past two weeks, the Japanese have been padding their radio messages with garbled or old messages to make decoding more difficult.

> • *Three days ago, the Japanese Imperial Navy changed its ship call signs. This is an unprecedented change, since they had just been changed. Normally they are switched every six months.*
>
> • *Two days ago, the Japanese Foreign Ministry ordered its consulates in six cities—including Washington—to destroy all but the most important codes, ciphers, and classified material.*
>
> • *Three days ago, the U.S. became unable to locate previously tracked Japanese submarines.*
>
> • *Scattered, unconfirmed reports indicate naval air units in southern Japan have been practicing simulated torpedo attacks against ships there.*
>
> *These warning signs justify immediate, extraordinary steps, including placing the Pacific commands on immediate alert.*[93]

IF THE CIA HAD BEEN AROUND AT THE TIME, THIS IS WHAT the agency's Directorate of Intelligence might have handed President Roosevelt three days before Japanese forces attacked Pearl Harbor. As Dr. Harold P. Ford, a former acting chairman of the CIA's National Intelligence Council, has pointed out in his book *Estimative Intelligence,* all of the facts listed above were known to the U.S. government—three days before the disastrous attack on Pearl Harbor. If such an intelligence estimate had been presented to the president, defensive action would almost certainly have been taken. But the government had no central agency for marshaling all the information, making sense of it, and presenting strategic assessments to the president.

The only existing intelligence agencies at the time were those operated by the military, and they were often considered dumping grounds for the least qualified military personnel. Each of the services was at the others' throats, and fiefdoms within the services often suppressed whatever intelligence assessments were made. The government had no tradition of assessing the intentions—as distinguished from capabilities—of other countries. Those officials who did look at the question of Japanese intentions decided that Japan would never attack, because to do so would be irrational. Yet what might seem irrational to one country may seem perfectly logical to another country that has different goals, values, and traditions. Finally, many in the government looked with disdain on Japanese capabilities. As one admiral said after the attack, "I never thought those little yellow sons of bitches could pull off such an attack, so far from home."[94]

An alert was finally sent at the very last minute on the morning of December 7, but it did not reach its destination before the attack. The Army officer given the job of notifying the command at Pearl Harbor sent the message by Western Union, instead of through Navy channels, when he found the Army's circuits to Hawaii were down. But this was just the last in a series of bungles. The result was the Japanese sank 5 of the Navy's 8 battleships based at Pearl Harbor, damaged 200 of the 300 aircraft based there, and killed 2,330 servicemen and 100 civilians, bringing the U.S. into World War II.

"We just didn't have an intelligence system," Dr. Ray S. Cline, who was an analyst in the Navy and Office of Strategic Services before becoming deputy CIA director for intelligence, said. "Franklin Roosevelt had lots of information, but he didn't have an intelligence system to present it to him. There was plenty of information about the attack on Pearl Harbor, but it was not handled bureaucratically in a way that would alert the armed services and the White House what was going on. There was no central system at that time."[95]

These failures led indirectly to the creation of the CIA in 1947. The idea of a CIA was the brainchild of Col. William J. ("Wild Bill") Donovan. A New York lawyer and politician, Donovan had served heroically in World War I, commanding a battalion and winning the Medal of Honor. During World War II, he headed the Office of Strategic Services (OSS). Back in 1941, Donovan submitted a plan to President Roosevelt outlining the need for a government-wide organization that would pool and coordinate existing intelligence. Following Donovan's advice, Roosevelt created a Coordinator of Information as part of the Executive Office of the President in July 1941.

After a year, the Coordinator of Information evolved into the OSS, which became the model for the CIA. During the war, OSS organized resistance movements and sabotage operations behind enemy lines. The OSS also tried unsuccessfully to centralize intelligence functions within the government through an analytical section known as Research and Analysis.

At the end of the war, OSS was disbanded, and the State Department absorbed many of its functions. But again at Donovan's urging, it was reconstituted when President Truman agreed to the creation first of the Central Intelligence Group and then, a year later, the CIA. The National Security Act of 1947 establishing the agency took effect on September 18, 1947, a birthday celebrated by the modern CIA with a family day. While Donovan never served as director of the CIA, the new agency absorbed the institutional values of the OSS, including the "can do, try anything" approach that Donovan had instilled.

Both before and after Pearl Harbor, the idea of centralized intelligence drew stiff opposition from many in the War Department, who saw it as an infringement on their turf. As one general said, a central agency would be "very disadvantageous, if not calamitous" from the point of view of the Pentagon. That was why it was so important to Truman that the new intelligence agency be independent and not tied to the interests of the military. When the Defense Intelligence Agency was later created in 1961 to focus more on tactical questions, it often exaggerated Soviet prowess, reflecting biases of a military that constantly sought bigger budgets.

This concept of a centralized intelligence agency—one that would bring together all the available information on a subject and analyze it objectively—is embodied in the CIA's Directorate of Intelligence. With three thousand employees, it is the CIA's smallest directorate.

The directorate is the analytical side of the house, where Ph.D.'s who could just as easily be college professors pore over all the available information and produce estimates on what they think will be the future course of events. Eggheads rather than spooks, the analysts openly identify themselves as CIA employees and contribute to academic publications and attend conferences in their field just like university professors.

"Most of us on the estimative side had little or no knowledge of the techniques of clandestine work and were prone to scoff at the excessively tight security about operations and to sneer at the bumbling of 'the spooks.' They were doers, not contemplators, and they approached foreign affairs from precisely the opposite vantage point,'' R. Jack Smith, a former deputy director for intelligence, said in his book *The Unknown CIA.* "Also, they could point to several loose-lipped indiscretions by one or more senior estimative people that they claimed had blown operations. So there was a wall between the two sides on all operational matters.''[96]

Typically, the analysts want to disseminate material obtained by the operations side, and the operations officers object because they are afraid it will expose a source.

The intelligence directorate brings together information from all sources—satellites, human spies, intercepts of communications, the press, foreign broadcasts, trade publications, newsletters, computer bulletin boards, and scientific publications. That information—at least 80 percent of it from open sources—is used to prepare daily research and intelligence reports, as well as long-range analyses. In addition, the information is used by the National Intelligence Council, a component of the intelligence community that reports directly to the director of Central Intelligence, to prepare estimates of future events that are presented to the president. While each of the agencies in the intelligence community may contribute to the estimates, the most important source of information generally is the Directorate of Intelligence. Therefore, the work of the directorate is critical. The other directorates can do marvelous work, but it will languish if it is not presented to the president and policymakers. If the analysis is wrong, the foreign policy of the U.S. will suffer.

In the early days, there were a number of failures. In Korea, despite ample evidence, the CIA did not clearly alert senior policymakers in June 1950 that North Korea was about to invade the Republic of Korea. Nor did the CIA warn that tens of thousands of Communist Chinese troops, who had been infiltrating North Korea, were about to attack U.S. and United Nations troops.

In September 1962, the CIA said placing ballistic missiles

in Cuba would not fit into the Soviet Union's known behavior patterns, and Nikita Khrushchev "would not do anything so uncharacteristic, provocative, and unrewarding." Prompted by contradictory and fragmentary eyewitness reports that such a deployment might be taking place, the estimate was produced just before photographs taken by a U-2 on October 14, 1962, showed conclusively that the Soviets were moving missiles into Cuba.

This was a good example of "mirror-imaging"—assuming that another country would think the same way America thinks. While an estimate cannot predict with absolute certainty events that have not yet taken place, they can lay out the possibilities and assign probabilities. This allows smart policymakers to ready options to cope with the most likely outcomes. Yet it is not unusual for heads of state to ignore intelligence, as Joseph Stalin did in 1941 when told that the Nazis were about to invade the Soviet Union, costing the Soviets tens of thousands of lives.[97]

"The most important thing was not whether we were right or wrong about the occurrence of events, but to help the people making policy decisions by giving them background information," Edward W. Proctor, a former CIA deputy director for intelligence, said. "Sometimes you give them information that is right, and they make the wrong decisions. Sometimes you give them information that is wrong, and they make the right decisions for different reasons. Sometimes you give them information that is right, and they make the right decisions. Sometimes you make a prediction on something coming up, and the policymakers take an action which, in effect, makes your prediction wrong, but it was the right thing to do based on your prediction. The whole purpose is to help these people make better decisions."[98]

Another example of mirror-imaging occurred in 1973, when the CIA and the rest of the U.S. government failed to warn that Egypt and Syria were about to launch major attacks on Israel in what came to be known as the Yom Kippur War.

"We did not predict it, period. We had seen the same thing occur several times before, including a year before, and nothing had happened," Proctor, then deputy director for intelligence, said. "It was a buildup of forces and threats. We did not understand what the purpose was from the Egyptians' point of view. They knew they couldn't win, but it was one way of breaking the deadlock."[99]

Probably the most well-known failure came in February 1979, when the CIA did not foresee that the shah of Iran might be overthrown. In fact, in mid-August 1978, a CIA analyst reported to President Carter, "Iran is not in a revolutionary or even prerevolutionary situation."[100]

In this case, the Directorate of Intelligence disregarded reports coming in to the CIA from the operations officers in Iran, who were reporting growing opposition to the shah. The analysts assumed that the shah would crush the opposition, as he had in the past. But the shah's bout with cancer had weakened his resolve.

"We were aware the shah had opposition," Stansfield Turner, who was director of Central Intelligence at the time, said. "One difficulty was it was hard to appreciate that a man with the military and SAVAK [the shah's secret police] would be toppled by people parading in the streets. When you make an intelligence forecast, you make an assumption. We thought he would use the powers he had, but he didn't."[101]

It is always easier, of course, to assume that the status quo will continue. Far less risk is involved. Without hard data on Mikhail Gorbachev's intentions, for example, anyone who predicted that Gorbachev would release the Soviet grip on Eastern Europe and allow East Germany to reunite with West Germany may well have been referred to the agency's Office of Medical Services for psychiatric consultations. Anyone who said the Soviet people would vote to change the name of Leningrad back to the original St. Petersburg would have been thought to be similarly mad.

"There is almost never enough firm intelligence to support a solid, definitive statement," Smith, the former deputy director for intelligence, said. "If there were, there would be no need for an estimate; the threat would be self-evident."[102]

Unless prodded from within or without, organizations tend to become more bureaucratic as they mature and less willing to take risks. The CIA is no exception.

"It takes more people to get things done, and they don't do them as well," a former CIA analyst said. "There is a concern with warm bodies, production schedules, concern with pleasing the boss and not getting out of line, a process of homogenization so strong personalities or characters get shunted aside."

In those cases, the former analyst said, "the going evaluation is such and such, and the head of the office and his boss has said so. Someone says, 'This is one hundred and eighty degrees different.' In the coming days or weeks, the situation plays out, and the dissident is shown to be right. Often, instead of being rewarded, he is put off to the side." It is a case, the former analyst said, of causing embarrassment by being "too accurate too soon."

"One thread that runs through the whole story from the beginning of the CIA to the present is the gradual bureaucratization of the CIA," Russell J. Bowen, a retired analyst who continues to consult for the CIA, said. "There is a certain momentum that carried from World War II and OSS type thinking into the early sixties. The idea was you had a job to do, and you go out and do the job, and you clean up the problems later. Now we say, 'If we do this job, what are all the problems we might get into?' So the motivation for go-go-go is long gone."[103]

Another perennial problem is the way CIA reports are written. Often, they do not state conclusions clearly enough to attract attention. Besides the president, the National Security Council is the CIA's major customer. Staffers there often complain that they find CIA estimates too balanced or boring compared with those by the State Department's Bureau of Intelligence and Research, a much smaller outfit that prepares analyses for the State Department. Since the State Department is engaged in making policy, its analysts tend to tailor their work to the specific needs of the moment. In effect, State has the inside track on what the president and his aides want to read—aides who are already burdened with too much material.

"You have a super editor at State, who says, 'These are the subjects I am interested in. The secretary of state is involved in these issues,' " an NSC staff member from the Reagan administration said. "They [the State Department] share the same short-term interests as the NSC and White House.

"You have overload," the former NSC staff member said. "There is a limit to what those people [at the NSC] can handle. So you go with what is really relevant. You get a mediocre report, but it's relevant, and you read it. If it's a super report but not relevant, it doesn't get read very much."

Because of the size of its analytical side—more than two thousand analysts—the CIA tends to have more specialists who become immersed in their subjects.

"Steeped in the minutiae of their field, in this instance the daily flow of events in a country, they frequently mistake back-page filler items for front-page banner-headline stories," according to Smith. "Moreover, they have a persistent tendency to believe that their sometimes arcane thought processes will be transparent to their readers."[104]

In contrast to President Reagan, President Bush read CIA reports avidly. In part, that has contributed to a sharpening of the CIA's writing style.

"One of the things that has changed for the better over the last several years is they write it more to the point," said Robert Gates when he was still deputy assistant to the president for national security under Bush. "The president reads the estimates and rereads them, which is a change from the past."[105]

Still, Army General H. Norman Schwarzkopf complained to Congress after the Persian Gulf War that while intelligence during the war was excellent, the analyses on the Iraqi military had been "caveated, footnoted, and watered down" to the point that they became useless.[106] He thus appeared to distinguish between the hard facts provided by intelligence and the analyses that sought to draw conclusions from the facts and predict the future. Schwarzkopf did not specify whether he was referring to CIA or military analysis.

William Webster encountered the same problem when confronting the question of whether economic sanctions would drive Saddam Hussein out of Kuwait. According to an aide, he had to beat the analysts into being more precise about the effect of the sanctions. The analysts were being too vague. One said sanctions would cause "belt tightening." What did that mean? Webster wanted specifics on when they would work. In six months? In a year? he wanted to know. If an estimate covers all bases, it will always be right—but also close to useless. Webster finally got what he wanted, a statement that the sanctions would take at least a year to have any chance of working.

Webster also browbeat Dr. Fritz W. Ermarth, then chairman of the National Intelligence Council, over the use of the words *probably, likely,* and *possible* in estimates. Webster wanted to know what these words meant in terms of the percentage chance that certain events would occur.

Over the years, the national estimating structure has been changed several times to try to sharpen its work. After the CIA failed to predict the North Korean invasion of the South, CIA director Walter Bedell Smith established an Office of National Estimates to focus more attention on the process. The estimates were developed collegially, based on information presented by CIA analysts and the entire intelligence community. In the fall of 1973, Colby replaced the old board with the National Intelligence Council.

"I changed the board because I thought the estimates and analysis were much too generalized," Colby said.

Under the new system, each of the sixteen members of the board is called a national intelligence officer and is given responsibility for a specific issue or geographic area. The idea was to make each officer accountable for his or her area, rather than to develop estimates by consensus of the board members. There is a national intelligence officer for warning, one for nuclear proliferation, one for strategic weapons, and then one for each area of the world, such as Latin America and the Near East and South Asia. The NIO for warning, for example, has the primary responsibility for sounding the alarm if a military attack is about to take place.

Generally, the NIO officers are veteran CIA officers, former high-ranking State Department officials, or former generals or admirals—people with enough standing to buck the bureaucracy. Typically, they serve for two-year terms to guarantee that the position will constantly be replenished with new blood. They are supposed to spend more time with policymakers than did the old members of the Office of National Estimates.

In drawing up estimates, the NIOs rely on their own staffs and on analysis presented by the Directorate of Intelligence.[107] The final draft of a National Intelligence Estimate is written by the appropriate NIO. Changes may be made all the way along the line up to the president. The chairman of the council, the DCI, and other agencies within the intelligence community can and do add their views. The council itself reports through its chairman directly to the director of Central Intelligence, who presents estimates to the president representing the collective judgment of the dozen agencies that make up the intelligence community.

In some cases, CIA directors have disagreed with their own estimates, as John A. McCone did when he took issue with the agency's judgments on the meaning of Soviet activity in Cuba before the Cuban missile crisis. McCone met with President Kennedy and said "something new and different was going on in Cuba." He flatly said the Soviets were introducing offensive missiles on the island. McCone had nothing to go on except his own intuition about Khrushchev. After the CIA issued its estimate discounting the buildup, he cabled the agency while on his one-month honeymoon in Europe, urging a reassessment. By then, events had shown that McCone was right.[108]

William Casey and Stansfield Turner also tended to act as analysts and offered their own opinions, which sometimes differed with what the CIA was saying. If a DCI disagrees with all or part of an estimate, he may choose to submit it anyway and signify his disagreement on the document or in a note attached to it, or he may reject it outright. Individual agencies within the intelligence community often disagree with all or part of the estimates. Their dissent is carried in the document also.

Besides national intelligence estimates, which look at fundamental issues and often take a year to complete, the council issues special national intelligence estimates, which are generally more urgent and completed in a matter of days or weeks, as well as a variety of memos that may be completed within a few days in response to particular concerns.[109] In addition, the analysts prepare hundreds of additional reports on everything from wheat harvests to the political standing of world leaders.

In 1976, the CIA experimented with creating competing teams for developing national estimates on Soviet intentions and capabilities. In all, the CIA had six teams look at three different questions. The A teams represented the intelligence community, while the B teams were composed of a panel of outside experts. In one area—Soviet strategic intentions—the B team shone. It said the Soviet Union was seeking a first-strike capability in the 1970s, while the A team discounted the possibility. Recent Soviet statements have validated the B team's judgment. But not all of the B teams were superior, and the CIA abandoned the system. In effect, it was like letting an outside group submit competing editorials for publication in a newspaper. If the editorials did not represent the opinion of the newspaper, their value was diminished.

In 1980, Stansfield Turner gave the chairman of the National Intelligence Council greater authority over the individual officers to better supervise their work. In the view of Dr. Ford, a distinguished expert on estimating, this system has worked better than any previous one. With the exception of the failure of the CIA to predict sharply worsening economic conditions in the Soviet Union, there have been no significant intelligence failures since then. While the CIA reported on growing destabilization within the Eastern bloc, it would have been impossible to predict that Gorbachev would relinquish the Soviet grip on Eastern Europe before he himself had made that decision.

Despite the occasional failures, the CIA, as the representative of the intelligence community, has registered a more than respectable batting average over the years.

Sen. Frank Church, one of the CIA's severest critics, acknowledged in 1975 when he became the first chairman of the Senate Select Committee on Intelligence, "In the last twenty-five years, no important new Soviet weapons system, from their H-bomb to their most recent missiles, has appeared which had not been heralded in advance by NIEs [National Intelligence Estimates]."

Among other events, the CIA predicted that the Soviets would launch an earth satellite before the U.S., that the Chinese Communists would detonate an atomic bomb, and that the Soviets would produce a ballistic missile. The agency predicted the 1967 Arab-Israeli war, the India-Pakistan war, and the Soviet invasion of Afghanistan.[110] Back in 1960, despite claims by James Angleton and his supporters that the split was a fraud, the CIA alerted the U.S. government to the causes and dimensions of the rift between the Soviet Union and Communist China.

Before the U-2 and imaging satellites, the CIA tended to overestimate Soviet progress in weapons development, but not nearly as much as did the military services. Yet overestimates of military strength are always preferable to underestimates. From the mid-1960s to the early 1970s, the CIA tended to underestimate the extent of the Soviet buildup, but not by enough to make an appreciable difference.[111]

During the Vietnam War, the CIA repeatedly asserted that the enemy was stronger than believed within the U.S. government and that the South Vietnamese government was weaker. The agency stated that other countries would not fall to communism if the North overran the South. For example, on June 11, 1964, in answer to whether the defeat of the South Vietnamese would lead to the feared domino effect, CIA director John A. McCone wrote to McGeorge Bundy, special assistant to President Johnson for national security affairs, "We do not believe that the loss of South Vietnam and Laos would be followed by the rapid, successive communization of the other states of the Far East."

On May 12, 1967, in a report entitled "The Current Status of Morale in North Vietnam," the CIA said, "With only a few exceptions, recent reports suggest a continued willingness on the part of the populace to abide by Hanoi's policy on the war." The report added that the mood is "one of resolute stoicism with a considerable reservoir of endurance still untapped."

"I remember once—in the Lyndon Johnson period—being asked by [McGeorge] Bundy to have the CIA prepare an objective analysis of the results of the U.S. Air Force bombing of North Vietnam," Dr. Ray S. Cline, then the CIA's deputy director for intelligence, said in his book *The CIA Under Reagan, Bush & Casey*. "He said, 'Everyone agrees your analysts are the only honest guys in town, and we need to know the truth.' A small group of analysts went to work making such evaluations. Over a period of time, their work demonstrated that little progress was being made in slowing down the North Vietnamese infiltration of the South. The CIA was the bearer of bad tidings throughout the Vietnam War and was not very happily received by any of the policymakers who tried to make the Vietnam intervention work."[112]

Ironically, the CIA, in classified reports, was saying exactly what the antiwar demonstrators were saying on the streets of Washington. The analysts gnashed their teeth as President Johnson turned a deaf ear to their warnings, preferring—like President Nixon after him—to believe that the Soviet Union or communists were behind the antiwar sentiment.

"The trouble was the Johnson and Nixon administrations did not really listen to intelligence," said Thomas Polgar, who was CIA station chief in Vietnam from 1972 to 1975. "They had their own policies and preconceptions."[113]

"Johnson only wanted to hear the good points about Vietnam," said R. Jack Smith, who was deputy director for intelligence at the end of the Johnson administration.[114]

By and large, the CIA stuck to its guns and continued to report unfavorable prognoses. But when William Casey became director of Central Intelligence in 1981, the CIA faced a different problem: What happens when the director of Central Intelligence himself has a political agenda?

13 | *Trying to Cook the Books*

OVER THE YEARS, THE CIA HAS RESISTED POLITICAL PRES-
sures to change its judgments. When the military pushed for
higher estimates of Soviet capability, the agency stuck to lower
estimates that by and large proved to be correct. While Richard Helms bowed to White House pressure to see if foreign
countries were financing dissident groups, he reported to Presidents Johnson and Nixon that there was no foreign involvement in the antiwar movement. When Nixon tried to enlist
the CIA to cover up Watergate, Helms refused, resulting in
his removal.[115]

The agency has protected the integrity of its personnel as
well. In the summer of 1953, Sen. Joseph McCarthy announced he had reason to believe there were more than a
hundred communists in the CIA. He aimed his sights at Cord
Meyer, a CIA officer hired by Allen Dulles himself. Meyer
had a liberal background; before coming to the CIA, he had
headed the United World Federalists, a group opposed to

national armament. McCarthy got J. Edgar Hoover's FBI to investigate Meyer and came up with lurid charges: that he was, for example, an associate of Cass Canfield, who was described in an FBI report as sympathizing with communist causes. In fact, Canfield, then the chairman of Harper and Brothers, the New York publishing firm, was a moderate Democrat who had no interest in communism.

Dulles opposed an FBI request to interrogate Meyer and said the CIA itself would investigate the charges. On Thanksgiving Day, Dulles called Meyer at home to say he had been cleared of any security problems.[116]

McCarthy also tried to railroad William P. Bundy, then assistant to the deputy director for intelligence, but Dulles repulsed those efforts as well.[117] In contrast, most government bureaucrats were afraid to stand up to McCarthy for fear they would be tainted as well.

Probably the best example of CIA independence came during the Vietnam War. When President Johnson pushed the CIA to ratify his policies in pursuing the war, the agency did just the opposite: it warned that the "domino theory," the claim that the rest of Southeast Asia would fall to communism if the North took over South Vietnam, was fallacious, thereby undercutting one of the administration's principal justifications for prosecuting the war. Repeatedly, the agency questioned the policymakers' continuing reassurances that progress was being made there.

That is why the CIA was established in the first place, to provide candid, independent, and objective information and analysis about world events. If the agency lost that reputation, it would have nothing.

But all that began to change when William J. Casey became DCI on January 28, 1981—or so it seemed. Casey was a brilliant man, a lawyer by training and a student by avocation. From 1944 to 1945, he was chief of the Special Intelligence Branch of the OSS in the European Theater of Operations. From 1971 to 1973, he was chairman of the Securities and Exchange Commission. In 1980, Ronald Reagan asked him to head his first presidential campaign.

A voracious reader, Casey read every book he could get

his hands on about world affairs and economics. He haunted Washington bookstores, especially Sidney Kramer Books, searching for the most obscure books he could find on Soviet issues and world affairs. Mostly, it was to satisfy his intellectual curiosity. Casey bought so many books at a time that his security guards usually had to help him carry them all. One aide estimated he spent $40,000 a year on books and magazines alone.[118]

"He was the brightest person I've ever met," said Stanley Sporkin, who was Casey's general counsel at the CIA and is now a federal judge in Washington. "He had a photographic memory. He didn't tolerate fools. He couldn't stand long meetings. He would tell people, 'Don't repeat things. I understand,' and he did."[119]

But there was another side to Casey, that of the politician and policymaker, the dealmaker and ideologue. When he took the job of DCI, Casey asked President Reagan if he could have cabinet status, and Reagan agreed to give him that extra degree of prestige and clout. It was a critical break from the past, when directors of Central Intelligence were considered impartial purveyors of information. As a member of the cabinet, Casey became an integral part of the Reagan administration, responsible not only for running the CIA and presenting intelligence estimates to the president, but also for making policy.

Casey was convinced that the Soviets were far more mendacious and powerful than the U.S. government collectively thought. In showing that the Soviet Union was an "evil empire," he sought to outdo Ronald Reagan, to hit them where it hurt, to show them for what they were. Casey's approach to the CIA was shaped not only by his political conservatism but also by his days in the OSS, known not only for its daring but also for its cowboylike ventures.

While Casey was generally pleased with the work of the Directorate of Operations, he was not at all pleased with the work of the Directorate of Intelligence. To Casey, the analysts were a bunch of liberals—fuzzy-headed thinkers who did not know about the hard realities in the world and were afraid to venture opinions.

"Casey's first priority was to improve the estimating process," said John A. Bross, a longtime CIA operative whom Casey brought out from retirement to be one of his assistants. "He found a very disorganized system. Estimates had gotten very thinned down. Bill's priority was to get the estimates back into a stronger posture and let people take stronger positions."[120]

Yet the direction Casey took was always in line with his conservative worldview. Soon, he found himself colliding with the CIA's most hallowed commandment: thou shalt not cook the books.

To goad the bureaucracy, Casey hired Herbert E. Meyer, a thirty-six-year-old editor of *Fortune* whose book, *War Against Progress,* had been widely cited during Reagan's 1980 presidential campaign. The book was an attack on opponents of real estate and technological development. At first, Meyer, a cigar-smoking, smart, cocky man, was Casey's special assistant. In 1983, he got a much larger role as a vice chairman of the National Intelligence Council, the group of national intelligence officers who prepare the national intelligence estimates. In that job, Meyer helped manage production of all the CIA's estimates. At the same time, he continued to act as Casey's assistant.

Meyer brought to the job both a conservative bent and a journalist's probing mind. He decided CIA analysts were too isolated from the rest of the world, too insular in their approach. Meyer had contacts abroad with politicians, statesmen, and chief executive officers of major corporations. While it was the job of the Directorate of Operations to obtain information in the field, it seemed to Meyer that the analysts should also have their own contacts and sources.

"In New York, when I was at *Fortune,* you would walk around at lunch and pick up a book," Meyer would say. "The people at that agency have had lunch in the executive dining room for years. That is very destructive. You don't take an intelligence engine and put it out in the woods. It breeds ignorance, arrogance."[121]

"If you are in the business of seeing trends, of seeing the future, government is not one of the places where one would be likely to work," he would say. "The rewards are much greater in journalism, politics, business, academia, and think tanks. The moment you start taking the C and maybe B students, they will hire other C and B students. Over time, you have an institution that is not operating the way it should. They want consensus rather than dissent. That isn't good enough in a fast-changing world."

Thus when Meyer suggested exploring a new issue that happened to support his conservative worldview, it was hard for anyone to accuse him of trying to distort the estimating process. His approach was to question, to probe, and to argue. Moreover, much as his views seemed out of place with prevailing thought, he sometimes was right.

Whether Meyer actually changed analysts' lunch habits so they began seeing outsiders more, and whether that had any effect, is a matter that can be argued. But his feisty approach clearly produced fresh thinking.

"He [Meyer] brought a considerable freshness as an outsider to the organization, although he probably ruffled professional feathers because of his nontraditional approach and because many people did not like his political views, which are conservative," Graham E. Fuller, who was a national intelligence officer at the time and succeeded Meyer as a vice chairman, said. "But he did nothing but ask tough questions of people and engage them in debate. He did not dictate what our office would say. He would say, 'Have you considered this or that?'[122]

A lot of people disagreed with Meyer, including me," Fuller said. "But I heard him out. I think he had some useful things to say. Because of his conservative background, a lot of people dismissed what he said."

In much the same way, Casey would question and fulminate. Because he was the director, his views were taken much more seriously than Meyer's. But Casey soon learned that there was only so far he could go. He could not push the CIA officers into saying something they did not want to say or that they felt they could not support. But Casey tried, and the result was a series of spats—some public, some private—that created the appearance during Casey's tenure that the agency's analytical side was losing its integrity.

It began on March 1, 1981, when the *New York Times Magazine* ran an excerpt of Claire Sterling's book *The Terror Network: The Secret War of International Terrorism*, which suggested that the Soviets were providing the weapons, training, and sanctuary for terrorists as part of the Soviet effort to undermine Western democracy. The CIA had never said anything like this. Casey wanted the agency's analysts to follow up and discover if Sterling's facts were right. The CIA director had long suspected that the Soviets were in control of world terrorism, using thugs from all over the world as fronts for their own devious purposes.

What came out in the form of a draft estimate was ambiguous and not at all what Casey had wanted. According to those involved in preparing the estimate, the evidence available to the CIA at the time did not support Casey's or Claire Sterling's views.

"It was a question of semantics," said David D. Whipple, later national intelligence officer for terrorism. "He [Casey] would say, 'They [the Soviets] support them, and therefore they are responsible.' We would both go before a congressional committee. Casey would say, 'They are responsible,' and go back to work at noon and leave me to face the committee in the afternoon. I would try to erase what he said, because I was trying to differentiate between Soviet support for so-called national liberation struggles and actual direction of terrorist activities.[123]

"There was pressure internally to say more than we could professionally justify, and most of us resisted that," Whipple said. "Casey was on the right. An NIO can't be as far forward leaning as he was. . . . Everything you say has to be supported by intelligence. You can't sit there and interpret facts. Casey had a way of going beyond that sometimes." Whipple said that despite more recent revelations of East-bloc support of terrorists, "I don't think they'll ever prove that the Soviets instigated actions of terrorism, but they certainly supported people and groups who did engage in terrorism."

"The analysts were afraid they would be accused of engaging in some political act," said Adm. Bobby R. Inman, who was deputy director of Central Intelligence at the time. "The first draft bent over backward to avoid that. In any intelligence report, you identify assumptions. It said there is not conclusive evidence that this or that. I read it and put a note on it saying, 'This sounds like the prosecutor's argument on why he decided not to prosecute the case.' "[124]

Casey was more blunt. He wrote on the draft, "This is a bunch of shit." According to Inman, Casey was concerned more with the lack of logic and flow than with the conclusion.

"I've seen other instances where he [Casey] had strongly different personal views, but the paper in those cases was very well written. He would say it was well composed or well done," Inman said. "He then attached a memo on it to the president saying, 'I don't agree with this,' or, 'I think they are too bashful and my own view is this.' He never took off his very conservative lenses about how he made his own valuation. But he was the most cautious DCI I've seen about not trying to change somebody else's words to shape a view."

"I think Casey sensitized—that's an understatement—the intelligence community to that possibility [that the Soviets directed terrorists]," Fuller said. "The community was required to think more carefully about it. In the end, the community did not feel there was a sufficient case. . . . In the end, he didn't fight the problem."

Casey's intervention, his fervently conservative viewpoint, and his repeated involvement in the politics of the Reagan administration made him suspect in the eyes of CIA professionals—suspicions that sharpened after it turned out Casey had improperly and disastrously embroiled the agency's Directorate of Operations in the Iran-contra affair.

Another major flap came on September 28, 1984, when the *Washington Post* reported that John R. Horton, who had been national intelligence officer for Latin America, had resigned when Casey rewrote an estimate on Mexico to fit U.S. policy. According to the article, Horton had taken a moderate view about prospects in Mexico, and Casey wanted a hard-line approach that said the Mexican government would move to the left and become destabilized.

The newspaper story made good copy, but the facts were quite different. The impetus for the estimate had come from Meyer and Casey when they began hearing anecdotes from friends in Mexico about worsening conditions there. For example, the owner of an executive search firm said everyone he knew was sending his kids to the U.S. Middle managers were said to be leaving the country.

Brian Latell, a respected CIA analyst, was assigned to write a draft of the estimate. Usually, analysts base their conclusions on material available at headquarters, including traffic from stations. But Latell also traveled to Mexico, where Meyer kept in touch with him. Latell then wrote a draft of an estimate that concluded there was a possibility—later set at one in five—that Mexico would become destabilized in the next three to five years. That view coincided with the concerns of Meyer and Casey, who felt U.S. policymakers should at least be alerted to the possibility that Mexico could become a serious problem.

Meyer put a copy in his safe. Horton, a former station chief in Mexico City, disagreed with the draft. He exercised his right as the national intelligence officer in charge of the area to write a final version that disagreed with Latell's conclusions. Instead, he took a somewhat more sanguine view of developments in the country. But Meyer, as a vice chairman of the National Intelligence Council, exercised his right to change the estimate essentially back to Latell's draft.

"Horton's problem was we exercised our right to edit what he said," Meyer later said. "He never said the draft [he wrote] was the second one. He turned the expert's draft around. We turned it back. He had a right. I also had a right."[125]

"It was a fresh and provocative approach written by an analyst on Mexico which suggested a sharp recasting of our thoughts about Mexico," Fuller said. "This analyst, who is immensely respected and knows the field, suggested this was not the only approach, but it deserved real consideration. Casey insisted that this aspect of analysis be given reasonable credence within the body of the overall estimate."[126]

Said Fuller, "If you say things will be the same, you'll probably be right seventy-five percent of the time. When credible analysts come up with fresh approaches, it behooves managers of intelligence to pay special attention."

"Casey ironically thought Horton was trying to suppress what the analyst had said. You had a bitter debate about it. But it was an honest estimate. It began on the first page of the finished estimate with virtually half the community dissenting from the pessimistic view," Robert Gates, who was then chairman of the National Intelligence Council, said.

As events unfolded in Mexico, they turned out to fall somewhere in between Horton's approach and Latell and Meyer's, but the incident further strengthened the perception that Casey was cooking the books. The truth was Casey did listen to facts and would back down if given a good argument. For the CIA's top officials, Casey's conservative bent was never any problem. They had enough standing to take him on.

"I felt when I went into Casey, there was a first-class intellect at work who would listen and argue and respond, which was extremely gratifying to senior intelligence analysts, as opposed to people who are weak and not particularly seized with the substance of the thing," Fuller said.

Yet no one can say for sure how much effect Casey's ideology might have had on lower-level analysts, any more than one can demonstrate the effect of a conservative or liberal newspaper publisher on the way his reporters cover the news. While Casey's constant questioning was stimulating, it all pointed in the same direction. Unlike his successor, William Webster, Casey was an observer with a political agenda. He was therefore at odds with the purposes of the CIA—to present the facts and just the facts, as they are, rather than how policymakers may want them to be.

While it turned out that Casey and Meyer were right on a number of issues, they also turned out to be wrong a number of times. In 1983, Meyer wrote a series of memos saying the Soviet economy was in a shambles, which proved to be far closer to the truth than what the CIA's estimates were saying. Casey handed the memos to Reagan. On the other hand, the same series suggested that the shootdown of a Korean Airlines passenger jet on September 1, 1983, was a dire Soviet plot.

Meyer's memo predicted that there would be more such incidents.

The majority report of the congressional Iran-contra committees later said Casey "misrepresented or selectively used" available intelligence to win support for the Nicaraguan contras in certain limited areas. It said he pressured operations officers—as opposed to analysts in the Directorate of Intelligence—to change some reports on the contras, overstated their supply problems in one high-level meeting, and wrote a letter to President Reagan that distorted the attitudes of Central American leaders toward the American contra policy.

Certainly Casey's intervention created an *appearance* of lack of objectivity. In a business where integrity is critical, such an impression can be just as damaging as an outright effort to cook the books. Yet overall, the CIA continued to produce estimates that conflicted with Casey's views, demonstrating that ultimately, he had little or no effect on the process.

In 1983, the CIA said the rate of growth of Soviet defense spending was declining. The estimate conflicted with the agenda of the Reagan White House and Caspar Weinberger's Defense Department. Nor did Casey have any impact on the CIA's estimates on the prospects for the Nicaraguan contra rebels—the Reagan administration's pet project. A June 1985 estimate on Nicaragua said, "The Sandinista military . . . cannot by itself destroy the guerrillas, but neither can the insurgents destroy the Sandinista military."

Not that Casey didn't try to alter that judgment.

"I argued with him [Casey] and others in this building, because for a number of years, the argument of the intelligence community was that the contras would not win the war in Nicaragua," said Richard J. Kerr, then the CIA's deputy director for intelligence and later deputy director of Central Intelligence under Webster. "They did not have the force, they did not have the confidence of the people, they did not have the capability to carry Nicaragua. He [Casey] did not believe that at all. But if you look at our product, it consistently said they would *not* win by force of arms. They weren't going to make a strong political movement. All they would do is cause the Sandinistas to modify their behavior. He didn't really agree with that, and he never came down and said, 'You change that.' "[127]

Robert Gates, who was deputy director for intelligence, chairman of the National Intelligence Council, and deputy director for Central Intelligence under Casey, said Casey never influenced the analysts.

"The analytical side of the agency was always more pessimistic about the prospects for the contras than the policy side of the government or the clandestine service," Gates said. "At the same time, we were probably overly pessimistic about the Salvadoran military.[128]

"The bottom line," Gates said, "is that throughout that period, the agency did a lot of analytical work that was very unpopular with the policy side. The notion of analysis being influenced politically is dead wrong."

"He never told me to write something different than what I wrote," Kerr said. "What he did do is say, 'I don't believe this. I don't think this is what was reported. I don't think it's well documented. I don't think you've done a good analytic job on it, and I think you've missed what I consider to be the major issue.'

There are other people who say in that process, he did that [bring political pressure to bear], because he was the boss and he could intimidate you. He tended to be more hard-line, but not always. He had views, and they were strong views. They weren't necessarily always identical with conservative issues. If you were not willing to defend yourself, you could be rolled over by him, no question," Kerr said.

But by and large, CIA remained impervious.

"It's not because we are better than other people, although we are good, but part of it is we believe there is no alternative to being impartial," Kerr said. "That's what we do, and that's the only reason people read us. It's because they believe we have some contribution to make that is not tied to departmental policy. We may not understand it, we may be wrong, but it's not because we are pushing a line that is somebody's policy. If you vary from that, you lose your access, and you lose people who read you. For us, you are doomed if you do that.

"Ideally," Kerr said, "you don't have a DCI like that, but you do need one who forces you to test things. He can have strong opinions. He needs to have different views to get people to develop their arguments."[129]

Nowhere was that better demonstrated than on the question of the Soviet economy.

14 | *Too Little, Too Late*

SINCE THE END OF WORLD WAR II, THE CIA'S DIRECTORATE of Intelligence has struggled with a close to impossible task: estimating the size of the Soviet economy and the amount of money spent on defense. It is difficult because of the nature of Soviet society. Until the end of the Cold War, the Soviet Union was closed to the outside world, but that was only part of the problem. The larger difficulty was that the economy of the Soviet Union defied all common sense. In theory, it was a planned, centralized economy where production, price, and quantity were dictated by Moscow. But in practice, because of this artificial control, it was larded with under-the-table transactions and fraud that were impossible to measure.

From massive waste to black-marketing, the Soviet economy operated on many levels. Under the planned economy, Soviets had no incentive to work hard or to produce anything. They got paid the same regardless of whether they did anything or not. Because prices of goods bore no relation to their actual cost or to their value to consumers, they did not serve the normal function of regulating supply and demand. In a free economy, if sneakers or chocolate are in short supply and in demand, their prices rise, spurring entrepreneurs to produce more of them. That was missing in the Soviet economy, where ponderous bureaucracies regulated supply. Even if it were possible to regulate millions of transactions from Moscow, the bureaucrats had no incentive to keep up with changes in demand. No matter how much chocolate or how many sneakers consumers wanted, the price and the supply remained the same.

The Soviets themselves did not know the true size or shape of the Soviet economy. Much of the economic activity took place off the books—in bartering transactions that ate up a good chunk of each citizen's day. And the Soviets did not want to know about the huge amount of waste and fraud that consumed so much of the country's output. If the Soviets did not know, how was the CIA to know?

The answers were critical. In order to better judge the strength of its adversary, the U.S. needed to know how much the Soviets were spending on defense and how long they could continue to do it. If the Soviet economy was strong, the Soviets could continue to pour massive amounts into defense indefinitely. If it was weak, the Soviets could be expected to cut down on defense spending. The two questions were interrelated: If the Soviet gross national product was higher than generally thought, the proportion it spent on defense was lower. If the GNP was lower, then defense spending was proportionately higher. In either case, the amount spent by the Soviets on defense was considered to be roughly the same amount spent by the U.S.

For years, the CIA estimated that the Soviet economy was expanding by an average of 2.4 percent a year. Beginning in 1980, the CIA signaled that the Soviet economy was in trouble and "losing momentum." It revised its estimate of annual growth slightly downward, suggesting it was averaging 2.1 percent a year.[130] But the CIA's figures on the Soviet gross national product did not fully reflect how serious the problems were. According to CIA estimates, the Soviet per capita GNP was roughly half that of the U.S. Yet one did not need a Ph.D. in economics to see that that clearly could not be. Any visitor to the Soviet Union was shocked to find that, with the exception of its military, the USSR was a Third World country.

Going into a grocery store was like walking into a tomb. On most days, they had literally nothing to sell except potatoes and onions. If they had some meat, it was almost entirely fat and invariably previously frozen. Chickens appeared to be a different species—virtually all skin and bones. Milk was sour when it was purchased. Often, milk sold as fresh was actually powdered. Apples were tiny and shriveled. The oranges were still green. Grapes, if available, were rotten. To meet plan quotas, tea was mixed with tiny branches and leaves of other plants to increase its bulk. Most Third World countries at least had enough to feed their people.

To get an apple, one would have to try to wedge one's way into a crowd to get a peek at the prices. Then one would have to stand in line for a half an hour to get to the cashier to pay in advance for it. Finally, one waited in another line for another half hour to present the chit to a second clerk who weighed the apples and gave them to the customer without any bags or wrappings.

Everything was made so cheaply and maintained so poorly that virtually nothing worked. A hotel such as the National across from Red Square in Moscow—supposedly high quality, used by foreigners—confronted guests entering the lobby with a moldy smell and carpets that were threadbare and soiled. Standing at the reception desk was like going back to the nineteenth century. There was a wooden Teletype machine that looked like one of the first radio sets. The guest rooms were out of the American West, circa 1890. The furnishings were about what one would expect in an American prison, with two beds the size of cots that sank like pedestrian underpasses in the middle. They were covered with tattered spreads with holes in them. The sheets had small rust stains. The pine dresser was so battered it would not be sold at a rummage sale in the West. A table was covered with a cloth that looked as if it had been used for wrapping fish.

But that was nothing compared with the bathroom. The

tiles were coming off, nothing was plumb, the toilet seat was as thin as the skin of a toy airplane, the sink was old and rusting, there was only one small piece of soap, and the toilet paper was coarser than the coarsest Western writing paper. The towels were so thin and worn from repeated washings they could barely absorb any moisture.

Downstairs in the dining room, there was at least one waiter for each table. Yet the service dragged on for hours because most of the time the waiters remained in the hallway chattering with each other. There was no incentive to do a good job or to cut down on extra workers because everything was owned by the government, which decided from Moscow how many waiters should work in each hotel, what prices should be charged, and how much food was needed.

Souvenir shops had three saleswomen who helped each other ring up a sale. One would hand each item in turn to the cashier. The cashier rang up the sale, while the third employee milled around and eventually wrapped the items. All three took more time to ring up a sale than the usual one American cashier.

In the same vein, five or six taxi cabs would pass by before one would pick up a passenger. The drivers got paid the same regardless of whether they picked up riders or not, so they continued driving without bothering to pick up anyone.

After Soviet leader Mikhail Gorbachev took over in 1985, the already fragile Soviet economy began to crumble. His policy of perestroika, or restructuring, had the effect of destroying much of the existing system, without replacing it with a new one. It was then that the CIA was blamed for failing to predict that the Soviet economy would collapse and for clinging to estimates of the Soviet gross national product that clearly did not portray how bad off it was. Yet for decades, the CIA's method worked.

Because official statistics could not be trusted, the CIA developed a model of every facet of the Soviet economy, from the steel and transportation industries to production of coal and oil. Based wherever possible on visual evidence from satellites, the CIA determined the quantity and value of each item produced. For example, the CIA estimated the cost of producing a Soviet fighter plane by adding the value of the labor and the cost of the steel. Where satellite coverage would not work, the CIA used the observations of Soviet émigrés or information obtained by intercepting Soviet communications. Then the CIA translated the findings into rubles and dollars. Since rubles could not be exchanged for dollars, the CIA had to estimate the conversion rate based on what each currency could buy—how many BTUs of coal, for example.

The task was awesome. The CIA contracted out estimating the cost of reproducing each Soviet armament. As many as fifty CIA officers worked on the military questions alone. Every now and then, they got a break—a Soviet book that listed shipbuilding costs, an overheard conversation about the size of the Soviet military budget, or a defector such as Nicholas Shadrin. Shadrin was a Soviet Navy commander who knew the costs of building destroyers.

In 1975, a Soviet émigré who claimed to have seen the defense budget cited figures that tended to indicate Soviet military spending was higher than the CIA thought. Lt. Gen. Daniel O. Graham, then director of the Defense Intelligence Agency, decided the CIA was ignoring him. Although the man had failed lie detector tests, Graham thought the CIA had botched the tests by making the man nervous. Graham interviewed the man himself and decided he was telling the truth. He said he wanted the CIA to polygraph him again, this time using questions he prepared. The man passed.[131]

The CIA's estimates of military spending doubled the next year—from 5 to 6 percent of the Soviet GNP to 11 to 12 percent. CIA officials said the émigré's information played a role in the revision, which they claimed would have occurred anyway.

In the early 1960s, William T. Lee, an analyst at the CIA, had devised a different estimating system that made use of Soviet statistics. It showed an even higher proportion of military spending. In 1964, Lee left the CIA over disagreements about his method. He later joined the DIA, but he continues to testify before Congress that the CIA's estimates—still based on methods developed when Lee was with the agency—are unrealistic. As of 1990, Lee was estimating Soviet defense spending at 25 percent of the Soviet GNP.[132]

"They [the CIA] wanted me to recant, and I left in disgust," Lee said. "I was saying that the method I was using is a better method than what they were using."[133]

The CIA said its method was superior because it was based wherever possible on what could be seen, rather than on Soviet statistics, which were notoriously fallacious and self-serving. Yet in the end, Lee's figures seemed to be closer to the truth than the CIA's.

Igor Birman, a Soviet émigré and economist, also concluded early on that the Soviet economy was in much poorer shape than the CIA was claiming. According to Birman's figures, the Soviet GNP was only a third of U.S. GNP—more in line with that of a Third World country such as Mexico.

In 1980, Birman described the Soviet economy in *Soviet Studies* as being in a state of "crisis."[134] On October 27, 1980, Birman said in an op-ed page piece in the *Washington Post* that the CIA's estimates of the Soviet economy were far too rosy. Birman said the Soviet standard of living was "only a fourth or even a fifth the American level." Birman said Soviet military spending is "very likely about 20 percent" of the Soviet GNP, a proportion then almost double the CIA's estimate.[135]

"I was alone in the world, saying the huge CIA is wrong," Birman said. "The wonderful American press has criticized the CIA for spy operations, but never their analysis. I did. I knew I was alone, and if I say the truth, nobody would believe me."[136]

More recently, the CIA has said the Soviets spend 15 percent to 17 percent of their GNP on the military, compared with a figure of 25 percent cited by many of the critics.

As the Soviet economy continued to deteriorate, Henry S. Rowen, a former chairman of the National Intelligence Council and later assistant secretary of defense for international security affairs, and Andrew W. Marshall, director of net assessments at the Defense Department, began sounding similar warnings. In 1986, they and Charles Wolf, Jr., dean of the RAND School of Graduate Studies, met with President

Reagan to tell him the Soviet economy was in worse shape than the CIA was saying.

"Your advisers have seriously underestimated the difficulties of the Soviet economy," Rowen told Reagan. "We are in a much stronger bargaining position."

Their position coincided with memos William Casey had given to Reagan from Herb Meyer saying the Soviet economy was in much worse shape than the CIA was saying.

Still, the CIA clung to its position. Indeed, that same year, the CIA said the Soviet economy was improving. Later, the agency took note of problems in the Soviet economy but did not significantly revise its estimates of the GNP. For example, in 1987, the CIA said, "The Soviet economy has made solid gains since 1960 . . . but its growth has slowed, especially in the last decade."[137]

In retrospect, the critics' characterization of the Soviet economy as a system in serious trouble has proven to be correct. Their estimates that Soviet military spending takes up a far greater chunk of Soviet output than the CIA thought are undoubtedly true as well. That individual economists, working with practically no funding, could come out closer to the truth than CIA analysts with their immense resources is cause for concern.

At the same time, no one knows the true figures. How does one account for the fact that, because the Soviet system measures output by square yards of glass produced, glass-manufacturing plants make plate glass that is so thin that most of it breaks before it leaves the plant? Or that ornamental vases made of lead are produced in vast quantities but no one buys them? They are therefore stacked in a yard and melted down to go into the next year's supply of unwanted vases.

Trainloads of new tractors are delivered in a cannibalized state because people cannot obtain spare parts. People therefore steal the wheels and transmissions right off the tractors after they leave the factory. Likewise, up to a third of the Soviet wheat harvest has been estimated to consist of rubbish, weeds, and moisture. At the same time, because of poor transportation and storage facilities, as much as half of Soviet farm production never gets to market. Gorbachev himself estimated in June 1985 that a fifth of the overall agricultural harvest was being lost.

According to Swedish economist Anders Åslund, if Soviet manufactured goods were sold in the West, the prices they would fetch would be lower than the prices of the raw products used to manufacture them.

"It is a startling experience to walk into Soviet stores, assess the Western value of Soviet-made commodities, and compare them with actual Soviet prices," Åslund has written. "In the vast majority of cases, the Western market value of a Soviet commodity—food as well as industrial goods—would be nil or close to nil, since their quality is so poor that they could not be sold in the West."[138]

Meanwhile, a large chunk of consumer needs is met on the black market, still another quagmire that is impossible for economists—in or out of the country—to measure accurately.

"We try to account for fraudulent production like glass that breaks," a CIA analyst involved in producing the agency's Soviet figures said. "Sometimes we succeed, sometimes we fail."

By April 1990, John L. Helgerson, the CIA's deputy director for intelligence, was finally venturing that the Soviet economy was in an "unstable state" and could be "pushed over the edge into sharp deterioration" by further strikes or ethnic unrest. Still, "the most likely outcome for 1990 is that the Soviet economy will stagnate or decline slightly," the CIA said.[139]

It was too little, too late. By then, the CIA had clearly blown it.

With some exaggeration, William Safire wrote in *The New York Times*, "The central mission of U.S. intelligence is to gather and evaluate data on the economic and military strength of the Soviet Union in comparison with the U.S. We are now discovering how the CIA has botched that assignment."[140]

Even Abram Bergson, the Harvard economist who helped develop the model used by the CIA while working for the RAND Corp., has said recently, "I think the GNP is overstated [by the CIA]. How much is controversial."[141]

But given the difficulty of the job, the CIA over the years had done remarkably well. Predicting even the American economy correctly is a daunting task. For every five economists, as the aphorism goes, there are six opinions. In the early days of the Cold War, the CIA gave U.S. policymakers a rough indication of the strength of the Soviet economy and the amount being spent on armaments. Contrary to Safire's comment, the agency accurately catalogued the size and shape of the Soviet military. This was far more important than predicting the proportion of the Soviet economy spent on defense. It was only when the Soviet economy began to disintegrate that the CIA moved too slowly to recognize the change.

Whether through the CIA, Herb Meyer's memos from Casey, or his meeting with the critics in 1986, the word got through to President Reagan. In his book *An American Life,* Reagan wrote, "As president I learned the Soviet economy was in even worse shape than I'd realized. It was a basket case, partly because of massive spending on armaments."[142]

"Did they get the numbers wrong? Yes. Did they underestimate the percentage of Soviet GNP going to defense? I'd bet my life on it," Robert Gates, who oversaw the CIA's estimates as deputy director for intelligence, said when he was President Bush's deputy assistant for national security affairs. "But did they generally portray a Soviet economy in trouble and one less and less able to support this superstructure of the military and intelligence? I think they did."[143]

As the stories about the CIA's tardy response to the changes in the Soviet economy faded from memory, the CIA's intelligence directorate was faced with a new and much more critical challenge: predicting what Iraq was doing as it moved troops toward Kuwait.

15 ‖ *Triumph*

As the Cold War ended and the Soviet Union became less of a threat, the press began to question the need for a CIA. But those who raised the issue had only a limited perception of what the CIA does. By spying on friendly countries, the agency prepares for threats that may develop when those countries turn hostile. There could be no better example than Iraq's invasion of Kuwait on August 1, 1990.

During Iraq's ten-year war with Iran, the United States had tilted toward Iraq as the lesser of two evils. The Reagan administration approved giving Iraq the data from satellite reconnaissance to help it fight Iran, along with U.S. agricultural credit guarantees and Export-Import Bank financing. When the war ended, Iraq had $80 billion in debts and dwindling oil income. As his money problems worsened, Saddam Hussein, the Iraqi president, became belligerent toward the West.

By February 1990, Hussein was calling for the U.S. fleet,

which had been in the Persian Gulf for forty years, to return to the United States. On March 15, over British protests, Iraq executed Farzad Bazoft, an Iranian-born journalist working for the British press, for spying. On April 1, Saddam Hussein threatened to "make the fire to eat up half of Israel." On April 12, he told five U.S. senators that an "all-out campaign is being waged against us in America and the countries of Europe." At the end of May, he charged that Kuwait was waging "economic warfare" against him. He complained that Kuwait would not agree to lower oil production in order to raise oil prices—increases that Iraq needed to pay off its mounting debts.

Analysts at the Directorate of Intelligence watched these developments with keen interest. During Iraq's war with Iran, the CIA had built up an extensive data base on Iraq and its military and industry, including its chemical and biological weapons plants. The CIA also knew what kinds of movements the Iraqi military made before taking offensive action. However, in part because the CIA had been ordered to help Iraq during the war, the Directorate of Operations had not had much interest in developing an extensive array of agents or human spies within the government. Moreover, since Saddam Hussein trusted only close friends and family members, it would have been extremely difficult to do so under any circumstances.

In November 1989, the CIA prepared a National Intelligence Estimate that said Saddam Hussein wanted to be the "bully of the Middle East." Going with what a reasonable man would think, the estimate said it would take three years before he had recovered enough from the war with Iran to take any action. In 1990, an analyst wrote a "think piece" suggesting that the Iraqi leader might invade islands coveted by Iraq off the Kuwaiti coast, and that he might go on to invade Kuwait itself.

Three weeks before Iraq's invasion of Kuwait, the CIA's Directorate of Science and Technology began receiving hard evidence of a military buildup near the Kuwaiti border. The question was whether Iraq meant to invade Kuwait or merely to threaten it. The State Department's Bureau of Intelligence and Research thought Saddam Hussein was probably bluffing. But as days wore on, the CIA began warning the president that Iraq would most likely invade.

"Strong words could threaten them [the Kuwaitis], let alone one hundred thousand troops," Richard J. Kerr, the CIA's deputy director for Central Intelligence, said.[144] "It was clear there was more there than was needed [to bluster], and there was a serious military option, and given the forces, there was an increasing possibility—and probability as we walked down to the last several days—that he would actually move at least partway into Kuwait," Kerr said. "There was a probability he would take the northern area and the oil fields and islands, and a possibility he would go much farther and take the whole thing."

On August 1, the CIA said it was more likely than not that Iraq would invade within twenty-four hours.

By predicting the invasion, the CIA had given President Bush and his policymakers additional time to plan a response, which came almost immediately in the form of a demand that Iraq pull out of Kuwait. Whether the early information could have been used, or should have been used, as the basis for a stronger warning to Iraq before the invasion is debatable. In now famous remarks, April Glaspie, the U.S. ambassador to Iraq, told Saddam Hussein on July 25 that the United States had "no opinion" on Iraq's border dispute with Kuwait. But she also warned, according to her later statement before Congress, that the United States would protect its vital interests in the area. Glaspie's cables reporting on her meeting with Saddam Hussein did not support her testimony to Congress that she warned the Iraqi president that the U.S. would protect its interests in the area. However, a cable from President Bush to Saddam Hussein after the meeting said, "We believe that differences are best resolved by peaceful means and not by threats involving military force or conflict."[145]

Bush could have warned Iraq more bluntly that any invasion would be turned back by force. But the U.S. would have had to be in a position to back up any threat with action, and the administration was not yet ready to take that position. Indeed, Saddam Hussein asked Glaspie to assure Bush that he had no intention of attacking Kuwait. That reassurance was soon amplified by King Hussein of Jordan, President Hosni Mubarak of Egypt, and King Fahd of Saudi Arabia, who each told Bush that in their view, the Iraqi president would not attack.

Nevertheless, at three P.M. on August 1, Assistant Secretary of State John Kelly warned Iraq that its differences with Kuwait must be resolved peacefully. He asked Iraq to pull its forces back. Iraq denied any aggressive intentions.[146]

By eight P.M., the invasion had begun.

"If you go back through the meetings at the NSC [National Security Council] at the deputy level, you'll see a realistic assessment of Saddam Hussein in terms of a man who was pretty much a cutthroat bully," Kerr said. "The question was how do you deal with him. Do you deal with him by threatening him or do you try to engage him in some kind of a process? Threatening him without backing it up is not useful. Just saying you better not do it is not going to have much impact."

Ideally, the Bush administration would have threatened Saddam Hussein with force if he moved into Kuwait. But whether that would have worked is highly debatable. Over the ensuing months, Saddam Hussein refused to budge even when threatened with massive military force by the U.S. and its allies. In the end, only military action against Iraq's forces worked. The CIA collected most of the intelligence used.

First the CIA reassigned at least four photo reconnaissance satellites to orbit over the Middle East. Costing $1 billion to $1.5 billion apiece, the satellites were from the KH-11 and KH-12 series. They orbited 200 to 500 miles above the earth's surface. In addition to relaying photographic images in real time, the satellites transmitted images based on heat emissions. LACROSSE, a satellite system using radar imaging, saw through cloud cover, darkness, and smoke from 500 miles above the earth. Finally, satellites code-named MAGNUM and VORTEX intercepted Iraqi communications from 22,000 miles above the earth.

The Directorate of Operations formed a wartime task force of more than two hundred officers. Among other things, they worked to free Americans held by Iraq during the early stages of the conflict, established a clandestine radio station that urged Iraqi troops to surrender, and helped the U.S. Army design leaflets urging surrender.

Through the National Collection Division within the Directorate of Operations, the CIA was able to obtain the plans for weapons plants and other military installations from American businessmen. The Soviet/East Europe Division obtained similar information from Poland and Hungary, countries that had formerly worked with the Soviets to supply Iraq its armaments.

Meanwhile, the CIA's Counterterrorism Center sifted through more than one hundred terrorist threats that came in against the countries allied against Iraq just after the invasion of Kuwait. After war broke out, the CIA recorded one hundred and twenty terrorist acts—not threats—against the allies. Working with law enforcement agencies throughout the world, the CIA helped to foil a number of the efforts.[147]

The Directorate of Intelligence established a task force of one hundred analysts who pored over the images, intercepts, and reports from agents. Before the war began on January 16, 1991, they issued some five hundred reports to the White House on the effect of economic sanctions against Iraq and on Saddam Hussein's preparations for war. After DESERT STORM began, the CIA issued hundreds of additional reports to the White House and the military. Among them were analyses of Saddam Hussein, who was judged to be sane and operating according to the values and traditions of his society.

Dr. Jerrold M. Post, a former CIA psychiatrist who analyzed personalities of world leaders, described Saddam Hussein as a man who is not "suffering from a psychotic disorder. He is not impulsive, acts only after judicious consideration, and can be extremely patient, indeed uses time as a weapon. While he is psychologically in touch with reality, he is often politically out of touch. Saddam's advisers do not lightly contradict his views or his plans."

According to Dr. Post, the Iraqi leader is able "to justify extremes of aggression on the basis of revolutionary needs. If the aggression is counterproductive, he has always shown a pattern of reversing his course when he has miscalculated, waiting until a later day to achieve his revolutionary destiny."[148]

Dr. Post later expanded his evaluation of the Iraqi leader, saying he suffers from "malignant narcissism," a severe personality disorder that manifests itself in paranoia, ruthlessness, and grandiose ideas.

The CIA presented most of its key findings to President Bush at daily eight A.M. briefings, when the agency gave him the President's Daily Brief (PDB), a compendium of the CIA's best intelligence and analysis. From the day the CIA began, the agency had prepared a daily current intelligence summary, which evolved into the National Intelligence Daily, now given to 250 senior government officials in Washington and hundreds of other U.S. officials around the world. However, President Kennedy asked for a publication that would more directly address his needs and interests. The result was the PDB.

Each president designates who should receive the PDB within his administration. Bush wanted it distributed only to the secretaries of defense and state and to the chairman of the joint chiefs of staff. The PDB also goes to other members of the intelligence community besides the CIA.

Some presidents, such as Ronald Reagan, did not read the PDB themselves, preferring to have their national security advisers read the document and brief them. Others, such as George Bush and Gerald Ford, read the PDB themselves. When they are reading it, they receive a briefing from a CIA analyst. The briefer jots down questions the president has as he reads the PDB and listens to the briefing. The briefer brings back answers the next morning, or sooner if necessary.

The PDB is prepared by the CIA's Office of Current Production and Analytic Support. Located on the seventh floor of the old CIA headquarters building, it is part of the Directorate of Intelligence and includes the CIA's operations center that keeps track of minute-to-minute developments around the world. The center looks very much like the news anchor studio of a major television network. Like many CIA offices, the windows are protected with devices that vibrate, making it impossible for laser beams from outside to pick up sound from within. Like the offices of most high-ranking CIA officials, it has a television monitor tuned constantly to Cable News Network (CNN).

The PDB is prepared by ten officers, including a chief and deputy chief who also take turns briefing the president each morning. The officer who will brief the president the next day usually stays until eight P.M. the night before to read a draft of the next day's PDB. He comes back to the CIA before the PDB's five-thirty A.M. deadline to insert any late-breaking developments. The CIA's printing plant, at the northwest end of the CIA compound, then prints the top-secret document. The director of Central Intelligence receives a draft of the PDB at the end of the day so he can read it on the way home. A final copy is delivered when the CIA security guards pick him up in the morning.

The PDB is usually eight to ten letter-size pages arranged in newspaper column format. The pages on the left are usually reserved for photographs, charts, and tables. Like a newspaper, the PDB presents the most important news near the front, while longer analyses appear near the end. For example, before the war began, the PDB carried an analysis of Saddam Hussein's personality. The PDB staff refers to it as the "book."

As a rule, about half of what are known as "key facts" in the PDB are not yet publicly known. For example, during the war, the PDB addressed the question of whether Israel would respond to Iraq's Scud missile attacks. Other material, while rumored, was reported with more authority than what appeared in the press at the time. The PDB also conveyed analysis. For example, it summarized William Webster's prediction in December 1990 that Saddam Hussein would not withdraw until faced with "imminent military attack." In January 1991, Webster said that economic sanctions alone would not force Saddam Hussein to withdraw his forces from Kuwait for at least a year.[149]

The agency thus dismissed the possibility that economic sanctions would work in the foreseeable future, a judgment proven correct by later events. The PDB also correctly predicted that Saddam Hussein would use scorched-earth tactics and spill oil on the Persian Gulf before withdrawing from Kuwait.

When William Webster was DCI, he briefed the president himself, along with the officer from the PDB, three to four times a week. During the war, he briefed him virtually daily. First Webster met with Bush's national security advisers and gave them a copy of the PDB. Then, for the next fifteen to twenty minutes, they all met with Bush to review it and take questions. The briefer then returned the document to the CIA. If Bush was out of town, he received a copy of the PDB by secure fax.

"What has been unique in the Bush administration, and was done only once before with Gerald Ford, is that we have daily personal contact with the president when he is in town," a member of the PDB staff said. "The normal pattern has been for the person we call the PDB briefer to go downtown and see the national security adviser and sit with him while he goes through the book and asks questions, hand over any supplemental material, late-breaking news, and photography that illustrates the point and that came in too late to get in the book. The national security adviser would then see the president."

Both Ford and Bush had read the PDB when they were vice president and had come to rely on it. As a former CIA director and someone who was intimately familiar with the foreign policy issues addressed, Bush took a particular interest in the briefing.

"Bush, after he was elected, I think the first day, said he would like to continue to have someone from CIA brief him," the staffer said. "He reads it, and the others read it at the same time. The president asks questions: 'How confident are we of this particular information? Might we be able to get additional information on this using one or another kind of collection technique?' Then usually the briefer leaves, and usually the director leaves. Occasionally, he'll stay behind to discuss a sensitive program, or the president will ask him something."

In reporting on Iraq, the CIA's efforts were not without

flaws. The agency vastly overestimated the number of Iraqi soldiers in Kuwait. Many had defected from their units, and the agency assumed each unit in place had a full complement of men. The CIA underestimated the number of Iraqi mobile Scud launchers. And the agency did not know that the bunker in the Amariya district in Baghdad used as a secret military command post during the day was packed with hundreds of women and children at night. The reason was that most of the spy satellites passed over Iraq during the day. Many women and children died when an American jet attacked the bunker.

But overall, the performance of the CIA and related intelligence agencies was a "triumph," as the *Wall Street Journal* later called it in a feature article by Walter S. Mossberg. The military was able to see its targets from space in real time, a war-winning advantage. With few exceptions, the CIA pinpointed every tank, every gun emplacement, and every chemical and biological weapons facility. When a defector reported that contrary to earlier reports, not all of Iraq's equipment for making nuclear explosives had been destroyed, the CIA provided photographs of out-of-date uranium-enrichment machinery being moved around on trucks or being buried to evade United Nations inspections. Most important, the CIA had predicted the outbreak of the war in the first place.

"The Central Intelligence Agency and its sister services, especially the code-breaking National Security Agency, supplied U.S. military commanders with an immense quantity of timely information," the *Wall Street Journal* said. "Spy-satellite photos, intercepted Iraqi military communications, and other data gave U.S. generals a capability their predecessors could only dream about—the ability to track just about every important military action Iraq undertook."[150]

A later story by George Lardner, Jr., of the *Washington Post* sounded a similar theme. "U.S. intelligence during the Persian Gulf War has been widely rated by government officials as superb in many respects, but the conflict also produced hard evidence of the breakdowns that can occur," the July 5, 1991, story said.

While Army General H. Norman Schwarzkopf later complained that analyses were too qualified, he said intelligence during the war was excellent, contributing to the allied success. He also singled out for criticism bomb-damage assessments, which conflicted with higher reports of damage from pilots. Which assessments were closest to the truth is still not clear. Like any witnesses, pilots are often wrong. On the other hand, the analysts back in Washington had little experience tracking the kind of destruction wreaked by "smart" weapons. From the air, a tank may appear undamaged because it has not exploded in flames and appears to have only a tiny hole where a missile entered it. But today's missiles can wipe out the inside of a tank and its occupants without creating outside damage. For that reason, the analysts could very well have underestimated damage, contributing to unnecessary loss of lives from bombing missions that were not militarily necessary. But that kind of analysis, for the most part, was done by military intelligence analysts, not by the CIA.

Some publications trumpeted what they called "failures" of intelligence during the war. They cited the fact that the CIA had overestimated the number of Iraqi soldiers in Kuwait and had predicted that Saddam Hussein would use chemical weapons. Yet overestimates of opposing forces can never be a failure if the idea is to win the war. Where it overestimated the enemy, the CIA contributed to the allied success by suggesting the need for a large military offensive able to swiftly overrun the enemy.

"If you know others and know yourself, you will not be imperiled in a hundred battles," the Chinese warrior-philosopher Sun Tzu said more than two thousand years ago.[151]

The fact is that Saddam Hussein, who should have known more about his own forces than did the CIA, also overstated their capabilities and did not take desertions into account. To expect that anyone can predict every tactic that an enemy will use—including use of chemical weapons—is unrealistic.

Some media critics and a few members of Congress said the CIA should have known earlier on that Saddam Hussein would invade Kuwait.

"The president could have had very many options" if the plans to invade Kuwait were known weeks earlier, Sen. David

L. Boren, the Oklahoma Democrat who headed the Senate Select Committee on Intelligence, said. Only "in the last few days" before the invasion did U.S. intelligence agencies forecast its occurrence, Boren said.[152]

Again, the criticism was unfounded. If there were evidence that Saddam Hussein knew what his own plans were well before the CIA knew about them, the criticism might have been justified. Certainly his officers did not know his plans. In interviewing captured Iraqi officers, the CIA found that the military did not know more than twenty-four hours before the invasion what their leader's intentions were. Tariq Aziz, Iraq's foreign minister during the war, told Milton Viorst, on assignment for the *New Yorker,* that Saddam Hussein did not decide to invade Kuwait until August 1, when talks on oil disputes between Iraq and Kuwait collapsed in Jidda.[153]

In effect, the critics were saying that the agency should have known that Saddam Hussein was going to invade Kuwait before he knew it. To suggest that the CIA should have known more than the enemy knew is to require clairvoyance, something that no one has yet been able to achieve. Intelligence is nothing more than information, and to insist that the CIA should have it before it exists is unfair. Unless there is reason to believe that an event is going to happen, the CIA has no business saying it might happen. After all, anything might happen.

Three weeks before the military offensive took place, the CIA raised the possibility that Iraq would invade. In doing so, the CIA fulfilled its role, which is to take the first cut at world events, to filter out important developments, to bring them to the attention of the White House, and to sound a warning about the possible outcomes so that policymakers can prepare.

Absent hard evidence, the CIA would have been irresponsible if it had said flatly that Saddam Hussein would invade. Even if the CIA had had hard evidence of Saddam Hussein's intentions early on, no one—including the Iraqi leader—knew for sure that he would go ahead with the plan until he did. The fact is the CIA did raise the possibility that Iraq would invade Kuwait three weeks before the invasion. It could not have stated the case more strongly than it did because, even to this day, there is no evidence that Saddam Hussein knew then he would order an invasion. Even when the CIA did sound the alarm, the Bush administration did very little about it.

"People make critical comments about us all the time," Kerr observed. "A lot of it is out of frustration. We don't do what they would like us to do, or we are doing something they would just as soon we didn't do."[154]

The fact is the U.S. could not have won the war, with its outflanking maneuvers and precise bombing, as quickly and effectively as it did if it had not had good intelligence. In this case, the intelligence overall was nothing short of spectacular. Yet even when the CIA does well, its success is often portrayed as failure.

Meanwhile, an entire directorate of the CIA goes on about its business largely unaffected by the crisis of the moment. This is the Directorate of Administration, which supports the CIA. Yet in many ways, this is the most fascinating of all the CIA's directorates. Because it contains the Office of Security, it is also the one with the most problems.

PART IV

The Directorate of Administration

16 | *Laundering Money*

THE DIRECTORATE OF ADMINISTRATION, WHILE ONLY A support element, is no different from the other directorates in thinking that its job is the most essential. It is this directorate that keeps the other pieces of the agency in place. Without it, no one in the CIA would get paid, no one would be hired, and no one would have any computers, communications, heat, or electricity. Most important, without the directorate's Office of Security, opposing spy agencies could infiltrate moles into the CIA or bug the office of the CIA director himself. With nine thousand employees, it is the CIA's largest directorate.

This is the directorate that buys the pencils and paper clips, orders the phones, and processes new employee applications. These are normally prosaic duties. But because it services the CIA, the Directorate of Administration can be as exciting as any James Bond thriller. It has its covert side, its cover stories and cutouts, which often rival those of the operations side of the agency.

Within the directorate, the Office of Security is responsible for the physical security of the CIA. It conducts background investigations of new CIA employees and CIA contractors, administers polygraph tests to employees and agents, debugs offices at Langley and overseas stations, patrols the buildings and grounds, protects the director and other key CIA officials, and investigates security problems. With the help of the FBI, it also investigates espionage. Some of the CIA's most serious abuses have been perpetrated by this office.

Besides administering the finances of the agency, the Office of Financial Management launders money using dummy corporations and multiple bank accounts worldwide in order to further the work of the clandestine side of the agency.

The Office of Medical Services administers physicals to employees and supplies security-cleared psychiatrists to help them with psychiatric problems. It operates a psychological profiling unit that issues psychological analyses of world leaders such as Saddam Hussein. It also helps out in analyzing specimens—from feces to hair—of world leaders to determine if they have any health problems that might affect their longevity or judgment. Finally, at various times it has gotten involved in such esoteric matters as determining if ESP would help uncover drop sites of the KGB.

The Office of Training and Education trains CIA employees. It operates Camp Peary, a supposedly still secret CIA compound near Williamsburg, Virginia, that teaches the tools of the spy trade—how to recruit and handle agents, how to avoid surveillance. The office's courses include instruction in area studies and twenty-five languages. It also manages publication of *Studies in Intelligence,* a classified CIA quarterly journal.

The Office of Communications not only orders phones but provides top-secret coded communications by satellite throughout the world. The Office of Information Technology runs the vast array of computers needed to keep each of the directorates functioning. Overseas, it arranges for quick-burn devices to destroy computers in case an embassy is taken over.

Laundering Money

The History Staff within the directorate consists of three historians who obtain recollections of officers who have retired and write a continuing classified history of the CIA. A Freedom of Information Office processes requests for documents under the provisions of the Freedom of Information Act.

The Office of Personnel keeps the agency staffed by recruiting on college campuses, running ads in newspapers, overseeing hiring, and administering psychological and other tests to applicants. Recently, it began a new program to assist retired CIA officers adjust professionally, economically, and psychologically to life in the private sector.

The Office of Logistics not only moves employees and offices and provides couriers for delivering top-secret documents but also buys guns and ammunition and runs so-called proprietaries, companies such as Air America that are owned by the CIA. Through Fairways Corporation, a longtime CIA proprietary, the office operates the CIA's planes, including regular flights to Camp Peary, the training center. The office manages the agency's procurement system, the printing plant, photographic facility, mail system, motor pool, courier system, and food services. The entire monolith would grind to a halt without the office's Real Estate and Construction Branch, which runs the CIA's physical plant and maintains its grounds.

In this area, as in others, the most important goal is secrecy.

17 | *Langley*

FROM A DISTANCE, THE ONLY UNUSUAL FEATURE ABOUT the CIA's compound is Virginia Power Company's 113,000-volt transmission line, which is needed to power the agency's massive computers. It enters the agency's property at the left of the main gate on Dolley Madison Boulevard at Georgetown Pike in McLean.

Originally, highway signs marked the location of the CIA from George Washington Memorial Parkway in Virginia, but Robert F. Kennedy, who was attorney general at the time and lived nearby at the family's Hickory Hill estate, asked the CIA to take them down.

"Bobby Kennedy said, 'This is the silliest thing I've seen. Please take the signs down,' " William Colby, director of Central Intelligence from 1973 to 1976, said.[155] "We pretended that the building wasn't there, even though every pilot uses it as a checkpoint going down [to National Airport]."

When James R. Schlesinger became director of Central

Intelligence in 1973, he asked Colby why the CIA had no signs. Colby told him the story.

"I think we should have signs," Schlesinger said.

After Schlesinger checked with the White House, the signs went back up.[156] Today, highway markers along Dolley Madison Boulevard going northwest say, "CIA Next Right." But sometimes they temporarily disappear again when souvenir hunters snatch them.

Closer up, one can see double chain-link fences topped with barbed wire surrounding the compound. The fence is marked with the standard signs: "U.S. Government Property, No Trespassing." Each segment of fence is fitted with a tiny black plastic box, part of a system that sounds an alarm in the Office of Security's duty office when the fence vibrates.

"All nonbadged visitors must keep right," a sign says along the access drive. Other signs warn that the speed limit is twenty-five miles per hour—speed is checked by radar—explosives are prohibited.

Visitors turn into a separate lane, where another sign tells them to drive up to a post equipped with an intercom and closed-circuit television camera. Just as in a drive-in hamburger stand, a visitor tells the guard at the other end what he wants. The guard asks for his social security number. If the visitor has an appointment, his social security number will already be registered on a computer list. The guard then instructs the visitor to pull up to the main guard gate, a concrete-and-glass structure twenty-five feet beyond the intercom. There, the visitor must show picture identification. If everything matches, the guard gives him a visitor's badge, a parking permit with a map of the parking lots, and a form to sign. The form gives the CIA the right to search the visitor.

If anyone tries to enter the compound without permission, the guard can flip a switch and raise a steel barrier that revolves out of the ground. Just in case, the guards, who wear broad-brimmed hats that make them look like park rangers, have machine guns and guard dogs.

Just after Webster appointed William M. Baker to be the CIA's director of public affairs, Baker returned to Washington's National Airport from a trip. Baker's wife, Robin, a flight attendant, had just gotten off a plane herself at National. It was ten P.M., and they had to drive back to the CIA's compound to pick up Baker's car.

Robin Baker viewed her husband's new job with trepidation. Baker had spent his career at the FBI, where he had been Webster's director of public and congressional affairs. When Webster asked her husband to take the CIA job, Robin Baker was apprehensive. Like most people, she wanted nothing to do with the CIA. This was to be her first encounter with the agency.

Robin Baker drove to the CIA's main gate. Mercury-vapor lights blinded her as she drove up to the concrete guard gate. From the passenger side, Baker showed his CIA building pass.

"Lady," the guard snarled at Baker's wife, "you dim your lights when you come up here."

Robin Baker had not seen a small sign that said, "Parking Lights Only."

"I don't like this place," Robin Baker muttered as they drove into the parking lot.

During the two years that Baker assisted Webster, Robin Baker visited her husband's place of employment again only once—the day he left.[157]

The CIA compound is indeed a spooky place. Even its location—Langley, Virginia—is not what it seems. In fact, it does not exist.

Langley is the name of an estate that was owned by a member of the family of Robert E. Lee, who led Confederate forces in the Civil War. Originally, Langley was the name of the Lee family's estate in Shropshire, England. The estate in Virginia bordered Georgetown Pike, originally an animal trail formed by the hooves of buffalo on their way to feeding grounds in Maryland and the Blue Ridge Mountains of Virginia. Later, the Susquehannoc Indians used the trail when they brought furs to English traders who anchored their ships in the Potomac River. The Lee estate included part of what is now the CIA compound.[158]

Langley later became a village with its own post office inside a country store, an inn with a tavern or ordinary where stagecoaches stopped to rest their horses, a blacksmith, and a weigh station where farmers could weigh their hay before taking it to market in Washington. By 1910, the village had been merged into nearby McLean, named for the then publisher of the *Washington Post* and the principal stockholder in an electric rail line that linked the area with Washington. Because of the rail line, there was no need for a separate village so close to McLean. The Langley post office was closed. Today, Langley does not exist, yet because the CIA is located in the area once called Langley, it is commonly described as being in Langley. The agency as a whole is often referred to as Langley as well.[159]

When the agency was started in 1947, the CIA had its offices in some twenty-five buildings all over Washington, many of them temporary wooden structures around the Reflecting Pool in front of the Lincoln Memorial. The buildings were so rickety that it was not uncommon for safes used to hold classified documents to come crashing down from the upper floors. Headquarters was a brick building with white Ionic columns next to a Navy medical building at 2430 E Street NW in Washington.

Allen Dulles, who became director of Central Intelligence in 1953, wanted a permanent headquarters in the suburbs. For public consumption, he would say he wanted a campuslike atmosphere to symbolize the agency's scholarly pursuits. But the primary reason was security. The government's emergency plans called for locating sensitive facilities away from Washington, which would presumably bear the brunt of any atomic attack. A secluded area would be easier to police as well. At the same time, the agency had to be close enough to the White House to make it easy for the CIA director to see the president.[160]

Since 1940, what was then known as the federal Public Roads Administration had been assembling 742.9 acres of land off Georgetown Pike for its research facilities. This agency, now known as the Federal Highway Administration, was not using most of it. The land was seven miles northwest of the White House, an ideal compromise between the need to get away from Washington and the need to be near the president.

"Dulles saw the property and fell in love with it," Walter N. Elder, an assistant to Dulles at the time, said.[161]

The CIA obtained 225.5 acres of the land for its headquarters. The Federal Highway Administration's Turner-Fairbank Highway Research Center, which tests highway barriers and cars for crashworthiness, still occupies a tract that the roads agency retained outside the CIA's acres.

On a map, the CIA's compound looks like a giant weather balloon, with its top jutting toward the northeast just below a crook in the Potomac River. The mouth of the balloon forms the entrance to the compound, which is where Dolley Madison Boulevard and Georgetown Pike come together, forming the apex of a triangle.

In the records of Fairfax County, the CIA is part of Parcel 22-3-01-00-40, with land assessed at $235,932,200. This parcel extends northeast well beyond the CIA compound to the Potomac River and includes the highway research center, which is northwest of the CIA. Because it is all held in the name of the U.S. government, the assessors do not distinguish between the portion held by the CIA and the portion used by the roads agency.

In 1955, President Dwight D. Eisenhower signed a bill authorizing $46 million for the construction of the CIA headquarters complex. On September 20, 1961, the first employees began to move into the new building, a concrete and glass structure that consists of 1.4 million square feet. There was one problem. The Public Roads Administration, in assembling the original land, had been unable to obtain a last 32.5 acres that jutted like an iceberg into the tract where the CIA planned its compound. Moreover, it was right at the mouth of the property, just to the left of the access drive that the CIA wanted as its main entrance off Dolley Madison Boulevard.

The land had been purchased in 1933 by Margaret Scattergood, a graduate of Bryn Mawr College who had worked for the original American Federation of Labor doing economics research. With Florence C. Thorne, a friend and co-worker, she purchased the home, along with a tenant farmer's house and a maid's house that sat on the property.

When the federal government tried to take the property, she got a private law passed allowing her to stay there undisturbed until she died. In the meantime, title passed to the government, and she received $54,189 for the property immediately.[162] In the records of the Fairfax County assessor, this parcel is designated as 22-3-01-00-40A and is assessed at $6,492,000.

When they came to work each day, CIA employees drove past Scattergood's home with its wide front porch and columns. Few knew anything about her and what she stood for. The daughter of a wealthy dye maker in Philadelphia, Scattergood was a Quaker and a pacifist. The CIA, in her view, meant war and killing—everything she was against. Scattergood helped civil rights organizations and was corresponding clerk of the Langley Hill Friends Meeting in McLean. But she spent most of her time doling out money from a trust fund left by her father to antiwar and other liberal causes. Meanwhile, she wrote letters to members of Congress urging cuts in the military and intelligence budgets. She also gave sanctuary to refugees from Nicaragua and Guatemala—illegal aliens fleeing the turmoil in the two countries where the CIA was heavily involved. Occasionally they ended up at the CIA's gate as they tried to find Scattergood's driveway, which was off an access drive to the CIA's rear entrances.

"She had an income of $100,000 to $125,000 a year perhaps. But she had no mortgage, no taxes. She lived a simple life, she and Miss Thorne. So she gave away between a third and a half of her money each year," Nancy H. Blanchet, a grandniece and executor of her will, said.[163]

When the CIA began widening its front access drive in 1983, Harry E. Fitzwater, the CIA's deputy director for administration under William Casey, learned that Scattergood was worried that the agency would intrude on her property. For some time, Fitzwater had been concerned about Scattergood's welfare. Since her home extended into the CIA's grounds, it was probably more secure than the White House. But Scattergood was advancing in age. Since Thorne's death in 1973, she had lived alone. Fitzwater had had the CIA's guards patrol her property to make sure she was okay.[164]

Fitzwater invited Scattergood and a grandniece, Sylvia Blanchet, to have lunch in the director's dining room and to tour the CIA. After they sipped sherry, Casey dropped in, and they had lunch with him. When the subject turned to the American Revolution, the subject of Casey's 1976 book, *Where and How the War Was Fought: An Armchair Tour of the American Revolution,* Scattergood said, "My relatives were in jail at the time."

"What do you mean?" one of the CIA people asked.

"They were Quakers and were doing civil disobedience. They don't believe in war and don't believe in killing other people and would rather go to jail and lose everything rather than participate in war," Scattergood replied.[165]

Scattergood died on November 7, 1986, at the age of ninety-two, after a stroke. She had lived on the property twenty-five years after the CIA occupied its headquarters building—a last show of disobedience.[166]

After Scattergood's death, the CIA extended its chain-link fence to include her property. The house is used for training sessions and will eventually be used for CIA conferences. On part of the property just to the left of the front gate the CIA built a day-care center for 104 of its employees' offspring. Each child is enrolled by code number. From Soviet satellites, it looks like the CIA is training midgets, or so the joke goes.

To the right of the CIA's front access ramp stands a massive, nineteen-room brick home. Built in 1988, the home at 1124 Savile Lanes sat unsold for two years. A new broker, Cathie Gill, got a bright idea: Why not sell it to the CIA as the home of the director? She approached both the CIA and members of Congress, who took up the cause with William Webster. But the agency wanted no part of it, and a Saudi diplomat eventually bought it in 1991.

Besides the main entrance, the CIA has two rear entrances off Georgetown Pike and a side entrance off the George Washington Memorial Parkway that runs along the Potomac River. In 1977, three Marine officers saw the security measures as a challenge. They got drunk in Washington's Georgetown section and decided to prove their manhood by scaling the CIA's fence. Well past midnight, they parked their car along the

George Washington Memorial Parkway and made a run for the fence near the side entrance.

Alarms went off in the duty office just behind the CIA's main lobby, pinpointing the exact location of the intrusion. By the time armed security guards reached the area, one of the Marines was already inside the compound. The guards drew their guns and stopped the Marine. With the help of Fairfax County police, they caught the other two as they ran back toward their car. The CIA reported the incident to Quantico Marine base, where the officers were assigned. Each got two weeks in the brig.

Organizations opposed to the CIA occasionally station members near the CIA's entrances so they can write down or photograph employees' license plates. In the 1970s, these efforts led to publication of some names of CIA employees. Soviets masquerading as picnickers did the same thing. Since then, state motor vehicle departments have made it tougher to obtain the names of owners of motor vehicles.

The CIA's rear entrances are off an access drive that leads from Georgetown Pike to the Federal Highway Administration's Turner-Fairbank Highway Research Center. Trucks with deliveries for the CIA use the first entrance. Across the street from the second rear entrance is Claude Moore Colonial Farm at Turkey Run, a 100-acre replica of a Virginia colonial homestead that is open to the public. Occasionally, 250-pound razorback hogs, denizens of the farm that resemble boar, squeeze out of their pens and amble past the CIA's guard posts onto CIA property.

Other lost souls may get less gentle treatment. At the height of the Persian Gulf War, motorists who wound up at the CIA's rear entrances while looking for the Turner-Fairbank Research Center or the Claude Moore Farm found themselves confronted by CIA guards, who ordered them out of their cars before they would give them directions. Guard dogs, normally inside the guard posts, stood at the ready outside the gates.

In 1985, construction began on an addition to the CIA at the rear of the compound behind the old building. The first employees began moving into the addition in June 1988. The new building has 1.1 million square feet. Unlike the old building, which has tiny slits for windows, the new building makes use of large expanses of green-tinted glass, giving it the appearance of a multicolored silicon chip. With the new building, the CIA's land and structures, along with the Turner-Fairbank Research Center, are assessed at just over half a billion dollars.

Just over half the CIA's 22,000 employees work at Langley. Fifteen percent work overseas, and the rest work in some twenty-two CIA offices scattered throughout Washington, or in the CIA's domestic stations.

Visitors to the CIA may be directed either to a lot on top of a parking garage in front of the new building, or to the VIP parking lot in front and slightly to the left of the old or original building. Inside the compound, there are tall oak trees that occasionally sprout closed-circuit television cameras. Near the front entrance of the old building are weeping cherry, magnolia, and tulip trees. At various times, azaleas and rhododendron bloom near the old building, and daffodils and tiger lilies adorn the beds.

A futuristic concrete bus shelter rises in front and slightly to the right of the old building. Here, blue and white shuttle buses pause on their way to other CIA offices around Washington, and Metro buses let off employees who take the McLean–Crystal City line. In the late 1970s, a Soviet diplomat got off the bus in an apparent attempt to test CIA security. A CIA guard who checks building passes as passengers alight put the man back on the bus.

Just behind the bus stop is the CIA's 7,000-square-foot auditorium. Because of its globular appearance, the auditorium is known as the "bubble." A tunnel connects it to the old building. Next to the auditorium stands a statue of Nathan Hale. During the American Revolution, Hale volunteered to go behind British lines and spy. The British captured him on September 21, 1776, and hanged him the next day. His last words were said to be, "I only regret that I have but one life to lose for my country."

Fifteen doors at the main entrance lead to a lobby of different shades of gray and white Georgia marble. Along the left wall is a statue of William J. ("Wild Bill") Donovan, director of the Office of Strategic Services, the forerunner of the CIA. On the wall is a biblical inscription from John 8:32: "And ye shall know the truth and the truth shall make you free."

Along the right wall are fifty-three gold stars flanked by an American flag on the left and a flag with the seal of the CIA on the right. Each star represents a CIA officer who lost his or her life in the service of the agency. Beneath the memorial stars is a glass case that displays a book listing the years when the officers died. In some cases, the names of the officers are listed—Richard Welch, for example, who was killed by terrorists in Athens in December 1975, after the English-language *Athens News* published his name and home address. Most of the names are not listed because the officers were operating under cover, and their affiliation never came out.

When Adm. Stansfield Turner was director of Central Intelligence, the memorial book disappeared for two weeks. Turner's assistants were frantic. Could someone have stolen one of the CIA's most revered possessions, a symbol of the dedication and sacrifice of every CIA officer? The Office of Security was called in to investigate, but it could find no clues. Finally, just as suddenly as it had disappeared, the book reappeared in the display case. It turned out that a CIA employee who was supposed to add a new name to the book had gotten tired of waiting for the Office of Security to give him the key to the case. So he pried it open without telling anyone.

Visitors present their signed visitor forms to one of the receptionists at the far end of the lobby. The receptionist calls the employee listed on the form, and the employee comes down to escort the visitor. If the visitor is going to the director's suite on the seventh floor, he is usually taken to the director's elevator to the left of the lobby. From the elevator, the director can descend to the garage, where thirty of the agency's top officials are allowed to park.

In July 1991, Dr. Stanley Moskowitz, the agency's director of congressional affairs and formerly associate deputy director for intelligence, left his car in the garage. Later in the day, the Office of Security called him. Would he mind stepping into the garage and opening his trunk?

It seems a dog trained to sense explosives had fingered his trunk for harboring a bomb. Because of Dr. Moskowitz's status, a second dog was called in. The dog confirmed the diagnosis.

No problem, Moskowitz said. He opened the trunk to reveal the item that had offended the dogs' senses—workout clothes concealed in a gym bag.

The director's elevator operates only with a key that is given to those who report to the director. Other visitors—and employees routinely going to work—use one of six turnstiles to enter the rest of the building.

Armed guards watch as the escort first inserts his or her identification card in the turnstile and punches in a code. Then the visitor inserts his or her visitor card. The card must be inserted again when leaving the building. Each time a card is inserted, a second bar closes behind the person using the machine. If there is anything wrong, he or she is trapped.

Every hour or two, there is the sound of a buzzer and nervous laughter as a quirky turnstile malfunctions and traps an employee or visitor trying to enter or leave the building. The guards usually explain that the turnstiles are malfunctioning. They lower the gate to let the embarrassed employee pass.

The new building has its own entrance, with sixteen turnstiles at the end of an arched skylight of green-tinted glass. The addition is airy, with escalators and an atrium filled with potted palms. Because the new building is on higher land, the fourth floor of the old building connects to the lobby of the new building.

Many of the offices in the new building—and the director's offices in the old building—are so-called vaulted areas, where less sensitive classified documents can be left on desks overnight. When the last person leaves, he or she calls security, flips a switch, and locks the door.

For all the high-tech gadgets, employees who want to place calls between the old and the new buildings on nonsecure lines must dial a seven-digit number, just as if they were calling outside the CIA. However, practically everyone uses the secure, green touch-tone phones to make calls within the agency, even when making lunch dates. The secure phones require five digits when calling within the CIA.

The corridors inside both old and new buildings are lined with artwork—formal portraits of each of the directors of Central Intelligence, signed photographs of American presidents since the agency was established, and a rotating exhibit of the work of local artists under the auspices of the CIA Fine Arts Commission. Recently, the exhibit featured the Vincent Melzac collection of Washington Color School Painters. Mainly geometrics—polka dots and stripes and other repeated patterns—they were by Tom Downing, Howard Mehring, Gene Davis, Alma Thomas, Norman Bluhm.

Occasionally, employees leave their belongings on the floor as they gaze at the exhibits or bulletin boards listing cars for sale or houses for rent. When one man forgot to take his briefcase after resting it on the floor, the Office of Security confiscated it and took it to a concrete-lined bomb-disposal enclosure on the grounds. Fearing it might be a bomb, the guards blew it up, depriving the man of his lunch and some papers he had been working on.

The architects who designed the old building wanted it to be state-of-the-art, so they included a conveyer belt in the walls for carrying packages from one office to another. When officials of the Office of Security saw it, they threw up their hands. The system would make it too easy to distribute bombs throughout the building. The system was never used, and the passageways inside the walls are now used to store backup batteries for the CIA's vast banks of computers.

Where the new and old buildings meet is a rectangular courtyard dotted with black plastic picnic tables. In one corner of the courtyard is a part of an installation by Washington artist Jim Sanborn, who was chosen after a competition among two hundred entrants. It took Sanborn two years to build the work, which includes three other pieces within the courtyard and at the entrance to the new building. The cost was $250,000.

The main piece is a sculpture that stands more than six feet high and looks like a scroll. Constructed over a pool of water, it is made of petrified wood, granite, red slate, green quartz, and copper. The petrified wood symbolizes the trees that once stood on the CIA's site and the fact they are used to make paper and record language. Letters carved in a curved copper plate at the right of the installation represent a table that can be used to decipher the encoded text cut into the plate at the top left. The text can be deciphered only by using the table and a key word, which is *kryptos*. Another plate at the bottom left contains more text, which can only be deciphered by computer.

Sanborn composed the message in the encoded text with the help of a fiction writer. Totaling two thousand words, the combined messages describe the information-gathering role of the CIA. Sanborn entrusted only Webster, as the then director of Central Intelligence, with a deciphered copy of the text at the opening for the artwork in November 1990.[167]

Sanborn found the experience of working on CIA grounds unnerving. One day, he showed up to work on the installation only to find that his art material—twenty-five tons of granite—had disappeared. Was the agency checking the stone for bugs? Was it part of some nefarious plot to stifle his creativity? The CIA never explained. It simply issued him a check for $5,000 so he could buy new stone to replace it. Agency officials speculate that maintenance workers, thinking the rock was left over from construction of the new building, simply hauled it away.

Off the courtyard in the new building is a plum-colored employee cafeteria, separated into two dining areas: one for undercover officers, and the other for everyone else. The old building has another, gray-accented cafeteria where employees can take visitors. The tuna sandwich is just $2.25.

Also off the courtyard in the old building is the CIA's National Historical Collection, two rooms enclosed in glass and crammed with memorabilia of a bygone era. Here is the first United States flag to fly over CIA headquarters, the razor that William Donovan used during World War II, Russian railway schedules purloined by the CIA in the late 1940s, a camera the size of a matchbox, a device that detects move-

The CIA's main gate off Dolley Madison Drive is one of four entrances to the CIA compound in McLean, Virginia. *(CIA photo)*

The main entrance at the front of the CIA's old building is just to the right of the director's suite of offices on the seventh floor. *(CIA photo)*

The CIA's old building and main entrance, in the lower right, were completed in 1961, while the new building, in the upper left, was completed in 1988. *(CIA photo)*

The entrance to the CIA's 1.1-million-square-foot new building is sheathed in glass. *(CIA photo)*

The CIA's main lobby includes a memorial to fallen CIA officers. *(CIA photo)*

William J. Donovan, whose statue stands to the left as one enters the CIA's lobby, urged creation of an agency that would centralize intelligence gathering and served as the director of the Office of Strategic Services (OSS), the forerunner of the CIA. *(CIA photo)*

The installation by Jim Sanborn in the courtyard between the old and new buildings carries secret messages encoded in copper plates outlining the CIA's mission. *(CIA photo)*

William H. Webster met Nancy McGregor's son Ben in May 1987, just before she became his special assistant at the CIA. *(FBI photo)*

William Webster equipped William M. Baker with a Sherlock Holmes outfit when Baker left the CIA as public affairs director in May 1989 to become the FBI's assistant director in charge of the criminal investigation division. *(CIA photo)*

The CIA and FBI jointly recruited a KGB officer in the Soviet embassy in Washington while operating out of a building at 6551 Loisdale Court in Springfield, Virginia. *(Ronald Kessler)*

The CIA's Foreign Resources Division recruited foreign diplomats and intelligence officers in the Washington area from a suite at 7101 Wisconsin Avenue in Bethesda, Maryland.
(Ronald Kessler)

William M. Colby began CIA reforms.
(Wide World)

Stansfield Turner emphasized technical collection. *(Wide World)*

William J. Casey embroiled the CIA in the Iran-Contra scandal. *(Wide World)*

George Bush, himself a former CIA director, met with William Webster at the new CIA building for a working lunch in August 1990. At left is Richard J. Kerr, deputy director for Central Intelligence. *(Wide World)*

President Bush applauded after Supreme Court Justice Sandra Day O'Connor swore in Robert M. Gates as the fifteenth Director of Central Intelligence on November 12, 1991. *(Wide World)*

ment and is disguised as dog feces, and a lantern that was to be used to guide planes landing in Cuba during the Bay of Pigs invasion.

One of the cases holds a .22-caliber pistol with silencer that Donovan showed to President Roosevelt in the White House. To demonstrate how quiet it was, Donovan shot a round into a sandbag that he'd brought along for the purpose, then handed the hot muzzle to the startled president.

A day after the United States began the war to liberate Kuwait in January 1991, Linda McCarthy, the CIA exhibits officer, donned a pair of white gloves and carried a Civil War Colt .44 to the ladies' room to clean it. Around a bend in a corridor came an excited CIA security guard.

"We had a report of a weapon!" he said.

"The worst I could do with this is throw it at you," she said dryly.

"I was about to call in backup," he said.

Not far from the museum on the first floor of the old building is the CIA's main library. With smaller specialized libraries in each directorate, the CIA has 146,000 volumes, including 25,000 books on intelligence. This is the largest collection of intelligence books in the United States. A lower level of the library has 1,700 newspapers and periodicals on file.[168]

Below the first floor in the old building are a gym and a barbershop. When he was director, this is where Webster got his hair cut by one of two barbers. The new building also has a gym.

When he first came to the CIA, Baker, Webster's director of public affairs, went to work out in the gym in the old building around lunchtime. He had just finished his routine and was taking a shower when he heard women's voices. They sounded angry. It turned out the locker room had separate hours for men and women. While Baker was taking a shower, the hours had changed. The women were irate because he was cutting into their time.

In his FBI career, Baker had arrested armed robbers and had participated in shootouts. J. Edgar Hoover, the FBI director, had commended him for arresting more fugitives in one day than any other special agent. But the locker room situation was a new one.

As he ran to his locker to get a towel to wrap around himself, Baker identified himself.

"Sorry, sorry," he said as he scurried into a closet to get dressed.[169]

At the rear of the compound, behind the new building, is the CIA's electrical substation, printing plant, a helipad, a car wash for the agency's motor pool, and a loading dock for receiving mail and supplies. Looming over the electrical substation is a water tower that helps maintain water pressure in the area. Because of new construction in McLean, the pressure changed one afternoon, sending a geyser of water twenty feet into the air. As the water rained down, CIA workers went scurrying to find the shut-off valve, only to learn to their horror that it was buried underground. Using shovels, they frantically dug holes in the area until they found the valve and shut it off.

Despite backup generators, the CIA's power supply has also gone on the fritz. At least twice, electrical components have malfunctioned, shutting off even emergency power to the agency and its computers. Nonetheless, when this happened under Stansfield Turner's regime, the only complaint the engineers got was that Turner had not been able to eat breakfast.[170]

The agency has its own zip code—20505—at the Washington, D.C., post office. Because mail to the CIA is screened at the post office by X-ray equipment, the McLean post office is too small to handle the load. A second X-ray machine at the loading dock checks packages when they arrive.

These are under the control of the Office of Security, in many ways the most controversial office in the CIA.

18 | *Keystone Cops*

WHEN PEOPLE PICTURE THE OLD CIA, THEY ARE MOST likely thinking of the Office of Security. It was the CIA's Office of Security, starting in 1967, that illegally infiltrated and spied on dissident groups in Washington, D.C., in order to protect agency buildings. It was the Office of Security that illegally wiretapped the telephones of three newsmen in 1959 and in 1962 in order to determine their sources. It was the Office of Security that illegally incarcerated Soviet defector Yuri I. Nosenko, who defected from the Soviet Union after the assassination of John F. Kennedy, for three and a half years beginning in 1964. It was Office of Security that arranged for the Mafia to try to assassinate Fidel Castro and that ordered poison pills for him to take. And while investigating CIA employees, the Office of Security illegally conducted twelve break-ins and installed thirty-two wiretaps and thirty-two bugs.

Nor has the office's heavy-handed approach changed appreciably. As recently as 1985, it contributed to the decision of KGB colonel Vitaly Yurchenko to redefect to the Soviet Union by treating him as a prisoner. When Yurchenko's handlers complained to the Office of Security about the treatment, they were told that was the way things were; there was nothing to be done about it.[171]

As director of Central Intelligence, William Webster had more problems with the Office of Security than any other office. He found it to be still operating in the dark ages and most resistant to change. Sometimes, Webster's aides felt that perhaps the Office of Security considered *Webster* to be a security risk.

"Their attitude is, 'This is the way we do things, and we aren't going to change,' " a former Office of Security official said.

Even letters sent out by the Office of Security to notify employees that they had failed polygraph tests were clumsy. The letters said "you have been deemed deceptive" on the issue of providing information to a foreign government. At the suggestion of an assistant, Webster had the office change the letter to say "you evinced physiological reactions" and the matter was resolved "in favor of the national security." In plain English, that meant, "You're fired."

Of all the office's functions, none is more important than preventing espionage. While the CIA's Counterintelligence Center works overseas to thwart opposing intelligence services that try to recruit CIA officers, the Office of Security is charged with protecting CIA facilities and people from penetration.

It is, to be sure, an impossible task. No one can expect that the KGB and other hostile intelligence services will never have any successes in the silent espionage battle. Nor are statistics meaningful. Since 1975, the Justice Department has prosecuted fifty-six spy cases, of which six involved CIA employees or employees of CIA contractors. A seventh case, that of Edward Lee Howard, a former CIA officer, has never been prosecuted because Howard fled to Moscow, where he now lives. A warrant has been issued for his arrest. Of the fifty-six prosecutions, all but one has brought a conviction.

The fact that an espionage case has occurred does not automatically mean that the Office of Security has failed. One can always wish that the office had done better, that it might have gotten lucky and caught a spy who decided to sell out his country. But just as the FBI cannot be expected to stop all bank robberies simply because that is the bureau's job, the Office of Security cannot be expected to stop all espionage against the CIA. What can be expected is that the Office of Security will follow its own procedures and will have enough understanding of the law to preserve suspects' rights so they can be convicted if guilty. In all too many cases, the Office of Security has failed in these areas.

Indeed, of all the CIA's offices, the Office of Security is the one most likely to be heavy-handed where sensitivity is called for, most likely to overlook proper legal procedure, and most apt to yearn for the days before the Church Committee hearings when the CIA was far less accountable to Congress.

Nowhere is this attitude better illustrated than in a talk that Jerry G. Brown has given often to new CIA employees. Brown joined the Office of Security in 1956 and most recently headed its Clearance Division. Heaping ridicule on the efforts of the Church Committee and the presidentially appointed Rockefeller Commission that investigated the abuses, Brown said the CIA's Operation Chaos—the effort to investigate domestic dissidents—was seen by our "unsophisticated detractors" as "a purposeful attempt by the agency and the Nixon administration to subvert the domestic political process by spying on American citizens."

This was not the case at all, Brown claimed. In fact, he said, Operation Chaos represented an effort to address "serious national security questions." In saying this, he overlooked the fact that by spying on American citizens, the CIA had violated its own charter.

"Those who would destroy us and our efforts were not the Soviets and our other worldwide enemies but our own elected legislative representatives," Brown declared.

While Brown acknowledged that some reforms were

needed, the investigators did not want to hear the truth, he said.

"The tragedy of the congressional and Rockefeller Commission inquiries into Operation Chaos was that none of the staff investigators bothered to find out how the operation began," Brown said. If they had, they would have found that it began with what Brown called a serious problem—the leak in 1967 to *Ramparts* magazine of the fact that the CIA was secretly funding the National Student Association.

According to Brown, this funding was essential so that the National Student Association could fight Soviet efforts to control international youth organizations. The tip to *Ramparts*, he said, was "one of the most flagrant leaks of classified information ever known to the agency."

And who leaked the information? According to Brown, it was the KGB, which obtained the information directly from the CIA and gave it "through individuals peripherally connected with the magazine" to *Ramparts*.

"The exposure of the agency's involvement with the National Student Association by *Ramparts* was totally inspired by the KGB," Brown said.

Brown claimed the CIA learned this information from a Soviet defector. The claim fit in neatly with his theme that the Church Committee investigations into CIA abuses were misdirected. The leak contributed to greater scrutiny of the agency, and that led to investigations that threatened CIA employees who had participated in the abuses. The only problem was, he was wrong.

In order to fund the student organization, the CIA had had to tell hundreds of National Student Association officers over the years about the secret program. As the source of the story, the *Ramparts* article named Michael Wood, a National Student Association employee who had been told about the funding by one of these officers. The author of the piece, Sol Stern, and Cord Meyer, the CIA officer in charge of the CIA funding operation, both corroborated the fact that Wood was the source of the story.[172]

"Having learned about the secret funding as the result of a conversation with an excessively loquacious NSA officer who did know the facts [about the CIA's funding], this young man, Michael Wood, decided that it was his duty to expose the whole relationship," Meyer wrote in his book *Facing Reality: From World Federalism to the CIA*.[173]

The CIA's naïveté in thinking that it could inform successive generations of the association's officers about the funding without its leaking to the press had led to the scandal in the first place. In suggesting that the leak to *Ramparts* was a sinister KGB plot rather than the inevitable result of spreading the word among hundreds of young students, Brown had overlooked the obvious. But far more troubling is the failure by a senior official of the Office of Security entrusted with training new employees to recognize that by subverting the law, the CIA subverts the very freedoms it is trying to preserve, while failing to achieve its objectives.[174]

The same unfocused thinking led to one of the major screwups in the history of U.S. espionage investigations—another one where the Office of Security was involved. It was the case of Karl F. Koecher, a Czech Intelligence Service officer who managed to get a job at the CIA in 1973 as a translator. With his stunning wife, Hana, Koecher attended sex orgies and wife-swapping parties in Washington and New York. At the parties, Hana Koecher, also a Czech Intelligence Service officer, would take on four to five men at the same time. But it was all for the cause. Many of the partygoers were fellow CIA employees who swapped classified information as well as sex with the popular couple. Through his translation work, Koecher learned enough to compromise Aleksandr D. Ogorodnik, a high-ranking Soviet diplomat working as an agent for the CIA. When the KGB confronted him, Ogorodnik committed suicide by taking a poison pill concealed inside a fountain pen given to him by the CIA.[175]

After a Czech working for the FBI turned Koecher in, the bureau, which has responsibility for investigating espionage by Americans, followed him for two years without developing enough evidence to prosecute him. In an attempt to get him to confess, the CIA's Office of Security and the FBI devised a plan to approach him in the fall of 1984. As an officer of the Office of Security would later tell new CIA employees,

193

the FBI and CIA had "absolutely no thought of prosecution." Rather, the idea was to find out how much damage Koecher—who had become a U.S. citizen—had done.

This is a classic blunder. The agencies investigating espionage become so fixated on finding out what happened that they forget about an equally important goal: prosecuting suspects as a deterrent against future espionage. Often, there is another motive for avoiding this. Prosecution leads to publicity, which can be embarrassing to the agencies involved. A bank that has been defrauded would just as soon not see the case plastered all over the papers, but it has no choice. The CIA and other intelligence agencies can try to hide their mistakes by claiming that prosecutions would air secrets that would compromise the work of the agencies.

For twenty years, the CIA had a secret agreement with the Justice Department that if criminal conduct occurred within the agency, and it involved classified information that would have to be disclosed outside the CIA, the agency would resolve it internally. That changed under Attorney General Griffin Bell, who decided that no individual in government should be immune from criminal prosecution.

In 1978, the CIA strenuously objected to prosecuting William P. Kampiles, a former CIA watch officer assigned to analyze incoming traffic at the CIA's Operations Center. Kampiles had sold portions of a "top secret" technical manual on how to use the KH-11 surveillance satellite to a Soviet agent in Athens for $3,000. What the manual showed was that the satellite transmitted its data up to another satellite instead of down to earth, as would be expected. Because of this ruse, the Soviets thought it was a "dead" satellite.

Bell took the issue of prosecuting Kampiles to President Carter, who authorized it.

In 1980, the CIA argued against prosecuting David H. Barnett, a former CIA officer who had been over CIA operations in Jakarta. Barnett got $92,600 for letting the Soviets know that the CIA—through Operation Habrink—had found out how to control the guidance systems for their SA-2 surface-to-air missiles. As a result, Habrink was compromised. Barnett also identified for the Soviets thirty CIA officers and many of their agents.

The fact that the Soviets already knew that Barnett had given them the information did not deter CIA officials from insisting that Barnett should be let go. Somehow the CIA felt any public discussion of the case would damage the agency and its operations.

Very often, according to John L. Martin, chief of the Justice Department's internal security section, who supervised the case, the CIA simply wants to avoid the embarrassment that comes with publicity about its penetrations. Other CIA officials sincerely believe that *any* information about their operations can only help the other side, a throwback to the days when no highway signs marked the location of CIA's headquarters, even though airplanes used the building as a landmark when flying into National Airport.

"The intelligence community had come to believe that every time you prosecuted a spy, you would lose the secret, and that it was better public policy—the best of two evils—to let the spy go and keep the secret," Bell said. "But I had the idea that you could prosecute these cases without losing the secret."

In fact, with professional handling, investigators can prosecute suspects and find out what has been lost. The FBI, in investigating Ronald Pelton, a former National Security Agency employee, did just that. After conning Pelton into revealing what he gave away, the FBI turned the case over to Martin of the Justice Department for prosecution. Often, the Justice Department agrees to bring to the attention of the sentencing judge the fact that the suspect has cooperated, in return for a guilty plea and full disclosure of the spy's activities. That happened in Pelton's case, but he still got life in prison.

In the case of Czech Intelligence Service officer Karl Koecher, none of this was done. The Office of Security and the FBI in effect promised Koecher that he would not be prosecuted if he talked—that he could become a double agent for the CIA, pretending to work for Czech Intelligence while reporting to the CIA—and that he could return to Czechoslovakia if he wished. In fact, neither the FBI nor the CIA had any intention of making Koecher a double agent, thus making the offer improper. Koecher served time in prison waiting for his trial. But in the end, because of the false promise of immunity from prosecution, the Justice Department had to settle for trading Koecher rather than incarcerating him. As part of the deal, Koecher pleaded guilty to espionage.

When the CIA's Office of Security later examined how Koecher had been hired by the CIA in the first place, it discovered that his polygraph exam had been poorly conducted. When asked if he was under the control of a hostile intelligence service, Koecher showed some signs of deception. However, Koecher explained away his nervousness by claiming he had briefly tried to serve as a double agent for the FBI. Instead of asking more questions and administering a second test, the polygraph examiner moved on to the next question.

The same lack of care occurred when the Office of Security polygraphed Larry Wu-Tai Chin, who was hired as a CIA translator even though he was then working for the People's Republic of China. In a subsequent confession to the FBI, Chin said he had managed to avoid showing deception because the CIA asked all the questions in English instead of in Chinese, his native tongue. It was easier to lie in a foreign language, he said.

At least in part, the Office of Security was also responsible for the fact that nearly all of the Cuban agents recruited by the CIA over the years have been double agents. Of the thirty-eight Cuban agents working for the CIA at the time they were first exposed in 1987, nearly all had taken polygraph tests, and most had passed. The test results of many of the other agents were deemed inconclusive.

Polygraph tests are not infallible. The hoary aphorism that the machines are only as good as their operators is true. In this case, the operators had a major deficiency: they did not speak Spanish. In contrast, the FBI was able to avoid accepting many Cuban double agents because it generally administered polygraph tests to them in Spanish.

Only one CIA operations officer has ever been prosecuted for espionage. Laxness by the Office of Security contributed to the damage he did. Operations officer David H. Barnett began telling the Soviets about CIA operations in Indonesia in 1976, after he had left the agency to start his own business. Faced with mounting debts, he reapplied to the CIA and was hired. At that point, the Office of Security should have polygraphed him, just as all new hires are polygraphed. If he had been polygraphed, his earlier spy activity would presumably have come out. Instead, he was allowed to teach tradecraft to CIA officers who were about to go overseas. In this position, he had extremely valuable information to offer the KGB, which he offered to sell at a meeting with them in Vienna in April 1980.

When American government agents spotted him in Vienna, the FBI entered the case. However, when the agents first asked about Barnett at the Office of Security in February 1980, they were told he no longer worked for the agency. Later, it turned out that either the Office of Security or the Directorate of Operations had failed to record the fact that he was again working for the CIA. From February until March 1980, the FBI watched Barnett twenty-four hours a day. During that time, the CIA removed him from his sensitive job without letting him know why.

Barnett pleaded guilty in 1981 and was sentenced to eighteen years in prison.

Two other espionage cases—that of Christopher J. Boyce and his friend Andrew Daulton Lee, the protagonists in *The Falcon and the Snowman,* and William P. Kampiles, who sold the manual to the KH-11 spy satellite to the Soviets in Greece—also stemmed in part from laxity by the Office of Security.

Boyce held a relatively low-level, low-paid position with TRW Inc., which was a CIA contractor on the spy satellite program. He gave classified code material used to transmit photos from the RHYOLITE surveillance satellite to Lee, a drug addict. Lee sold it to the Soviets in Mexico City and shared the proceeds with Boyce.[176]

In congressional testimony, Boyce would later describe security at TRW as being so loose that he and his coworkers "regularly partied and boozed it up during working hours within the 'black vault,' " the supersecret room housing information on the CIA satellite project. "Bacardi rum was usually stored behind the crypto machines," he said, while a code-destruction machine similar to a blender "was used for making banana daiquiris and Mai Tais."

It was the CIA's Office of Security that was responsible for making sure security procedures were followed by CIA contractors. The Office of Security was also responsible for keeping tight control over classified documents.

To be sure, the Office of Security has helped to apprehend spies. But unfathomable screwups sometimes mar even those success stories. The best example is the case of Sharon M. Scranage, who was a thirty-year-old operations support assistant for the CIA in Ghana. She gave classified information to her Ghanian boyfriend, Michael Soussoudis, a first cousin of Jerry Rawlings, prime minister of Ghana.

The case began in Ghana in 1983 when Scranage invited an Office of Security officer to dinner at her home. On the way to the bathroom, he noticed a photo of a man taped to the vanity in her bedroom. The man turned out to be Soussoudis. The photo showed Soussoudis sitting in Scranage's bed, the covers drawn up to his naked chest.

The security officer returned to dinner and warned Scranage of the dangers of romances with local nationals, particularly one with a connection to the government. At the time, Ghana was pursuing a staunchly capitalist economic policy but a left-leaning foreign policy, cozying up to Cuba's Fidel Castro and Nicaragua's Daniel Ortega.

The security officer and a colleague told the CIA station chief about the romance, and the station chief warned Scranage to break off with Soussoudis. Scranage promised she would. Soussoudis subsequently stayed in the United States for almost a year. But when Soussoudis returned to Ghana, their affair resumed. It was not until Scranage returned to the U.S. for a new posting in the summer of 1985 that the Office of Security gave her a polygraph test.

When the test began to show signs of deception, Scranage at first denied any wrongdoing. Eventually, she admitted she had given her boyfriend extensive secret information. If she did not go along, he made it clear he would break up with her. In fact, she handed Soussoudis virtually everything there was to know about the CIA's activities in Ghana. She even gave him top-secret cables that she copied in shorthand, then recopied for her lover in longhand.

Her spying led to the compromise of eight CIA agents in Ghana, who were arrested and imprisoned. In addition, the pro-Marxist head of Ghanian intelligence is believed to have passed on information obtained through Scranage to the KGB and Cuban intelligence.

Scranage agreed to cooperate with the FBI and Jerry Brown of the Office of Security to catch Soussoudis, who was an agent of the Ghanian government. The FBI arrested him at a Holiday Inn in Springfield, Virginia.

After pleading guilty in 1985, Scranage was sentenced to five years in prison. Later, the sentence was reduced to two. Soussoudis was returned to Ghana in exchange for the release from prison of the CIA's eight agents. The CIA has resettled in the U.S. nearly two dozen Ghanians, including families, who were compromised as a result of the fiasco. The agency has since tightened its regulations on reporting relationships with foreign nationals.

While the Office of Security had helped apprehend Scranage, its delay in polygraphing her after it became clear she had been dating a relative of the prime minister was inexcusable. Unlike a failure to forecast a political event, this was an avoidable mistake. Indeed, of the six Justice Department espionage prosecutions of CIA employees or employees of contractors to date, only one—that of Edwin G. Moore II, who threw a package of CIA documents over the fence at a Soviet apartment house in Washington—did not involve any mistakes by the Office of Security.[177]

More recently, the Office of Security botched one of the biggest spy cases in history by insisting on treating KGB spy Vitaly Yurchenko as a prisoner. This contributed to his decision to redefect three months after he left the Soviet Union in 1985. As the most important KGB officer ever to defect to the U.S., Yurchenko had in his head information about dozens of cases of interest to the Office of Security and the FBI. While he gave away two major cases—that of Edward Lee Howard, the former CIA officer who defected to Moscow, and Ronald Pelton, the former NSA employee who spied for the Soviets—Yurchenko had clues to many more. The CIA and FBI had meant to debrief him for years. If they had, he would almost certainly have led them to a number of other spies.

When Webster became director of Central Intelligence in 1987, the lawyers that he brought with him from the FBI found that, of all the CIA offices that deal routinely with legal issues—the Office of General Counsel, the Counterintelligence Center, and the Office of Security—the Office of Security was most likely to flout legal procedures. One example was the great postage-stamp case, which involved nine workers in the Office of Security's mailroom who noticed that $1 U.S. postage stamps had been misprinted. They sold eighty-five of the stamps—now valued at $28,000 each—to a New Jersey stamp dealer for an undisclosed sum. When the Office of Security learned about it, they interrogated the suspects without warning them of their right to have counsel present.

Eventually, four of the employees were fired because they had made statements during the investigation that were technically true but misleading, or because they had not returned the stamps they had taken, or both.[178] If the cases had been criminally prosecuted, they would most likely have been thrown out because the employees had not been warned of their rights.

To improve the operations of the Office of Security, Webster appointed new directors who came from outside the office—one from the Directorate of Intelligence, another from administration. While they were not burdened by the Office of Security's mind-set, they did not have the experience in law enforcement needed to give them the confidence to make wholesale changes. For his part, Webster did not want to become heavily involved in the operations of the office, realizing that trying to micromanage its activities would only lead to more problems. In any case, much of what the office does would be done the same way regardless of who is in charge. Debugging is one example.

19 | *Getting the Bugs Out*

WITHIN THE OFFICE OF SECURITY, NEARLY A HUNDRED technicians engage in a never-ending battle to find wiretaps and other eavesdropping devices in the CIA's offices at Langley and around the globe. Besides helping to investigate espionage and other crimes, polygraphing people, taking care of the buildings and grounds and locks, and guarding defectors, the Office of Security looks for eavesdropping devices. Given the threat, this is one of the most important jobs in the CIA. Besides finding bugs, the Technical Security Division within the Office of Security installs white-sound systems to mask voices, as well as state-of-the-art alarm systems, safes, locks, and other security systems. But the main job of the office is finding bugs by conducting periodic sweeps of the agency's buildings in Washington and stations overseas. While usually based in Washington, the technicians spend most of their time traveling to CIA stations in their quest for elusive bugs.

Getting the Bugs Out

A standard office can present dozens of possibilities for bugging, and CIA technicians have to check them all. Any speaker in a radio or television set can be turned into a bugging device that radiates signals to a remote listening post. An electrical outlet can be replaced with one that contains a bugging device that transmits signals through the air or over the power line. A microphone in a thermostat can transmit signals to the furnace, where a transmitter can beam the signals outside. Rewiring of a telephone can turn it into an open microphone, transmitting sound in the room down the telephone line even when the receiver is on the hook.

Typewriters are not immune. The power supply used by an IBM Selectric typewriter can be used to pick up what the typewriter is typing. Each time the typing element moves, the motor inside the machine runs. The amount of time the motor operates depends on how far the typing element moves. In turn, the amount of movement is based on which letter is being typed. By measuring the amount of current drawn, a snooper can determine how far the typing element has traveled and thus which letter it typed.

A computer screen also radiates signals that denote which letter is being typed. A microphone in a room can also be used to pick up sounds from the keyboard. Each key, when struck, makes a different sound. That sound can be used to determine which key was depressed. Likewise, a daisy-wheel computer printer emits sounds that can be translated into the text that it is printing out. If a computer has a modem, so long as the computer is turned on, a snooper can obtain the entire contents of the computer's hard drive over the telephone line.

In checking for electronic eavesdropping devices, CIA technicians try to pick up any signals that might be transmitting sound from a room. This is not as easy as it sounds. In debugging the American embassy in Moscow, State Department technicians did not find the bugs implanted in the embassy's IBM Selectric typewriters in part because of the clever way the Soviets masked the signals. The bugs stored data and transmitted it only intermittently. The Soviets controlled when the bugs dumped information and could turn them off when a sweep might be in progress. Moreover, the coded signals used the same frequency as a Moscow television station. When the bugs transmitted, viewers heard momentary static. Since the signals were on the same wavelength as the television station, sweeps of the embassy detected nothing.

In debugging overseas stations, one of the biggest problems CIA technicians face is not bugs but insistent requests from ambassadors to sweep their offices.

"It's a status symbol," a former technician said. "If the chief of station gets his done, the ambassador wants his done, too."

The State Department sweeps its own offices, including those of ambassadors, but when CIA technicians visit stations overseas, many ambassadors insist their offices need a check as well. When that happens, CIA officers assigned to the stations often apply pressure to go along with the request. But according to a former technician, "We've been told we'll be canned if we do it. The State Department doesn't want to send men and equipment there if we have just been there."

Depending on the size of the station, two or three technicians take one to two weeks to perform their sweeps. Depending on their sensitivity and the degree of the threat, the stations are checked every six months to once a year. The director's office has devices that constantly detect any stray emanations that might come from bugs. In addition, the office is swept along with the office of the deputy director of Central Intelligence every six months.

To keep in top form, the technicians look for bugs that are placed by the CIA's buggers—the Office of Technical Service within the Directorate of Science and Technology. The bugs are placed in homes and apartments previously used as safe houses. There is rivalry between the two offices, and the positive buggers often do not want to share their latest techniques and devices with the debuggers.

The technicians find bugs at overseas stations only occasionally. In one case, while checking the airwaves at a station overseas, they heard the voice of the chief of the British intelligence station there. It turned out the British had given the local security service some outdated bugging devices. The first thing the local security service did was to install one of the devices in the office of the British officer who had supplied them.

The Office of Security performs sweeps of the office of the director of Central Intelligence, his car, and his home every three to six months. They also sweep the rest of headquarters. CIA technicians have never found a bug in Langley. Sometimes, they think they have found one in the director's office when they find a strange new wire. But in every case, it leads to a buzzer installed to signal a request for coffee and tea, or to some other newly installed gadget.

"It's like looking for a needle in a haystack," a former technician said. "It could be anywhere in a building. You can bust your chops looking, never find anything, and never be sure if it was behind the next wall. You are never sure."

To find technicians who can debug offices, as well as the dizzying array of other specialists needed by the CIA, the CIA has an agency-wide office of personnel that looks for practically every area of expertise listed in college and technical-school catalogues. But finding people who will become spies takes a special approach, which is the primary purpose of the CIA's Career Training Program.

20 | *Charisma*

"WE NEED PEOPLE WHO ARE DRIVEN, PEOPLE WHO ARE AG-gressive, manipulative—people who can manipulate people to get them to do what they want them to do."

It is nine A.M. on a Friday. Bob, as distinguished looking as Walter Cronkite, is telling a group of eager and very respectful applicants what the CIA looks for in a spy. The applicants are being considered for the CIA's Career Training Program, the training program for the agency's elite. Most of the applicants will go into the CIA's Directorate of Operations—the side of the agency that engages in human spying. Some will obtain management positions in the agency's three other directorates.

This has to be the strangest show in Washington—a place where the CIA uses a classroom setting to recruit people to become professional impostors.

Competition to work at the agency is keen. Each year, the CIA receives 150,000 to 200,000 résumés for only 2,000 full-time, part-time, and contract job openings. In all, the agency has 22,000 full-time employees and 4,000 part-time and contract employees.

About 12,000 applicants complete all the requirements, including taking polygraph tests. Many drop out along the way when they learn they will have to reveal prior drug usage, when they find out more about the job, or when they simply get tired of waiting. The CIA does not tell applicants why they were rejected. One common reason for rejection is evidence of psychological problems revealed in psychological tests. Psychiatric treatment is also frowned on. Occasionally, in the course of trying desperately to pass the polygraph test, applicants reveal they have committed rapes or other crimes—information that is passed along to the FBI and of course, disqualifies them for the job. So long as it is disclosed, homosexuality is no longer grounds for rejection.

The CIA advertises in local media in all fifty states and has twelve recruitment centers throughout the country. Each year CIA recruiters visit 450 college campuses. There, they play a videotape put together by an advertising agency.

In the video, William Webster, wearing a button-down blue shirt and a blue-and-rust-striped tie, looks earnestly into the camera. "There's hardly any more diverse, complex, and truly worldwide organization than the CIA," he tells potential applicants. "As our name indicates, our primary concern is intelligence, that is, information, information that helps protect the security interests of the United States. The scope of this intelligence includes virtually every kind of information from all parts of the world—economic, political, military, scientific information about people, places, and events. Events that have happened and might happen. Wars, coups, terrorist acts, crop failures, elections, famine, drug trafficking, and natural disasters. All of these events and many more worldwide are the concern of the CIA."

Based on the résumés, the CIA narrows the list of applicants to five thousand and invites them to a three-hour introduction to the Career Training Program. Nearly all of the agency's spies in the Directorate of Operations come through this program, and more than half of those who join the program become spies. Only a few hundred a year are finally hired as operations officers. Specialists such as biologists, physicists, engineers, and demolitions experts, along with clerks and secretaries, are hired directly.

The introduction to the Career Training Program takes place several times a year in Washington and other cities. In Washington, the session is held in the Ames Building at 1820 North Fort Meyer Drive in Rosslyn, Virginia. There is no sign on the building, and visitors must have an appointment to get in. CIA guards check identification.

After receiving their visitor's badges, candidates go to a gray-carpeted room on the first floor at the rear of the building. Beige curtains cover the floor-length windows. School desks, in rows of six across, fill the room. The applicants, thirty-nine in this case, sit expectantly at the desks, most appearing nervous as they clutch the yellow notebooks they have been given.

Serious, well-groomed, and well-dressed, the applicants could all pass for prep-school students. Most of them are in their early twenties, although a few are as old as thirty. The men wear blue suits with white shirts. For the most part, the women also wear conservative suits. A third of the class is women, and there is one black man. This is a homogeneous group, intent on projecting a wholesome image.

Some 22 percent of the agency's new hires are minorities, according to Eugene J. Horan, the CIA's director of employment. Overall, 15 percent of the CIA's employees are minorities and 44 percent are women.[179]

Bob, wearing a gray suit, a white shirt, and paisley tie, introduces himself. He is from the Directorate of Administration, the side of the CIA that supports the rest of the agency by providing supplies, security, computers, and other necessities.

"The agency has four directorates," Bob says. "The Directorate of Operations tries to recruit people. It's a little like a marketing job."[180]

The applicants are listening intently. Most of them have no idea what spying is all about, their conceptions shaped by movies and novels.

"The first thing a case officer has to do is answer a question," he says. "Someone wants to know how much wheat the Soviets produced. It starts with a collection requirement."

The example is not particularly apt. In the Soviet Union, CIA officers are usually after more sensitive classified material than harvesting techniques. It is left to State or Agriculture Department employees to obtain this sort of detail.

Bob says most case officers or operations officers—spies who are staff members of an intelligence organization—work under cover, pretending to work for another agency of the U.S. government. They may meet potential sources of information at diplomatic receptions, for example.

"You start tasking with information collection. 'I need to know about your harvesting techniques.' You use tradecraft, microfilm. You watch for surveillance," he says. "It's received in Washington. It goes to the policymakers. It's a continuing cycle.

"It's not a nine-to-five job," Bob says. "Mostly they do agency work evenings and weekends. So it's a very strenuous career, but a very rewarding one."

Bob says the Directorate of Science and Technology determines military capabilities through satellites, radar, and other sensors. The Directorate of Intelligence analyzes information collected by the other directorates.

"The analysts have to be extremely careful they do not cross into policymaking," he says. "You have to have a thick skin to be an analyst. The paper comes back with red marks on it."

Then there is the Directorate of Administration.

"That's my directorate," he says. "It arranges cars, ships air freight for the DO [Directorate of Operations]. We make sure they get their pencils. We arrange S and T [Science and Technology] contracts."

Bob introduces Cecil, a black man wearing gold-rimmed glasses and a blue suit. He ticks off the requirements to join the Career Training Program: applicants must be U.S. citizens, twenty-one to thirty-five years old, and have a college grade point average of 3.0 or better.

"However, other circumstances like supporting yourself are

taken into consideration," he says. "Exceptional oral and written communication skills are needed. A track record in extracurricular activities. A stable work record. Military experience is good.

"We look for brains, smarts. Charisma is always good. We want impeccable character and integrity. You are asking people to be spies—to commit espionage. At the same time, we expect you to obey U.S. laws."

The Career Training Program takes a year, Cecil says, including internships of eight to ten weeks in two or three of the directorates.

"Here is a profile of a CT," he says. "They come from all over the country, average age is twenty-seven. Forty percent are female, sixty percent male. One-half have advanced degrees, two-thirds have traveled overseas, twenty percent have good foreign-language skills, fifteen percent are from the military.

"As for salary, I'm sure most of you are interested in that. Or are you that patriotic that you don't care?" Cecil asks rhetorically. A few applicants chuckle.

"You start as a GS-8, step 5. It starts at $26,000," he says. Foreign languages, military experience, and/or living overseas for an extended period qualify a new employee for a higher salary.

"Any questions?"

An intense young man asks about the organizational chart in a CIA brochure distributed when they arrived. He observes that no detail is shown for the Directorate of Operations.

Cecil explains that the organization of the clandestine side of the agency is classified.

"Is training nine to five?" someone asks.

"You have a little night hiking," Cecil says with a laugh, referring to paramilitary training.

It is now nine-fifty A.M., and Cecil introduces the next speaker, Shirley, from the Directorate of Operations. Shirley is pregnant and wears a gray maternity dress and polka-dot blouse. She has short, graying hair.

Whatever preconceptions the applicants have had about

what spies look like, Shirley probably does not resemble any of them.

"I have been in the CIA eighteen years," Shirley says. "We like to think we recruit responsible people. We are the clandestine service. We recruit human sources."

If you are going to be a spy, she says, "you have to be certain how you feel on the moral issue."

She does not spell this out, but the issue is of more than passing concern. To be a spy, a CIA officer must spend much of his or her life living a lie, pretending to be someone he or she is not, persuading others to turn against their own countries to commit espionage and become traitors. Not a job for everyone.

Shirley says another part of working as a spy is carrying out covert action.

"Covert action is undertaken when diplomacy doesn't work," she says. "It's designed to conceal the hand of the U.S.

"We put a high premium on social skills. You have to write well—to answer the standard journalistic questions of who, why, where, what, when, how. It makes a difference.

"You are not going to get recognition," she warns. "You will not be in the newspapers. You have to have a passion for anonymity. Otherwise there are other kinds of careers—military or what have you, for you."

She does not say so, but the State Department is usually cited by CIA officers as the place where those who seek glory should go—and good riddance.

Working as a spy "can be a lot of fun," she says. She catches herself. "Maybe I shouldn't use that word." She quotes an introduction written by former CIA director William Colby to a book about how to apply to the CIA.

"Colby said that looking back over twenty-five years, he had good times. We want people who want to do something for their country. . . . You have to have a strong desire to do something for the security of the U.S."

"Is your spouse required to be a DO [Directorate of Operations] officer as well?" an applicant asks.

"Absolutely not," Shirley says.

211

In the old days, she says, the CIA showed new employees a training film depicting a wife chastising herself for asking her CIA husband where he was going. This was silly, she says. CIA employees can give their spouses a general idea of what they are doing or where they are going without revealing "sources and methods," the mantra of security-conscious CIA employees.

On the other hand, "you really ought to make sure your spouse does not have a jealous bone in his or her body."

"Is it extremely dangerous? Let's say you try to recruit the wrong person," an applicant asks.

Shirley says there is a distinction between CIA officers, who generally operate under official government cover and therefore have diplomatic immunity, and the foreign agents they recruit to give them information.

"If you are going to pitch a Cuban, you might wait until the end of your tour [in a country]," she says. But a recruited agent does not have diplomatic immunity. "Your agent may be hanged. You try not to pitch someone unless he is going to say yes."

"Do you recruit a friend?"

"Yes," she says.

"What if I look American?" someone asks.

"You can have a disguise. You can blend in. You don't have to swagger."

What about paramilitary operations?

"We place a low priority on paramilitary," she says. "We are not really recruiting paramilitary [personnel]."

"What if your mother or father is foreign?"

"That's America," Shirley says. "It's a big melting pot. We'll check them out. We give polygraphs."

Now Mark from the Directorate of Science and Technology takes over.

"Is there anyone who is not familiar with James Bond?" he asks.

Mark says Q hands devices to the fictional spy so he can do his job—install bugs in a meeting room, for example, or put on disguises.

"I could change my appearance to a Michael Jackson look," says Mark, who is black.

Mark lists the components of his directorate—the Office of SIGINT Operations, which deploys sensors and intercepts communications; the Office of Technical Service, which develops spy equipment; the Office of Special Projects, which determines locations of nuclear devices and facilities and does other special collection of intelligence; the National Photographic Interpretation Center, which analyzes satellite photos; and the Foreign Broadcast Information Service, which transcribes and translates foreign broadcasts.

The SR-71 Blackbird, a follow-on to the U-2 reconnaissance plane that flies more than three times the speed of sound, is an example of the work of his directorate, Mark says. The plane is no longer in use, supplanted by spy satellites.

Mark introduces Christina from the Directorate of Intelligence. Christina wears a forest-green suit. Her graying hair is swept back. She refers to notes written on white index cards.

"I work in Soviet analysis," she says, peering over her reading glasses. "We have the task of taking information, analyzing it, and addressing national security problems and bringing them to the policymakers.

"We take considerable pride in doing unbiased analysis— to say it the way we see it. We take all source information and write products and we give briefings. There is a premium on getting information current and in an easily readable form.

"Every day," she says, "we provide briefings to the president, vice president, cabinet members.

"There are six offices on areas of the world—Soviet/East Europe, Europe, Near East, East Asia, Africa, Latin America. There are functional offices—economic, technical, geographic, nuclear weapons, leadership analysis on players.

"We are looking for people with strong analytical skills— research skills, the ability to think through problems, and people with good judgment.

"You are working with a team of smart people. There is high esprit. It is tough, hard work. Short deadlines cause stress, tensions. It is very fast paced and competitive."

213

"It seems to me it would be impossible to work on the Soviet economy without going there," an applicant says.

"We have an embassy there. We read the papers and reports here. We have clandestine collection. A lot of Soviet economists now come here. We don't rule out travel," she says.

It is eleven-fifty A.M., and Bob draws the meeting to a close. Each individual who is still interested will be interviewed separately. At the end of the interview, those applicants who are right for the agency will be handed an application.

A look of shock passes over some of the faces.

"If we don't receive an application, we're not being considered for employment?" an applicant asks.

"Right," Bob says.

The application is thirty-four pages long, Bob says. But not to worry—some of the pages contain instructions or certifications. The application asks for a listing of residences for the past fifteen years, employment history back to age seventeen, brothers' and sisters' employers. Even birth dates and places of birth of mothers-in-law and fathers-in-law are required.

Applicants will also be asked to take a psychological and aptitude test. They will be asked to provide a sample of how they write.

"Tell us who you are as a person. What do your best friends think about you?"

It will take six to twelve months before security checks are completed and jobs offered to those who have passed all the hurdles.

A young man wants to know the extent of the background investigation.

"If I had dinner with friends in a summer in Yugoslavia, will you talk to them?" he asks.

"Probably not. But we develop our own leads," Bob says.

Bob raises the subject of drugs.

"There are no problems with a six-pack on a weekend in college. We look at drug use. If you inject something, that will cause a lot of strong concern. If it stopped a year earlier and can be explained by peer pressure, it might not be a problem. What also concerns us is having three to four credit cards, and you don't have a job or have declared bankruptcy."

Another applicant asks if every foreign national he has ever met must be listed. What if he cannot remember them all?

"If you can't, say you can't remember," Bob says.

It is just before noon, and the session is over. The applicants line up expectantly for their interviews near the front of the building.

Understandably, the session did not explain what it really means to be a spy for the CIA. That would give away too many secrets. Nor did the session touch on the office of the director of Central Intelligence, which constitutes the CIA's fifth and most powerful component.

PART V

The Office of the Director of Central Intelligence

21 | Three Hats

BECAUSE OF THE WAY AMERICA HAD BEEN CAUGHT OFF guard at Pearl Harbor, President Truman and Congress wanted to make sure that in the future U.S. intelligence would be coordinated. For that reason, Congress created a director of Central Intelligence who wore three hats: one as the head of the CIA, one as the coordinator of the other intelligence agencies in the government, and one as the primary adviser to the president, through the National Security Council, on foreign intelligence matters.[181]

Since the Eisenhower administration, the panoply of U.S. intelligence agencies has been known as the intelligence community, suggesting a benign gathering of neighbors. Besides the CIA, the intelligence community consists of the State Department's Bureau of Intelligence and Research, the intelligence components of the Energy and Treasury departments, the National Security Agency, the counterintelligence component of the FBI, the National Reconnaissance Office, the Defense Intelligence Agency, and the intelligence elements of the Army, Air Force, Navy, and the Marine Corps. Other agencies that have intelligence-related functions, such as the Commerce Department, participate in some community councils but are not considered full-fledged members of the community.

To help in coordinating the intelligence community, the director of Central Intelligence has a separate intelligence-community staff with its own director. The DCI also sits on a dizzying array of interagency groups and committees that coordinate specific activities of the intelligence agencies. The most important is the National Foreign Intelligence Board (NFIB), whose membership includes the senior official of each agency in the intelligence community. Through this group, the intelligence community approves National Intelligence Estimates that represent the views of the entire community. Through various committees, the board also decides what priorities to focus on and what classified information should be given to allies.

The DCI is appointed by the president with the advice and consent of the Senate. The president may also fire him. In carrying out his intelligence community role, the DCI has a deputy director of Central Intelligence. He serves both as deputy director of the CIA and as the DCI's deputy in co-ordinating the intelligence community. Like the DCI, he is appointed by the president with the advice and consent of the Senate.

In directing the CIA, the DCI has four deputy directors who head each of the four directorates. The DCI also has a number of staff offices that are not part of any directorate and report directly to him. These are the offices of General Counsel; Public Affairs; Congressional Affairs; Comptroller; the Special Assistant for Arms Control, who monitors compliance with arms control agreements; the National Intelligence Council, which prepares estimates; and the director of the Intelligence Community Staff, which coordinates a number of intelligence community committees on such matters as security, information handling, and counterintelligence. In addition, a deputy director for planning and coordination reports directly to the DCI and has a staff of sixteen people. Taken together, these staff offices represent the fifth segment of the CIA.

As a result of legislation passed in 1990, the CIA's inspector general is on the same level as the DCI on the agency's organization chart. Like the DCI, he is appointed by the president with the consent of the Senate. Overseeing the entire octopuslike community are not only the congressional oversight committees but the President's Foreign Intelligence Advisory Board (PFIAB), a citizen panel that investigates shortcomings and reports its findings to the president. Finally, the President's Intelligence Oversight Board, consisting of three members from outside the government appointed by the president, is supposed to report to the president any intelligence activities that appear to be improper or illegal.

Most of the directors of Central Intelligence had no previous intelligence experience. Two of those, John A. McCone and Walter Bedell Smith, are remembered as being among the best DCIs. Smith, who served from 1950 to 1953, established the machinery for preparing National Intelligence Estimates to better coordinate the analytical work of the agency. McCone, who served from 1961 to 1965, sharpened the process for preparing estimates and established a fourth directorate for Science and Technology. On the other hand, William F. Raborn, Jr., who served from 1965 to 1966, is remembered as one of the worst DCIs. Like McCone, Raborn had no previous intelligence experience beyond what he'd picked up during his career in the Navy.

Russell Jack Smith, a former deputy director for intelligence, recalled that when Lyndon Johnson intervened with U.S. forces in the Dominican Republic in 1965, Raborn decided that he could best contribute by rushing every piece of paper received by the CIA to the president. But Richard Helms, then deputy director of Central Intelligence, calmed him down.

"Dick Helms's smooth intervention prevented the disaster that is risked when raw, unevaluated intelligence reports are placed in a president's hand," Smith said.[182]

"I never worked for a nicer guy who was more out of his

element," said Walter N. Elder, who was executive assistant to Raborn. "I thought President Johnson did him a disservice by naming him DCI."[183]

Other DCIs, such as Sidney W. Souers, William J. Casey, and William H. Webster, had some intelligence experience in predecessors of the CIA or in other intelligence organizations. Only three, Allen W. Dulles, Richard Helms, and William Colby, had served in the CIA before being appointed director.

Each director approached the job differently. Dulles, who served from 1953 to 1961, and Casey, who was DCI from 1981 to 1987, became highly involved in clandestine operations.

"Dulles always thought he was an excellent practitioner," Robert T. Crowley, a CIA officer at the time, said. "I have no evidence to support that."[184]

Adm. Stansfield Turner, who served from 1977 to 1981, felt the CIA emphasized human spying too much, to the detriment of technical collection. Turner devoted a great deal of his time to the analytical side, sometimes substituting his own opinions for the estimates presented to him.

"They [the operations people] were the elite directorate—the untouchables," Herbert E. Hetu, Turner's director of public affairs, said. "I think he [Turner] felt we got more bang for the buck from technical intelligence. You can't get intentions through it, though. He thought they [the operations officers] were important but overblown. They totally overreacted to that."[185]

By his quiet, princely manner, Helms, who was DCI from 1966 to 1973, gave an impression of harboring vast knowledge. He supported his troops while doing his best to deflect White House pressures to involve the agency in cover-ups, politically inspired estimates, and illegal activities. On the other hand, he approved the incarceration of Yuri I. Nosenko, the KGB defector mistrusted by James Angleton.[186]

Aside from strongly supporting CIA operations and improving congressional relations, George Bush is remembered for doing very little during his one-year tenure as DCI, from 1976 to 1977.

Turner is roundly hated for trying to diminish the importance of the clandestine side of the CIA and for cutting the staff of the Directorate of Operations in a crude manner. While the directorate was overstaffed because of staff increases during the Vietnam War, the reductions could have been accomplished over five years through attrition. But Turner was impatient and decided to reduce the staff over two years. This meant 17 people were dismissed and 147 people were forced into early retirement. Many others were told to find jobs in other directorates or be fired. Those affected were told to find new jobs on October 31, 1977. The two-paragraph letter said, "It has been decided that your services are no longer needed." The action came to be known as the Halloween Massacre.[187]

In his book, *Secrecy and Democracy,* Turner admitted that the wording of the notices was unfortunate but defended speeding up the retirement process. He said complaints about the 147 forced into early retirement "were beside the point. Almost all of them would have retired within a year or two anyway."

Robert (Rusty) Williams, one of Turner's aides, spent his first few months at the agency looking into whether operations officers were having "nooners" or were drinking at work.[188]

"Rusty Williams asked [subordinates] who I was sleeping with," a former station chief said. "People said they presume my wife."

After creating tremendous resentment within the operations directorate, Williams decided the staff operated ethically and soundly.[189]

"I don't think people should be drinking at lunch," Turner said recently. "They can have one if they want to, but he [Williams] found people who couldn't come back. They were drinking when they came into the building. They were genuine alcoholics and were producing only a small percentage of the time."[190]

But even Turner's aides conceded that his approach created unnecessary resentment. Any organization has its share of alcoholics, and by assigning an assistant to investigate the problem—rather than handling it through the chain of command—Turner seemed to be suggesting that he thought the CIA was full of drunks.

"Stan was book smart but street dumb," one of his former assistants said. "He didn't understand how things would be perceived."

In his five months as DCI in 1973, James R. Schlesinger never had time to get a handle on the agency, but he opened it up to public scrutiny by ordering the compilation of the "family jewels," the list of the agency's past abuses. Colby ushered the agency into the modern era by emphasizing the need to operate lawfully and be accountable to Congress and the public. But Casey moved the agency backward by again involving it in illegal and improper activities. While he temporarily improved morale by acting as the agency's cheerleader, most CIA officers—including those in the Directorate of Operations—look back on his tenure overall as a blemish on the agency.

"Casey had a lot of problems and did a lot of things that didn't do a lot of people any good," a former CIA operations officer said. "He did care about the agency."

The amount of influence the DCIs have had with presidents has depended on their relationships with them. After the CIA foresaw the outbreak of the Arab-Israeli Six Day War in 1967 and predicted it would last seven to ten days, President Johnson invited Helms to attend his Tuesday lunches with his inner circle of foreign policy advisers. Casey served not only as an intelligence adviser to President Reagan but also—having worked in his presidential campaign—as a political adviser.

Unlike Casey, Webster specifically asked not to have cabinet rank, feeling that the DCI should be an impartial disseminator of intelligence rather than a policymaker. Colby had a distant relationship with President Ford, exacerbated when he did not inform Ford of the existence of the "family jewels" before congressional committees and the press found out about them.

To some extent, the business of the CIA goes on regardless of who is DCI. Like any bureaucracy, the agency has a life of its own, responding to events and pressures based on values instilled over time. But most of the DCIs have made their own marks on the agency, rearranging its various parts, establishing new offices, changing emphasis here or there, and in most cases, imposing new regulations and controls.

In that respect, William Webster, who took over as DCI in May 1987, was no different from his predecessors. What made his term distinctive was that he was the ultimate outsider, a lawyer who had been a federal judge prior to becoming FBI director. Webster had no political constituency, no political obligations, and no ties to the intelligence community. Because of that, what happened during Webster's four-year term as director of Central Intelligence provides an unusual opportunity to gain insight into the character of the modern CIA.

22 | 00-14

When a director of Central Intelligence is to be nominated, each directorate hopes that one of its own will get the job. If a former analyst is nominated, the operations people grumble. If an operations officer gets the nod, he can never satisfy the expectations of the other directorates.

As an outsider, William H. Webster—like most CIA directors—was from none of the directorates. Moreover, he had been FBI director for nearly ten years. There is an instinctive rivalry between the bureau and the CIA. Their jobs are similar and yet different, and bringing in someone from the FBI was like choosing the editor of the *New York Times* to head its natural competitor, the *Washington Post*.

The idea that a former judge could direct the activities of an agency whose mission was to break the laws of other countries sent shivers up the spines of many in the Directorate of Operations. For all the harm William Casey had done to the

CIA's reputation, Casey had still strongly supported the clandestine service.

At the FBI, Webster had done a first-rate job of putting into place procedures that would prevent abuses such as Cointelpro, a program approved by J. Edgar Hoover that included illegal mail openings and break-ins to gain information on the antiwar movement. Webster upgraded the bureau's counterintelligence program from a neglected and shunned sideline to one of the most respected lines of work in the FBI. He approved such controversial sting operations as Abscam, which targeted members of Congress, and he emphasized pursuit of white-collar and organized crime. While the FBI under Webster overreached its authority in investigating the Committee in Solidarity with the People of El Salvador (CISPES), the abuses never reached the point of illegality. The FBI investigated the group when it received allegations, which proved to be unfounded, that CISPES was involved in supporting terrorism. In the CISPES investigation, the abuses—which included inquiring into political beliefs—had not been approved by the director, as had been the case with abuses that took place under Hoover.

While black and Hispanic agents filed complaints of discrimination under Webster's tenure, Webster's emphasis was always on hiring and promoting more minorities.[191] Webster kept a card in his wallet with the latest minority statistics. From 1978 to 1987, while he was FBI director, the number of female special agents rose from 147 to 787. Black agents increased from 185 to 393. Hispanic agents rose from 173 to 400.[192]

Despite his impressive credentials in the law, Webster had no experience or special interest in foreign affairs. Born on March 6, 1924, in St. Louis, William Hedgcock Webster attended secondary school in Webster Groves, a suburb of St. Louis. He graduated from Amherst College in 1947 and from Washington University Law School in 1949. He served as a lieutenant in the U.S. Navy during World War II and in the Korean War, practiced law in St. Louis, and was appointed U.S. Attorney for the Eastern District of Missouri in 1960.

In 1961, Webster returned to the practice of law. In 1970,

he was appointed a judge for the U.S. District Court for the Eastern District of Missouri. In 1973, he was appointed to the U.S. Court of Appeals for the Eighth Circuit. Although Webster was a Republican, President Carter appointed him FBI director in 1978.

As the end of his ten-year term as FBI director approached, Webster was already evaluating offers from major law firms when then vice president Bush asked him if he would like to be DCI. After Webster's first wife, Drusilla, died in 1984, Bush and his wife, Barbara, had invited Webster to stay with them at their home in Kennebunkport, Maine. Webster and Bush had spent the weekend playing tennis.

While President Reagan never said so, it was plain that Webster had been chosen because of his reputation for imposing order on troubled agencies. Under William J. Casey, the CIA had become involved in the Iran-contra scandal and had failed to adequately inform Congress of the mining of the harbors in Nicaragua. The CIA had begun to project an image of being out of control, the inevitable result of Casey's penchant for thumbing his nose at Congress.

Webster was a first-class lawyer and judge whose integrity was beyond question—exactly what was needed to impose order on the CIA. For example, when the Carter White House asked the FBI to help guard the shah of Iran when he came to the U.S. for treatment for cancer, Webster questioned whether the FBI had the legal authority to comply. That sent White House lawyers scurrying to the law books to find a legal justification. Only when they found a law permitting the FBI to assist other agencies in guarding foreign dignitaries did Webster accede to the White House request.[193]

To underscore the fact that he was an outsider who would not tolerate past abuses, Webster preferred that others refer to him as "judge."

"When he went to the FBI, it was in a state of disarray," said John P. Austin, a friend who nominated him to be chairman of the American Bar Association's Banking and Business Law Section. "He decided that he didn't want to be known as the director. He wanted to be known as Judge Webster. The reason he did was he wanted to make it perfectly clear that his relationship to the FBI would be in a sense similar to his relationship as a judge to what came before him."[194]

"If you went looking for the résumé of the ideal DCI, it wouldn't be Bill Webster," one of his aides said. "And yet in January of 1987, I'm not sure there was a better choice in the whole country to be DCI than Bill Webster."

With President Reagan looking on, Webster became the fourteenth DCI on May 26, 1987. Then Supreme Court justice Lewis F. Powell, Jr., swore him in. Pledging "fidelity to the Constitution and the laws of our country," Webster observed, "Today I leave one proud institution in American life, the FBI, to join another one, the CIA."

Noting that Webster had been an officer in the Navy, Reagan said that when the bosun's whistle was blown, Webster had responded. To commemorate the event, William Baker, Webster's public affairs director from the FBI, gave him a bosun's whistle from the British battleship H.M.S. *Hood* engraved with the date he was sworn in.

Webster declined to take a polygraph examination as part of the hiring process. But he did take what is known as a repolygraph almost immediately after taking office. The repolygraph is administered after employees are hired and is the same as the initial exam, except it does not include a number of questions on lifestyle. To Webster, it was a matter of principle. The president had nominated him, and the Senate had confirmed him. He would not subject himself to a test on whether he should be hired. But Webster recognized that the agency lives and dies on the polygraph. While universally hated, it is an integral part of every employee's existence. To demonstrate that he knew what it meant to take the test, he took a polygraph exam given to employees once they are already working for the agency.

Casey had often popped into people's offices just to say hello. Webster was not that kind of guy. To be sure, he had a playful side. Besides playing tennis, he enjoyed the antics at the Alfalfa Club, which holds an annual stag dinner in Washington. A strictly "No Women/No Press Allowed" affair, it is "one of the last gasps of the cigar-chomping, back-slapping, boozy days of yore," as the *Washington Post* called it. "It's a night when the president, most of the Cabinet, and congressional heavy-hitters don't have to worry about public image."

Webster also visited the Bohemian Club, an exclusive men's club sixty-five miles north of San Francisco that lists Ronald Reagan and George Bush as members.

Webster liked American Indian art and other art of the American West. He liked country music, particularly the mother and daughter team known as the Judds, who became his friends. On his fifty-four-acre family farm near Fulton, Missouri, he rode horses. He read history and Civil War books and spent a great deal of time researching the life of his great-grandfather, Col. George P. Webster, a lawyer who led the Union's Twenty-fifth Ohio Volunteer infantry at the Civil War battle of Perryville, Kentucky, on October 8, 1862. It was one of the bloodiest battles of the war, and Colonel Webster became one of the casualties when he fell from his horse, mortally wounded.[195]

One of Webster's favorite possessions was a two-foot-high brown bear—Judge WeBear—given to him by Mary Spaeth, a former White House fellow who had worked for him at the FBI. The bear wears black-rimmed glasses, pin-striped pants, an FBI T-shirt, tennis shoes, and judicial robes, a tennis racket clutched in its hands.

Spaeth gave it to Webster after he gave her a locket when she left the FBI.

"There were thirty guys at the FBI looking on," she recalled. "I thought, 'What if he doesn't think it's funny? I'm going to die. They'll shoot me right here.' Webster opened the box, and he started to laugh. He began to laugh so hard he began to cry. He took out his handkerchief and took off his glasses to wipe the tears from his eyes. And everybody else began to howl with laughter."[196]

After Webster's wife died, he led an active social life, dating a number of attractive women. He had a number of male friends, usually fellow lawyers or judges. While at the CIA, he jocularly signed letters to some of them 00-14, doubling James Bond's code number because he was the fourteenth director of Central Intelligence. But Webster was not someone to go drinking with. In fact, as a Christian Scientist, he generally eschewed alcohol, although he occasionally had a glass of white wine at a party. Webster had never gone to a doctor—he never seemed to need one. His first wife, Drusilla, was also a Christian Scientist and died of breast cancer without receiving any medical attention.

When CIA officials recommended a smoking ban in the building, Webster hesitated. He did not want to seem to be imposing his personal views on the agency. Perhaps he should propose the rule and get comments, he told John B. Bellinger, his assistant. But he overcame his reservations and imposed the prohibition that had been recommended to him.[197] The result was a collection of cigarette butts outside the building from smokers who took drags on the front steps.

On the job, Webster was not someone who took off his jacket when others did. Rather, he inspired fear and respect. That was the way he wanted it, to be the judge who keeps his distance from the litigants, who reads all the pleadings and listens to all the arguments, but whose decision in the end is final. It was a style that was not calculated to win friends or loyalty. Rather, it won often grudging admiration.

Like a judge, Webster relied on clerks—called special assistants—to filter material that came in and offer their opinions. While every DCI had special assistants, none relied on them so heavily or used such a systematic process for screening issues before decisions were made. Nor did other special assistants have the impressive credentials Webster's had. They were all lawyers, and all came with résumés that looked as if they had been made up. Almost every one had graduated either magna cum laude or cum laude from Harvard, Yale, Princeton, or Columbia. They had clerked for Supreme Court justices or edited law reviews or had been Woodrow Wilson Foreign Affairs fellows.

Webster chose the special assistants the same way he chose tennis partners.

"You can count on William to get the best player there is as his partner," said Walter M. Clark, a friend from childhood who practiced law with him in St. Louis. "It's done very subtly but very precisely. He likes to win. . . . He is awfully good at maneuvering things to end up with the best player as his partner."[198]

Like the clerks that served him when he was on the bench, Webster wanted his special assistants to read through the material he received, investigate and do research, and make recommendations.

"The job was structured very much like what he had experienced on the bench," said Russell J. Bruemmer, one of his assistants who later became general counsel of the CIA. "It was clear early on he was not setting up a classic chief of staff role or line responsibility but rather a staff responsibility for information gathering, analyzing the way the decisions ought to be approached, and once made, assisting in getting decisions through the agency."[199]

In reviewing the assistants' recommendations, Webster wanted to know, "How have we done it in the past?" Then he asked, "Why do we do it that way?"

"You better have the answers to both, and you better have it right," Bruemmer said. "If you are changing precedent, the question is, 'Why are we changing it?' "[200]

Beyond that, the assistants were to eye proposals with the perspective of outsiders to see if the idea would make sense to the American people. For that reason, Webster as a rule wanted his assistants at the FBI and the CIA to stay with him only two years. That way, he said, they would not begin to reflect the views of the bureaucracy.

"I want you to ask every time something comes up, why is it being done this way?" Webster told John B. Bellinger, who was his special assistant at the CIA until 1991. "When you know why, it's time to go."[201]

There were two exceptions—Bruemmer, who was Webster's clerk at the federal appeals court when Webster got the job at the FBI in 1978, and John B. Hotis, an FBI agent who had a law degree. Bruemmer became Webster's first special assistant at the FBI in 1978 and stayed with him until he left to join Wilmer, Cutler & Pickering in Washington in 1981. In 1987, Webster appointed Bruemmer special counsel to investigate the Iran-contra affair at the CIA. A year later, he made him general counsel of the CIA.

Unlike Bruemmer and the other assistants, Hotis did not come from the outside. He was more senior than the others and stayed throughout most of Webster's tenure at the FBI and CIA. Hotis acted as a sort of superclerk, with status slightly above the other special assistants. At the CIA, Webster gave him the title of counselor to the DCI. Generally, Hotis worked on special projects rather than the day-to-day issues that Webster's other assistants addressed.

When he first came to the CIA, Webster brought with him William M. Baker, who had directed public and congressional affairs at the FBI. Baker became CIA director of public affairs, but he also functioned as another personal assistant to Webster. Finally, Webster brought Peggy Devine, his executive secretary at the FBI. She was known as the Dragon Lady because of the way she fiercely guarded access to her boss.

After weeks of briefings by each of the directorates, Webster took command. The first thing he encountered was outright hostility toward Congress, which was hardly surprising.

"Don't brief; limit disclosure," Casey once told a CIA associate, then uttered an expletive to describe all members of Congress, according to *Veil* by Bob Woodward.

According to one of Webster's assistants at the time, CIA officials urged him not to be open with Congress.

"Well, Judge, you don't want to say that; you can't say that," he was told. "Only say that if they ask that question."

Often, holdovers from the Casey era compiled briefing books with sample questions and answers. The suggested answers gave a narrow response to the questions, avoiding possibly negative information. That never failed to infuriate Webster.

Webster occasionally raised his voice with subordinates when he was mad. But to those who knew him, the most ominous sign was when his eyes became more steely blue than usual, and his lips became thinner, so that his mouth seemed to disappear. It meant Webster was even more enraged than when he raised his voice. It happened a number of times as he made it clear he would not tolerate anything except complete and honest disclosure.

"He just couldn't stand the CIA's disdain for Congress," a former assistant said. "He thought it was ridiculous, dated, not in the best interests of the agency, not smart, and not good government. He really believed that Congress was the elected representative of the people. He couldn't stand the grumbling about sharing information with Congress."

Webster never said anything negative about Casey, even in private. In fact, he had played golf with him and liked him personally more than Stansfield Turner, Casey's immediate predecessor. It was not Webster's style to express his true feelings even to his closest aides.

Webster followed the same pattern at the FBI, where he never denigrated J. Edgar Hoover. Unlike Hoover, Webster had purposely avoided creating a cult of personality, stressing that the FBI was an institution whose mission must remain the same regardless of who was director. When some FBI executives complained about criticisms of the bureau that came from Rep. Don Edwards, a California Democrat who sits on the Judiciary Committee, Webster said, "I don't agree with him, but he is a congressman, he has oversight over us, and we are going to refer to him in a respectful tone."[202]

Webster led by example. It soon became clear that much of what Casey stood for would not be tolerated at the CIA.

When subordinates at the CIA insisted that Webster should not tell Congress about a particular problem, Webster told them, "You're wrong. I do want to tell them that, and I am going to tell them that."

Webster did not want anyone prosecuted for his testimony to Congress, as had happened to Richard Helms. When asked by Sen. Stuart Symington on February 7, 1973, "Did you try in the Central Intelligence Agency to overthrow the government of Chile?" Helms answered, "No, sir." Helms also denied to the Senate Foreign Relations Committee that the agency had passed any money to opponents of Salvador Allende, a self-declared Marxist who had been elected president of Chile.[203]

In fact, at the direction of President Nixon, the CIA in September 1970 had tried to mount a military coup in Chile to prevent confirmation of Allende's victory in the Chilean presidential election. The agency had spent $8 million to prevent his confirmation.

Helms agreed to plead nolo contendere to two misdemeanor counts of violating a federal statue, which made it an offense not to testify "fully and completely" before Congress. He told U.S. District Court judge Barrington D. Parker on October 31, 1977, that he found himself in conflict between his oath to protect the CIA's secrets and the need to tell the truth to Congress. Parker fined him $2,000 and sentenced him to a jail term of two years, which was suspended.[204]

"I have thought about it many times, and I couldn't figure out another way. If I had it to do over, I don't think I would change it," Helms said recently.[205]

But Webster told the CIA there was another way.

"You don't be disingenuous or dance around the question," Webster would say. "You try to understand what they want to know and not confine yourself to what they actually ask you. But if they ask something you don't want to tell them, or are not authorized to tell them because it would expose sources or methods, you should say, 'I am not authorized to say that.' Then go back to headquarters [for further guidance]."[206]

If underlings did not catch on quickly, they were out.

One of the first casualties was Clair E. George, the deputy director for operations. Of all the jobs in the CIA, none is more sensitive than DDO. George had been Casey's liaison with the Hill when Casey was limiting disclosure to Congress about events in Nicaragua. Moreover, George's style was not compatible with Webster's. He had a cocky, secretive air about him—exactly the opposite of the responsible attitude Webster wanted to project.

"What was clear was he was not going to continue to be DDO for Webster," a Webster aide said. "It first struck me then how important it was that the DDO's philosophy and style fit with the DCI. He [George] is a professional and his troops thought he walked on water. But their styles did not match."

Webster told George he wanted him to resign.[207] At the end of 1987, he did, convinced that Congress had made a deal with Webster that he would have to go if Webster was to be confirmed.

In his place, Webster appointed Richard F. Stolz. At sixty-two, Stolz was one of the most respected operations officers in the agency, a man who had served thirty-one years in the Directorate of Operations. During that time, Stolz had been Moscow and London station chief and chief of the Soviet/East European Division.

In 1981, Stolz retired after Casey appointed Max Hugel to head the directorate. Hugel was one of Casey's political cronies who knew nothing about intelligence. Casey had called Stolz back from London and told him he wanted him to assist Hugel by running part of the directorate. Another assistant would run the rest. To Stolz, the plan was a throw-back to the days of OSS, when human collection was split between the area divisions and the rest of the clandestine service. Stolz didn't think that division of responsibility had worked well in the OSS, and he was stunned that Casey would appoint someone to the most sensitive job in the agency who knew nothing about intelligence. Stolz turned Casey down.

Webster had known Stolz briefly when they were both at Amherst, and the two had kept in touch since then. When Reagan asked Webster to become DCI, Webster consulted with Stolz. Stolz had pointed out the need to keep his distance from the president, to avoid becoming a crony. Webster had said he would specifically decline to have cabinet status for that very reason.

When Webster asked Stolz to rejoin the agency as the top spy, no one had any question about his ability, and there were no resignations over his appointment. A short man with a graying pompadour, he had a low-key style that served him well. When Stolz finally retired in 1990, Webster proudly pointed out during a ceremony in the director's conference room that he had brought Stolz back to the CIA.

"I did that. I did that," he said, motioning toward Stolz.

In contrast to dispatching Clair George, Webster wanted to keep Robert M. Gates as deputy director of Central Intelligence. After Casey's death from cancer on May 6, 1987, Gates had served as acting director of Central Intelligence.

When questions arose about his knowledge of the Iran-contra affair, Gates withdrew as President Reagan's nominee to be DCI but continued as the deputy DCI.

Gates was unusually well qualified for the job. Born on September 25, 1943, in Wichita, Kansas, Gates graduated from the College of William and Mary and obtained a master's degree in history from Indiana University and a doctorate in Soviet studies from Georgetown University in 1974. His first experience with intelligence was as an Air Force intelligence officer with a Minuteman missile wing.[208]

Gates started as an analyst at the CIA in 1969 and moved to the National Security Council under President Nixon. After continuing at the NSC under President Ford, he returned to the agency, then moved back to the NSC under President Carter. In 1979, Gates again returned to the CIA, becoming deputy director for intelligence in 1982. In that job, Gates developed the first system for holding analysts accountable for their record of forecasts and assessments.

In 1983, Gates became chairman of the National Intelligence Council. In 1986, he became deputy director for Central Intelligence and during that time, acting director. Brent Scowcroft, President Bush's national security adviser, brought him back to the White House in 1989 as his deputy for national security affairs.

Gates clashed with Secretary of State James A. Baker III over Baker's intention to give a speech in 1989 that was highly pessimistic about Mikhail S. Gorbachev's chances of delivering on his reform promises. Baker shelved the speech, but events proved him to be largely correct.

Gates was a brilliant analyst who never failed to come out forcefully on an issue. As DDI, he had moved to sharpen the estimates, never bowing to Casey's pressure to exaggerate the prospects for the contra rebels in Nicaragua, for example.

Webster respected Gates's intellect and later pushed him as his successor. But Gates left the CIA in March 1989, to become deputy assistant to President Bush for national security affairs. In his place, Webster appointed Richard J. Kerr as deputy director of Central Intelligence. Like Gates, Kerr had spent most of his career on the analytical side of the house. Under Casey, he had become deputy director for intelligence. While he was not the brilliant scholar that Gates was, Kerr had a practical, common-sense approach to problems, as well as a practical joker's mentality.

When a topic in the Middle East was hot, Kerr showed up one morning at a meeting of Webster's executive committee wearing Arab dress. At Christmas, he wore a tie that played "Jingle Bells." Around Halloween, he wore a gorilla outfit.

In sharp contrast to Webster, Kerr practically never wore a jacket. Even in winter, he wore short-sleeve shirts. When Webster wore a jacket at lunch in the director's dining room, Kerr appeared in shirtsleeves. Some thought he was purposely trying to offset Webster's formality.

Besides establishing centers for counterintelligence and counternarcotics, one of Webster's more enduring changes was to systematize approvals for undertaking covert action. In the past, a committee called the Covert Action Review Group (CARG) had been used to examine and approve any covert action proposals. However, the committee functioned largely as a rubber stamp, informally signing off on proposals that were hand-carried from office to office. Webster did not want to emasculate covert action and could not do so if he had wanted to. Generally, the broad proposals originated with the National Security Council and the president. Since the CIA only implements policy, it needs to know what the policy is before it does anything. That includes the question of whether to undertake covert action and what form it should take. The White House and NSC gave the proposals to the CIA to fine-tune. But Webster did want to make sure every proposal was legal and made sense.

Just as if he were determining if one of his proposed judicial decisions complied with established law and precedent, Webster wanted to make sure that every covert action proposal had been tested against a set of unvarying questions: Does it fall within U.S. law? What would happen if it became public? Will the public understand it?* Finally, will it work?

---

* Richard Stolz framed the question, "What will happen *when* it becomes public?"

Initially, Webster assigned two of his assistants, John Hotis and Nancy D. McGregor, to sit on the CARG committee as his representatives. Like Hotis, McGregor had moved over to the CIA from the FBI with Webster. After they left the agency, other aides sat on the committee, which met every two weeks in the office of the director of congressional affairs on the seventh floor of the original headquarters building.

To some of Webster's aides, it seemed the committee consisted of "old boys getting together."

"Once it got up to the CARG, they no longer questioned the program. They questioned how do we do this tiny part," McGregor said. "In general, we tried to have a little more analysis done. We thought by the time it got to the CARG, it was a little too pat, with not enough discussion and critical thinking about the underlying purposes. The big questions were not asked. We wanted them asked. Webster wanted us to make sure they were asked. They were annoyed about that."[209]

As a result of the questioning by Webster's assistants, some proposals were modified, either to limit their scope or to eliminate dubious aspects. Once they were approved by CARG, they went back for approval by the White House. Then, they were presented to the congressional oversight committees.

"Webster wanted the covert action proposals to be reviewed to make sure they would make sense to the American people if they were to be revealed," McGregor said. "It sounds simplistic, but if you think about it, this approach places good controls over the proposals. The people in the agency can't be the sole watchdogs because of the natural tendency to get too close to the programs and lose perspective. Webster's questions were: Would people understand why and how a particular program was being carried out or would they say this is crazy, ludicrous, how could our government be doing something like that?"[210]

"I think the changes he made in covert action proposals were not to say, 'We aren't going to do it,' but, 'We are going to approach this according to different procedures.' Or he would send things back for more work when he wasn't satisfied with how they looked or felt," Bruemmer said.[211]

Webster's assistants prepared a briefing book listing all the covert action programs with an analysis of their purposes. Enclosed in a black, three-ring binder, the material summarized each program—roughly twelve at any given time—with two or three pages of description. The idea was to give Webster a handy reference guide that he could keep in his office and refer to when questions arose, as they invariably did.

The idea provoked outrage within the Directorate of Operations, which thought the existence of the book would somehow create a greater possibility of leaks. But once the book had been put together and placed on Webster's desk, it seemed everyone wanted his own copy to validate his status. Only the deputy directors, the general counsel, and the inspector general received one.

Particularly after the invasion of Kuwait by Iraq, Webster decided that the Directorate of Operations, battered by both the Church Committee hearings and the Iran-contra affair, had become so cautious that it passed up chances it should have taken to recruit agents. The best example was in Iraq, where the CIA had practically no agents of value reporting on Saddam Hussein.

There is no scientific way to evaluate how well an intelligence agency is doing in recruiting agents. In the case of Saddam Hussein, the CIA was hampered by the fact that Saddam Hussein allowed only family members or those who had been loyal to the Iraqi leader since childhood into his inner circle. Webster did not want CIA officers to take needless risks in penetrating such a country. But Webster believed there was a middle ground, one that would allow the agency's spies to be more aggressive while not becoming cowboys. In talks with Directorate of Operations officials, he noted that he had never disapproved a covert action proposal or a major intelligence operation.

"I want people in the DO who are risk takers, not risk seekers," Webster said at Richard Stolz's retirement party at the end of 1990.

Particularly after Kuwait, Webster—like directors before

him—pushed for more foreign-language training. To upgrade training generally, he tried to promote officers who did a stint as CIA teachers. And he emphasized more reporting on economic issues.

Webster wanted more accountability in the agency and more clarity in its reports. He hated acronyms and he hated the word *feel*. People could *believe* or *state* or *conclude,* but they could never *feel.*

"We are not paid to feel," Webster wrote in a memo to CIA employees. "We are paid to think."

Webster could not stand it when CIA officials submitted papers to him without attributing where they had gotten the information. In answer to some questions, he was handed background papers that did not say who had written them or who had submitted them. He demanded that each paper he received carry the name of the author, the author's office, and his or her telephone extension.

Webster was used to having personable FBI agents as his security guards. At the CIA, the guards were from the Office of Security, and they were anything but personable. Indeed, the young men assigned to guard Webster seemed to think they were the gestapo. Ramrod stiff, they bristled if anyone asked them their names. At receptions attended by Webster, they clung to the walls, looking like rent-a-cops in a grade B movie.

One weekend, William Baker's wife, Robin, decided to surprise Baker when her husband and Webster were due in New Jersey to attend a party given by Malcolm Forbes. Originally from New Jersey, Robin Baker drove from her parents' home to the airport, her Labrador retriever on a leash. There, she saw Webster's security detail with squiggly wires sprouting from their ears. The plane had not yet arrived. When she approached her husband and Webster, she did not want to alarm the guards, so she introduced herself.

"Hello, I'm Mrs. Baker. I'm married to Bill Baker, who is flying in with the director," she said as the dog wagged his tail. "I just wanted you to know I'm here to greet my husband so you know who I am."[212]

The guard did not respond.

"I guess I'll go and find somebody else to talk to," she said. The man ignored her.

Several minutes later, two guards came over to her and brusquely asked her for identification. Then they demanded proof that she was married to Baker. Having just gotten married, she had trouble finding a credit card in her handbag with her husband's name on it. The guards acted as if they had just caught her breaking into a bank, and she was livid.

Baker never told Webster of the incident, but Webster himself had become unhappy with the guards' style. With Webster's approval, Baker met with the head of the security detail.

"We need to go to charm school together," Baker said.

He then met with all the guards.

"Look, this is what the director expects," he said. "In addition to the professionalism which you have, he expects a little more than that."

Baker said he did not want them to be so tight. He gave them a supply of his business cards.

"If you're at a function or party with him, and someone asks if you're CIA, and you can't quite tell them that, hand them my card," Baker said. "Say, 'If you have any questions, call this gentleman.' "[213]

Webster found one of the CIA's biggest problems was the fact that each directorate is a separate fiefdom, with the Directorate of Operations usually the most dominant. The DO tended to be suspicious of the Directorate of Intelligence, which in turn resented not being fully trusted. There were constant complaints from both sides. Meanwhile, the CIA's other two directorates resented being looked down upon.[214]

Webster wanted more cross-pollination, and he began to rotate people so that they worked for two or three of the directorates during their careers.

"At the CIA, they are kings of their own dominion," a former Webster assistant said. "It is set up so loyalties are within directorate. You make your career within that division. You make or break your career based on loyalty to a specific boss, not the head of an agency or the head of a different division."

Turner had encountered the same problem.

"I think the biggest problem is coordination among the various branches," he said.[215]

The attitude was entirely different from that of the FBI, where the FBI director and the special agent in charge of each field office were the unquestioned bosses. Like the FBI, the CIA was a semimilitary organization that obeyed orders. But the boss at the CIA was the head of one's own division, not the head of the agency.

The result was that the directorates were not eager to share information with each other. While some secrecy was necessary, Webster and his assistants found it was often used to enhance people's own importance, hampering everyone's work. Despite the fact that they had clearances for virtually every program, the assistants were sometimes prevented from knowing what they felt they needed to know.

"Very few people [at the CIA] know the complete picture because very few are allowed to know it," McGregor said. "That is what makes it so difficult to get at the whole truth. This is exacerbated by the fact that so very few feel any loyalty to the head of the agency. Rather, their loyalties are to the heads of their divisions or their directorates."[216]

These attitudes contributed to the agency's involvement in the Iran-contra affair.

"Agency people . . . from the director on down, actively shunned information," Robert Gates, then the deputy director for Central Intelligence, later told the Senate Select Committee on Intelligence. "We didn't want to know how the contras were being funded . . . we actively discouraged people from telling us things."[217]

Webster decided that the CIA's inspector general was not tough enough to do the job of policing the agency, a fact underscored by what happened during the Iran-contra affair. Historically, the office was the domain of amiable CIA officers who were at the end of their careers and did not want to rock the boat. If a CIA director did not like the inspector general's criticisms, he could remove him. Back in 1960, after a review of the Office of Security, the inspector general recommended that the CIA prepare a "cover story" if the agency's mail-opening program were ever uncovered. The report made no mention of the fact the program was illegal.

According to Tom Gilligan, a former CIA operations officer, "Operations officers seldom suffered permanent career damage for poor performance or incompetence, even when agents were killed or compromised." Yet when Gilligan appealed a decision not to give his station more officers, he found his performance was down-rated because of it. He felt he could not bring the problem to the attention of the CIA's inspector general because of the inspector general's lack of independence. What is needed, Gilligan said, is inspectors general who "come from outside the organization."[218]

Before Congress created an office of inspector general, Webster elevated the importance of the job. He appointed William F. Donnelly, a tough, respected officer who acted as one of Webster's advisers, to the position. At the same time, Webster did not favor the approach proposed by Congress. In response to the Iran-contra affair, the oversight committees decided that the inspector general should be appointed by the president with confirmation by the Senate. Then only the president could fire him. Congress also wanted access to the inspector general's reports, which generally went only to the director and the affected departments within the CIA. Even though nineteen other federal agencies had independent watchdogs approved by Congress, Webster saw the proposal as a reflection on his own performance. He was the director of Central Intelligence, and he was charged with making sure the CIA conformed to the laws. It was a question of accountability. If he failed, he should be replaced. But he insisted the inspector general should answer to him, not to Congress or to the president.

What most troubled Rep. Dave McCurdy, an Oklahoma Democrat who led the fight for the bill, was Congress's lack of access to reports prepared by the inspector general.

"I wanted to find out how effective they were, how much support they had," said McCurdy, who later became chairman of the House Permanent Select Committee on Intelligence. "The more I got into it, the more I was concerned. There was no way for us to find out. 'Let me see some of your reports.' 'You can't have them.' 'Can I have an index so I can pick a couple?' 'No.'

"I think Webster totally mishandled the whole situation," McCurdy said. "I said I believe we have a right to see the reports, not as to individuals, but on general policy considerations and how the Soviet division is doing. He said you are not entitled to it, kind of exerting executive privilege. The reason was more micromanagement. He didn't want us to invade his executive turf."[219]

Webster lost the battle, and Congress passed a law establishing an independent inspector general at the CIA. Frederick P. Hitz, a lawyer and former CIA officer who was Webster's choice, got the job and took office in November 1990.

Besides investigating allegations of wrongdoing or mismanagement, Hitz continued the practice of examining each office and station every five years to determine if they are doing their job. That entails reading reports and cable traffic to see how agents are being handled, whether good judgment is being exercised in recruiting agents, and whether resources are being used wisely.

The complaints examined by the office ranged from allegations of defalcations to matters of taste. Just before Hitz took over as inspector general, the office had received a complaint by some female employees that the unisex barbershop in the old building provided copies of *Playboy* and *Penthouse* for customers to read while waiting. Without issuing a formal ruling, the office quietly resolved the matter by telling the barbers to drop the offending magazines.

If Webster lost the battle over an independent inspector general, he won on most issues requiring congressional approval. While his credibility and cooperative approach contributed to that record, it was also a result of good staff work. In that arena, Webster had a secret weapon—his special assistants.

23 | *The Munchkins*

IT WAS THE JOB OF WILLIAM WEBSTER'S SPECIAL ASSISTANTS to clone themselves, to find similarly qualified and brilliant lawyers to replace them after their two-year stints were up. So in July 1986, Howard W. Gutman and William T. Hassler, then Webster's assistants at the FBI, began calling friends and contacts at prestigious law firms to find a good candidate to replace Gutman.

Like the rest of Webster's assistants, both men had dream résumés. Gutman, for example, had graduated fifth in a class of 650 from Columbia University. He had graduated magna cum laude from Harvard Law School. He was a member of Phi Beta Kappa. He had been a law clerk to Supreme Court justice Potter Stewart. Later, he joined Williams & Connolly, eventually becoming a partner.

The two assistants knew that Webster favored Ivy League graduates, particularly from Harvard or Yale. After extensive inquiries, Gutman called Nancy D. McGregor, a twenty-eight-year-old lawyer who had graduated from Barnard College and Harvard Law School.

Then at Steptoe & Johnson, McGregor was not only a very good lawyer but extremely personable and attractive. With green eyes and brown hair, she had a direct approach that allowed her to say exactly what she wanted without creating bad feelings. She could be persistent in her questioning, yet tactful. When she decided to do something, she pursued it relentlessly and courageously. Yet she could be disarmingly charming.

Born in Pittsburgh, McGregor was the daughter of Jack McGregor, a lawyer and former Pennsylvania state senator. Her father had treated her like a friend and colleague, keeping her informed on what he was doing and asking her advice. When McGregor was six, her family became worried when they couldn't find her one afternoon. It later turned out she had been canvassing the street, asking neighbors to vote for her father.

McGregor had been working for Steptoe & Johnson for two years, handling white-collar criminal cases, when a partner in the firm said Gutman had approached him asking for recommendations on candidates for Webster's special assistant. Within Washington legal circles, the job was a plum. Not only did it give lawyers access to government at the highest levels, it was also a stepping-stone to a partnership in one of the top law firms.

"We decided you are the person we would like to propose for this," the partner said.

Everything she had heard about the job made it sound very desirable—a chance to participate in the investigation rather than the defense of white-collar crimes, to see a lot of secret information very few people ever see, and to work for what she felt was a great institution with a lot of commitment. Yet she would not be leaving the career track.

McGregor said she would like to be considered. Besides Gutman and Hassler, John Hotis, Webster's third special assistant who stayed on as a superclerk, interviewed her at the FBI. Three weeks later, Gutman called her to say the judge would like to see her for breakfast.

McGregor attended the breakfast in the FBI's executive dining room hours after she learned she was pregnant with her first child. One of Webster's assistants had told her she was one of a number of attorneys being considered for the job, and that Webster still had others to interview. She had no idea Webster would offer her the job on the spot.

Webster explained the purpose of the special assistants. They were to be outsiders who would take a fresh look at the bureau's activities—a new set of eyes that would judge issues by the standards of the public and the community. As lawyers, Webster wanted them to measure proposals against guidelines and statutes. But he also wanted the assistants to look at the FBI like John Q. Public to see if things made sense.

At the end of the breakfast, Webster looked at her and said, "Well, I think I'm ready to make this decision. I'd like you to come and work for me."

McGregor had planned to inform Webster that she was pregnant before he offered her the job. Now that that was no longer possible, she wanted to tell him before she accepted. McGregor wanted to tell Webster in private, so that he could quietly withdraw the offer, if he chose to do so, without any embarrassment. She was aware that Webster employed two assistants, and if she were on maternity leave, he would be left stranded. Not only would she be the first woman in the job, but McGregor would be pregnant in a sea of macho FBI agents.* But both Gutman and Hassler were at the breakfast, and McGregor said she would have to think about it.

Webster was furious with his two assistants. He had understood that they would bring him only a candidate who wanted the job. He hated rejection, and after the breakfast, he raked them over the coals for not doing their homework.[220]

When she got back to her office, McGregor called Gutman.

"There is something I have to discuss personally with the judge," she said.

"Well, what is it?" he asked.

---

* Several White House fellows who were women had worked for Webster, but they were not considered on the same level as his special assistants.

"Something personal," she said, cringing.

Webster was on a flight to Atlanta. When he called back, McGregor was in a meeting of partners working on a federal criminal case. They did not know of her application to the FBI.

"Nancy, the director of the FBI is calling," a secretary announced.

The others at the table looked shocked.

McGregor excused herself and took the call in another office. She explained the problem, and Webster took it in stride.

"What a relief," he said. "I was afraid you were going to tell me that you were a drug addict. That would have caused a problem."

At the FBI, McGregor had to change from being a lawyer who kept a pile of papers on her desk to someone who locked up all her papers at night in a safe. She visited the FBI's shooting range at Quantico, Virginia, and rode with the director to conferences. She would wander into the executive dining room and munch on the superb chocolate chip cookies made by Ray, the chef. When she found the dining room served Webster eggs and bacon or sausages every morning, she got the chief to vary the menu with healthier food such as fruit and cereal.

McGregor reviewed such sensitive matters as requests for wiretaps in counterintelligence cases and proposals to arrest spies. Webster wanted every question answered before he signed off on such matters, and if all the material had not been presented, she sent the memos back for more work. If something went wrong, she was often the first person to tell Webster. Her rapport with him was so good that FBI executives joked that if they wanted to break any bad news to the director, they would do it either through her or with her present.

On the other hand, even though Webster had been using them ever since he came to the FBI, some of the more seasoned FBI executives questioned Webster's use of assistants. They had spent their careers building enough trust so they would be allowed to see the most sensitive secrets in the government. Now young lawyers with no experience in FBI work were being allowed to see even more than they were.

Phillip Parker, the deputy assistant FBI director for operations in the counterintelligence division, was one of the FBI executives who came to call the assistants "munchkins." It was not that he questioned their loyalty or trustworthiness; it was just that he found the thought of entrusting so much to inexperienced people unnerving.

On the other hand, James E. Nolan, who preceded Parker in the same job, saw no problem with them.

"It gave him a sounding board when he thought maybe the career people were stacking the deck on him. He could get somebody else to look at it," Nolan said.

When Webster moved to the CIA, McGregor went with him. By then, Hassler had been replaced by Mark E. Matthews, a magna cum laude graduate of Harvard College. McGregor's son, Ben, had just been born. McGregor took the required polygraph test at CIA headquarters. Since she was still nursing at the time, she had to leave the baby with a relative who lived near the compound so she could race back in time to feed him.

McGregor regarded the CIA with a healthy skepticism. In part because of turf battles, FBI agents often derided the CIA in private. They questioned its competence and its adherence to the law. She came to the new job with similar questions.

In turn, CIA officials treated McGregor and the other assistants with suspicion. She was the only woman among the top twenty CIA officials and aides who met with Webster every Tuesday morning. Early on, at one of the Tuesday meetings, Bill Baker turned to her and cracked, "You could be the answer to one of those 'What's Wrong with This Picture?' shows."

The assistants did not know the difference between an "agent" and an "officer." Yet in some cases, it seemed to operations officers that the assistants felt they knew more than the officers did about intelligence.

For the assistants, extracting information was like pulling teeth.

"When we first came to the agency, it was clear that we

would have to fight for our jobs," McGregor recalled. "So many of the employees were just unwilling to share information with anyone other than the director, and I'm not sure at the beginning they were always willing to share with the director. They are so used to compartmenting everything. We often got the impression that we had to ask precisely the right question to get the information we were looking for. But they were not going to help find the right one. That sort of attitude makes you uncertain whether you have ever gotten the whole story."

John Bellinger, who replaced McGregor as an assistant at the CIA, sensed alarm bells going off every time he called someone in the Directorate of Operations. Usually, a higher-level official called him back with the answer to his question, rather than the person he had called.

The assistants found they had to fight to get parking near the building and to be allowed to eat in the executive dining room, a prime perquisite. The food was prepared by graduates of the Culinary Institute of America. When members of Congress or heads of foreign intelligence services came to dine, Webster would joke that the CIA ran the dining room. The chefs served salmon fillet with béarnaise sauce and pork chops with caramelized apples and angel-hair pasta for just $4 to $5.50.

To the people around Webster, it seemed they had been tossed into a sea of Casey lovers. By its very nature, the CIA seemed less hospitable than the FBI, which was populated by garrulous agents. McGregor found the CIA types to be more intellectual, more book smart than FBI agents, who tended to be down-to-earth, unaffected people.

"I found the CIA people reticent and not very easy to socialize with," McGregor said. "There were few people who opened up. That's probably due to their training and the nature of the spy business. My guess is we were extremely unpopular, coming in as we did with the director and immediately having access to people and information that took others years to acquire. We bent over backwards to blend in, though, not to interject our personalities."

When Webster first came to the CIA, he visited each of

the agencies in the intelligence community. Often, he took McGregor along. During a briefing at the Defense Intelligence Agency, a military man looked her over, looked at Webster, and said, "Judge, you got a real pretty one here."

Webster stared back at him and said icily, "Yes, and she's smart as a whip."

McGregor could tell Webster was annoyed. McGregor was impressed by the way Webster handled it.

It was McGregor's mission to set up a system so that the paper that flowed to Webster was written in a format with which he was comfortable. It seemed to her that the quality of the internal paperwork was not as polished as that of the FBI. While the CIA did a magnificent job at writing reports and estimates for the policymakers, the agency was not used to writing papers and reports as logically and clearly for internal use. Moreover, everything was presented in jargon and acronyms. The special assistants could not figure them out. As a lawyer, Webster wanted everything presented in a clear, coherent, and cohesive way. McGregor began sending papers back with requests for more information, more clarity, and fewer acronyms.

"At first, I found it a somewhat confusing place," said Bruemmer, who had been Webster's assistant at the FBI and later became his chief counsel at the CIA. "There are a number of things that agency officers, particularly operations officers, view as second nature—living cover, compartmentation, the inscrutability. The notion of not talking to reporters and wondering why reporters quote things that give the Soviets a leg up."

Despite the problems, McGregor was uncomfortable with only one covert action proposal that came before the CARG committee. It seemed to her that the proposed action was a little risky. But it appeared the CIA was adhering strictly to the Constitution and the law.

As John Hotis, Webster's superclerk, would observe, many of the decisions at the CIA required a theologian rather than a lawyer, particularly when it came to the question of assassinations. Assassinations had long been banned, but not everyone was sure why.

"I never understood why bombing innocent people is more morally permissible than the assassination of a single one." said Thomas Polgar, a former CIA station chief, citing such situations as the bombing of Iraq.

But what if a group supported by the CIA decides to assassinate someone? Does that mean the CIA has violated the executive order? If so, the CIA would probably have to withdraw its support from dozens of groups around the world. At Webster's request, the Justice Department issued a legal opinion that said that under existing executive orders, the CIA is not precluded from supporting people who engage in violence that leads to the killing of a foreign leader, so long as the CIA does not support the plans and is not aware of them. In practice, the CIA warns such groups that it will not condone assassination and will cut off support if one occurs.

Still, because of compartmentation. McGregor did not feel she had a handle on what the entire agency was doing. Even though she was cleared for nearly every top-secret program in the agency. getting information out of CIA officials remained extremely difficult. The problem was not so much the higher-level officials, who understood that Webster needed accurate information. Rather, it tended to be the lower-level case officers who gave her a hard time.

The Directorate of Operations is like a wild animal in the woods, a senior lawyer in the agency told John Bellinger.

"You have to stand stock-still and let them sniff you all over before they come to accept you," he confided.

Slowly, the DO came to accept the assistants.

"I found them all doing their best to get along," said Clair George, who was deputy director for operations when Webster took over. "I think they did the best they could."[221]

If operations officers were taciturn, they also did not understand the need for taking disciplinary action against those who had violated the trust the agency placed in them. After Webster disciplined officers for not telling the truth to the inspector general and the Tower Commission about the agency's involvement in the Iran-contra scandal, an aide to Clair George visited McGregor in her office at the end of the director's suite of offices on the seventh floor of the old building.

The aide sat down on McGregor's couch and gave her a stricken look.

"This is the worst day in the history of the DO [Directorate of Operations]," the man said.

McGregor was unsympathetic. It seemed to her that the officer's thinking was myopic. As he saw it, it was an outrage for the DCI to take action against operations officers. It was demoralizing and devastating to the troops of the clandestine service.

"I can't believe that you see this as affecting just the DO," she said. "Look at how some of the actions of the DO have affected the image of the whole agency. The agency is being dragged through the mud by Congress and the media and the administration. It is taking the fall for the whole fiasco."

To McGregor, the encounter illustrated the extent to which some CIA officials felt loyalty foremost to their own directorate rather than to the agency as a whole.

McGregor also could not understand the criticism she sometimes heard in the building that Webster was anxious to please Congress and the public.

"That is exactly the way it should be," she thought. "The agency can be responsive to Congress without sacrificing its mission."

McGregor did not need to fight a lot of battles. She could find the information she needed one way or another. Only rarely did she bother Webster with one of her own problems. He had enough to do, she felt. Often people came to her with problems that they hoped she would pass along to the director. Seldom did she do so. Webster wanted his assistants to be his "eyes and ears," as he put it, but it was not her job to be a conduit for anything she was told. However, if she felt the complaint was legitimate, she passed it along to Webster or to Gates, then deputy director for Central Intelligence. It was a constant balancing act between acting as a facilitator and acting as an independent analyst.

McGregor had a hand in resurrecting moribund plans to build a day care center for children of agency employees. The idea had originated with Harry E. Fitzwater, a deputy director for administration under Casey. However, without some word that it was important to the director, the plans had been pushed aside. McGregor brought it up with Webster at one of his breakfast meetings with his assistants. He said to go ahead. The Langley Children's Center opened in its own 10,000-square-foot building in the fall of 1989, with 104 children enrolled.

One of McGregor's more fascinating projects entailed reading top-secret reports of cases that both the CIA and FBI had been involved in and had screwed up. For example, the CIA had provoked Edward Lee Howard into spying for the Soviets by firing him on the spot. Then the FBI fumbled by letting him slip past bureau agents watching him in Santa Fe, New Mexico. Reading the reports, McGregor saw how each agency justified its own actions.

Webster did not maintain an open-door policy, but certain aides and officials could walk in at will—the deputy director of Central Intelligence, the deputy directors for operations and intelligence, the general counsel, the director of public affairs, Webster's assistants, and Webster's secretary. The deputy director had a door that opened directly into Webster's office. Webster was not used to dealing with a deputy who had as much authority as the deputy does at the CIA. He felt somewhat uncomfortable with the ability of the DDCI to walk in at any moment. But it never bothered him enough to do anything about it.

Webster kept six wooden boxes on his desk and on the credenza behind it. Each was marked with a red plastic label. One was marked "Critical Action" for matters that required his immediate attention. On top of the box rested a black folder that contained personal papers such as party invitations. He received two to three of these a day.

Another box was marked "Signature/Approval" for letters and formal rulings or rule changes that required his approval. Another said "DCI reading" for miscellaneous articles and trip reports.

Webster had a fourth box for material relating to the management and coordination of the intelligence community. A fifth box contained briefing papers and biographical sketches of people he would be seeing at coming meetings. The sixth box contained intelligence estimates and other memos from the Directorate of Intelligence. In all, some two hundred to three hundred of these documents came in from the DI each week.

Despite all the organization, McGregor and the other assistants sometimes left documents requiring immediate action on top of Webster's desk, or on his chair, to make sure he saw them immediately. Each day, at least one hundred and fifty items came in for his attention.

Because Webster realized his attorney assistants would not be as familiar with the work of the CIA as they were with the FBI's, Webster appointed an intelligence analyst as his executive assistant to read all the material and keep track of it. If Webster wanted to know the status of an issue, he could turn to the assistant—Paul Pillar—for the answer.

The assistants had access to anything on Webster's desk and could sit in on almost any meeting. They knew as much about what was going on in the agency as practically anyone. Occasionally, on matters that were extremely sensitive, the DDO walked into Webster's office and told him privately of a development. At other times, the DDO asked the assistants to leave at the end of a meeting so he could talk with Webster alone.

The assistants made their recommendations on blue notepaper. Even though they carefully reviewed each proposal, Webster insisted on going over them. The assistants were always amazed at how Webster zoomed in on questions they had not addressed. He seemed to have a sixth sense for detecting areas that might prove troublesome.

Just as if he were a judge on the case, after reviewing the recommendations of his assistants, Webster spent eight hours reviewing the case of the purloined stamps within the Office of Security.

"This case is important to every employee in the agency because it gives a clearer picture of what is expected of us," Webster said in a statement distributed internally. "Public service is a special trust. It is not easy; it is not without temptations."

In conversation, the assistants found that if they mentioned another document, Webster would invariably ask why he had not seen it. They learned not to refer to other papers unless they had submitted them to him first.

When the assistants made mistakes, Webster could become just as angry at them as at CIA officials. During the Iran-contra hearings, one of the assistants prepared briefing papers that, because of an editing error, contained a sentence that was incorrect. Webster fixed his steely eyes on the man. He told him the work was not acceptable. To the others present, it seemed Webster was embarrassing the man beyond what was necessary.

As a rule, Webster did not socialize with the assistants. They might be invited for his annual Christmas party at his home, or he might chat with them at a social function they had been invited to anyway, but Webster generally kept them separate from his social life. Assistants found that Webster was formal and businesslike at the office but was warm and expansive at home.

One evening at ten, Bellinger decided he would have to call Webster at home with a problem. Bellinger was amazed at how warmly Webster greeted him. Apologetically, he explained why he needed to call at that hour. Webster made it a point to tell Bellinger he had done the right thing in calling.

In May 1988, roughly two years after she had begun working for Webster, McGregor left the CIA to move to Texas, where her husband, Neal Manne, a former chief of staff to Sen. Arlen Specter, had joined a Houston law firm. Despite all the frustrations she had felt, McGregor came away with respect for the CIA and its people. They had an important mission, they worked incredibly long hours, and they were smart and highly competent.[222]

After leaving the agency, McGregor picked up the *New York Times* on her doorstep. It was then that the realization hit her.

"This is it," McGregor thought to herself. "No more President's Daily Brief. No more inside information on pending terrorist threats. There will be no way to judge if an article is true or not. This is all I'm going to know."

24 | X-Rated Chowder

AFTER GEORGE BUSH BECAME PRESIDENT AND ASKED Webster to continue as director of Central Intelligence, rumors began to appear in the press that Webster was about to be replaced. The press reports said Bush only wanted him as an interim DCI until he could get his own man. Sometimes, the reports referred to indifferent work habits. Later in his four-year term, the press reports referred to his inexperience in foreign affairs or to the fact that he was not part of Bush's policy-making team during the Persian Gulf War.

Usually, the reports were attributed to unnamed White House sources. CIA officials, so good at finding out secrets in other countries, never learned the source of the leaks while Webster was in office.

While some White House officials were dissatisfied with Webster, most of the claims that appeared in the press were myths. After coming to Washington, Webster had quickly grasped the fact that Washington work and social life are intertwined. The best way to avoid being crushed by others envious of one's power was to keep a high profile on the social circuit and on the tennis courts.

"I have made more real friends in tennis than I have at cocktail parties," Webster told the *Washington Post*. "It's much nicer to get to know people on a tennis court than it is in a hearing room."[223]

Webster played tennis with the likes of Mike Wallace; Merv Griffin; Zsa Zsa Gabor; Jack Nelson, the Washington Bureau chief of the *Los Angeles Times;* William French Smith when he was attorney general; columnist Carl Rowan; Sen. Lloyd Bentsen; and Bush when he was vice president.

While at the FBI, Webster typically played tennis for an hour two or three times a week and on Saturday mornings, usually at St. Alban's Tennis Club in Washington. It was less time than most people spend going to health clubs before or after work. At the CIA, Webster had to cut back to Saturday and occasionally Wednesday-morning games. Typically, he was at the White House by eight A.M. to brief the president. He left the agency at six-thirty P.M. In the evening, he attended social functions that were often related to the business of the agency. He occasionally came in on Saturdays and kept in touch from home, where he had a safe so he could read classified reports. Peggy Devine, Webster's executive secretary, usually came in to work when Webster did. Each year, she put in for four hundred hours of overtime—the equivalent of more than two extra months of work.

In fact, Webster's hours were not that different from Casey's.

"Bill [Casey] was there by seven forty-five A.M., and he would leave between six and seven-thirty P.M., then go off to one or two things in the evening, and read in bed for one or two hours," said Herbert Meyer, his former special assistant. "He was there on Saturday until lunch. Then he would play golf."[224]

Supreme Court justice John Paul Stevens III played tennis three to four times a week, and no one complained. Likewise, independent counsel Lawrence E. Walsh, the special prosecutor, rarely came into the office before ten A.M. Yet nothing appeared in the press about his hours.

In part, the inconsistent treatment arose from the inherently imperfect way the press operates. In most cases, the media rely on tips and leaks for stories. If no one is motivated to create an issue, a story may never appear. On the other hand, a critical story may appear simply because a reporter happened to meet at a cocktail party someone who felt that night like making a disparaging remark about his boss.

In Webster's case, the complaints that he was an absentee director flowed from Webster's style, which was to weigh decisions carefully and if possible, to obtain consensus within the CIA. Sometimes, it took him weeks or months to sign off on a proposal, leading impatient subordinates to question whether he was asleep at the switch, particularly in his first years at the CIA.

"He is not the sort of person to say, 'I've been watching you from afar, and I have forty-seven things for you to do,' " Bruemmer said. "Casey did that. Webster's approach was to wait and make sure he understood the organization first.

"He is trying to find a way to find a solution that he can then both support and defend in a way that makes everyone say, 'I understand, although I may not agree.' He does his decision making based on the principles. It's a very judicial style. Gather information. Keep an open mind. Think about it. Identify a framework for making a decision. Then decide," Bruemmer said.[225]

After his wife died in 1984, Webster went through a period of mourning that affected his work. But during most of his tenure, most of those who worked with him saw a committed, involved manager—not a workaholic, but someone who devoted much more than the normal forty hours a week to the job.

The week of October 28, 1990—chosen at random—was typical of Webster's schedule at the CIA—a combination of weekly scheduled meetings, special briefings, ceremonies, public relations events, and social events. On Monday, October 29, Webster arrived at the CIA at seven forty-five A.M. and received a briefing on the latest developments in Iraq.

At eight-ten A.M., he had breakfast with former DCI Stans-field Turner. At nine-fifteen A.M., he talked with college deans who were visiting the agency as part of the CIA's efforts to expand its college recruiting program. At ten A.M., Webster had his weekly meeting with Richard F. Stolz, the deputy director for operations, and his fifty-five-year-old deputy, Thomas A. Twetten, who later took Stolz's place.

At eleven-twenty A.M., Webster met with the CIA's chief of station in Bangkok and his division chief to receive an update on events in the area. Appointments of chief of station or COS are approved by the director. Whenever a chief of station is appointed or leaves his or her post, Webster would meet with him.

At twelve-ten P.M., Webster met with Richard Kerr, the deputy director for Central Intelligence. At twelve-thirty, he had lunch with the college deans and with Joseph R. DeTrani, the CIA's director of public affairs. At three P.M., Webster met with Theodore Price, then chief of the Counterintelli-gence Center.

After reading briefing papers, Webster addressed visiting cartography professors at five-thirty P.M. At five after six, he met again with Kerr, then left for a reception given by Nuzhet Kandemir, the Turkish ambassador, to celebrate Turkish Na-tional Day. Like most of the events Webster attended at night, this had a dual purpose. Turkey was a strong supporter of the U.S. effort to remove Iraq from Kuwait, and both the CIA and the military had extensive dealings with the Turkish government. In the ensuing weeks, Webster would visit Tur-key as well, flying in an Air Force C-141 Starlifter cargo plane outfitted with special communications for his use.

The morning after the reception, Webster met with Bush at eight A.M. at the White House to give him his daily brief. At eight-forty A.M., he arrived at the CIA and had what is known as the executive breakfast. This is a staff meeting held every Tuesday with the deputy directors of the agency, their assistants, the heads of each office, and Webster's assistants —roughly twenty people in all. Because of the need for compartmentation, nothing substantive was usually discussed.

Instead, broader issues—such as the penetrations of the American embassy in Moscow—might be on the agenda.

On Wednesday, October 31, Webster arrived at the White House at eight-fifteen A.M., where he briefed National Security Adviser Brent Scowcroft and his then deputy, Robert Gates. At eight-fifty A.M., Webster briefed the president and arrived at the CIA at ten, when he met with representatives of Middle Eastern intelligence services.

That evening, Webster attended a dinner at the Georgetown home of Katharine Graham, chairwoman of the Washington Post Co., to honor Pehr Gyllenhammar, who was retiring as chief executive officer of A.B. Volvo Gothenburg of Sweden.

The next day at one P.M., Webster had his usual weekly luncheon meeting with Secretary of State James A. Baker III and his deputy, Lawrence Eagleburger. At four P.M., Webster met with the intelligence community staff, a meeting he had every Thursday afternoon. This was followed by a meeting with Scowcroft and Gates.

On Friday, November 2, Webster had his usual weekly breakfast at seven-fifty A.M. with Secretary of Defense Richard B. Cheney and his deputies. At eleven-twenty A.M., Webster received a briefing on his forthcoming trip to Hungary and other East European countries.

The following Monday, November 5, Webster arrived at the CIA at seven-fifty A.M. At nine A.M., he had his regular Monday-morning meeting with his special assistants. By then, Webster had decided to operate a leaner office. His own people were in charge, and he trusted the agency more. When John Hotis retired, Webster chose not to replace him. That left only his newest assistant, John B. Bellinger.

Having started as a special assistant in 1988, Bellinger was the first one to work solely at the CIA. Because it took so long to master the intricacies of the CIA, Webster kept him three years rather than the usual two.

Like the other assistants, Bellinger brought with him impressive credentials. He had graduated cum laude from Princeton University and become a Woodrow Wilson fellow at the University of Virginia. He had then graduated cum laude from Harvard Law School, where he was an editor of *Harvard International Law Journal*.

Besides attending meetings with the director, Bellinger worked on such items as covert action proposals, significant intelligence operations, defectors, inspector general reports and recommendations, significant legal decisions, security disapprovals, and congressional testimony and letters. Each year, some twenty people, including contractors, were fired as possible security risks in the intelligence community and appealed their dismissals to the DCI. In addition, one or two CIA employees were dismissed for security reasons each year. Bellinger reviewed these cases before Webster signed off on them.

Webster's schedule was grueling, and he led an active social life as well. After the death of his first wife in 1984, Webster began dating Sally Tompkins, a National Park Service architectural historian. Tompkins had been to several FBI receptions, and Webster had noticed her. She was a family friend of Roger Young, who was then in charge of public and congressional affairs for the FBI.[226] Young suggested her to Webster as a tennis partner. The two dated until Tompkins died of cancer at the age of fifty-five on November 27, 1989.[227]

Lynda Jo Clugston played tennis but dressed more conservatively than some of Webster's other dates. Webster first met her in December 1984, at a function for singles at the National Symphony Orchestra.[228]

Clugston is blond and extremely attractive, with light blue eyes and a clear complexion. The daughter of a funeral home director, she had applied to the CIA but had been rejected because of a minor health problem. She entered the hotel sales business—"I wanted to go into undercover work, and that's how I got into hotels," she would say—and became director of sales at the Willard Hotel in Washington. Later, she was director of sales and marketing at the Watergate Hotel.

A few weeks after they met, Webster called Clugston at her office at the Willard Hotel to ask her out.

"They thought I was in some terrible trouble because the FBI was calling," Clugston said. "I was in the bathroom and my secretary . . . was banging on the door saying, 'The FBI is calling. What have you done?' "

In late 1986, Webster invited her to a dinner given by Count Wilhelm Wachtmeister, the Swedish ambassador in Washington, and his wife, Ulla. After that, they began seeing each other off and on.

Dating the DCI was difficult. When Clugston met Webster occasionally during out-of-town trips, she found the security detail consisted of three cars. Every time she entered his hotel room—even for something as innocent as meeting him for breakfast—alarms went off.

"There was a guy sitting there and every time you went in and out it would beep, and people would come running," she said.

When they were in Boston, a cousin of Clugston's dropped off some New England clam chowder at the doorstep of the house she was staying in. As she was about to drive off, CIA security guards pulled their car up behind her and questioned her about the package she had left. Before they gave it to Webster, the security guards X-rayed it.

At times, the security came in handy. Babs, Webster's basset hound, had a habit of running out the door of Webster's Bethesda home whenever the door was opened. The CIA men caught Babs and brought him back inside. The fact that the CIA usually drove Webster was a blessing as well. When Webster drove his own BMW, it often wound up in a body shop for a week.

By 1990, Clugston had moved to Boston to take a job with the Four Seasons Hotel. But the relationship continued as Webster visited Clugston in Boston. Webster asked her to come back to Washington, and they both realized that marriage was likely. Webster told his children—William, Drusilla, and Katherine. On October 20, 1990, they were married in the Eisenhower Chapel of the National Presbyterian Center.

Roberta Peters, a friend of the bride's, sang at the wedding. At the reception afterward in the Riverview Room of the Watergate Hotel overlooking the Potomac River, she sang "Always," a cappella.

The seventy guests were limited to those the couple considered to be close friends or family, including FBI director William S. Sessions and the two senators from Missouri, John C. Danforth and Christopher Bond. The only work-related guests were Richard Stolz, then deputy director for operations; Richard Kerr, the deputy director of Central Intelligence; William Baker, who had been director of public affairs; Roger Young, the former FBI public affairs director; Robert Gates, then in the White House; and Russell Bruemmer, the former Webster special assistant and CIA general counsel.

Clugston, never married before, was thirty-four; Webster was sixty-six. Even after remarrying, Webster kept a photo of his late wife, Drusilla, in his office at the CIA.

Ten days after the wedding, President Bush and his wife, Barbara, attended a dinner in honor of Webster's marriage to Clugston. It was given in Georgetown by Betty Beale, a former gossip columnist, and her husband, George Graeber.

The other guests at the dinner were Supreme Court justice Sandra Day O'Connor and her husband, John; Antony Acland, the British ambassador, and his wife, Jennifer; James W. Symington, a former Missouri congressman who was U.S. chief of protocol, and his wife, Sylvia; and William Cafritz, a Washington real estate developer, and his wife, Buffy.

Beale had urged Webster to marry Lynda.

"What are you waiting for? You're going to lose her," she would say.[229]

Despite the CIA's success during the Gulf War and the support Webster received from Bush, press reports continued that Bush wanted the DCI out. Usually, the reports said the president wanted to replace Webster with James R. Lilley, who was about to leave his post as ambassador to the People's Republic of China.

Unlike Casey, Webster was not a foreign policy junkie. Nor did he want to be part of the policy-making team. He had taken the job on the specific condition that he would not have cabinet status. When he was with Bush, the two spoke in sentence fragments, as if in code, leading some to wonder if Webster could speak English. Yet Webster was a master at public speaking, and his assistants never failed to admire his crisp writing.

While foreign affairs did not come easily to him, Webster worked hard at mastering its complexities. He asked the right questions and digested all the facts. But he was a lawyer, not a foreign affairs expert. There was no way he could ever approach the facility of a Robert Gates in analyzing and commenting on world affairs.

The director of Central Intelligence did not have to be an expert in each of the disciplines under his command. No one could have the background in intelligence, science, political science, and the dozens of other specialties that the CIA makes use of. Webster's style was to manage by eliciting the opinions of the experts and making sure those opinions got to the right people. But to many of those around Bush, that was not good enough. People such as Brent Scowcroft, the president's assistant for national security affairs, wanted a foreign affairs guru like himself in the job.

Eventually, since Webster could not remain in office forever, the stories of his departure would have to prove correct, and so they did—four years after he became DCI. Webster had always wanted to return to the practice of law. At the age of sixty-seven, time was running out to get a lucrative offer from a law firm. With the Gulf War over and increasing pressure from the oversight committees to alter the structure of the intelligence community, Webster felt it would be a good time to leave. Moreover, having just remarried, he wanted time for fun.

"He hasn't taken a two-week vacation in twenty years," Lynda Webster said, more than four months before Webster announced that he was retiring. "My guess is Bill will at some point say, 'Enough.' You get bored with a job. He's been doing it four years. I'd get bored after four years. He wants to be able to take time off and play. We haven't been able to have a honeymoon."[230]

"I think the point will come where he says, 'I want to take a weekend off and go somewhere and not have nine [security] men trundling around,' " she said. "He's not twenty-two. You calculate the number of years he has to play. He has earned it."

If anything, according to those close to him, the repeated reports that he would leave the agency had only strengthened his determination to stay.

On May 8, 1991, Bush called a press conference to announce that Webster had decided to retire. Bush said the decision was Webster's, and he said Webster had done a "superb job," providing impartial intelligence rather than trying to shape policy. Calling U.S. intelligence during the Gulf War "outstanding," the president said the intelligence community had performed "fantastically."

"I hate to see him go," the president said.[231]

"We had in the person of Judge Webster a former federal judge who was a strong and deep believer in the rule of law who, as director, complied not only with the letter of the law but with the spirit of the law as well," said Rep. Anthony C. Beilenson, a Los Angeles Democrat who formerly was chairman of the House Permanent Select Committee on Intelligence. "After our experience with Director Casey, he was just what the doctor ordered."

"Under Webster, I would say the biggest change was bringing the clandestine service, along with the rest of the agency, toward recognizing the reality of congressional oversight and [instilling] a positive attitude toward working with the congressional side, in terms of being forthcoming in answers and being cooperative," Robert Gates said. "I think the rest of the agency was already there by 1987 [when Webster took over].

"Casey's attitude I think communicated itself to the clandestine service more. Virtually every dispute was in the clandestine service. I think Bill Webster has made the clandestine service catch up. He has also been forward-looking by responding to new threats with the counterintelligence center, the counternarcotics center, and some capabilities that reflect better ways of dealing with old issues," Gates said.[232]

In an outdoor ceremony on July 1, Kerr, his deputy, presented Webster with the Distinguished Intelligence Medal. Motioning to several of Webster's former assistants in the audience, Kerr said, "We don't take very well to outsiders, but Judge Webster chose his assistants judiciously."

By then, employees had grown to like Webster; the rumors that he was not on top of things had vanished.

President Bush nominated Robert Gates, the former deputy director of the agency under William Casey, to succeed Webster, touching off a major debate about Gates's knowledge—or lack thereof—about the Iran-contra affair. Webster had planned to leave by the end of July, but as the debate about Gates's qualifications intensified, Bush asked him to stay on until the end of August, giving the lie to press reports that Webster had been pushed out.

On July 25, 1991, Bush invited Webster, his family, and a small coterie of intelligence community officials to a cocktail party at the White House. Referring to Webster as a "true patriot" who performed in an "outstanding" manner during the Gulf War, Bush presented him with the National Security Medal and the Presidential Medal of Freedom, the highest civil award given by the U.S. government. Bush had previously awarded the medal to Gen. Colin Powell, Gen. Norman Schwarzkopf, Secretary of State James Baker, and Defense Secretary Richard Cheney in appreciation for their efforts during the Persian Gulf War.[233]

By September 1991, Webster had become a partner with Milbank, Tweed, Hadley & McCloy in Washington. Webster had served four years, longer than all but three of the DCIs —Allen Dulles, Richard Helms, and William Casey. During that time, he had restored to the CIA credibility, its most important asset.

It is always difficult to predict how much of a CIA director's contribution will remain with the agency. Certainly the counternarcotics and counterintelligence centers will remain, along with the more formal and stringent procedures for approving covert action proposals. Because it was so overdue, Webster's change in policy toward dealing with the press can be expected to continue as well.

25 | *Selling the Agency*

FROM THE CIA'S EARLIEST DAYS, THE AGENCY HAD A PRESS spokesman whose job was to say "no comment" to virtually every question. The job was handled by an assistant to the director, who usually had other duties as well, such as coordinating training or arranging for the director's congressional testimony or speeches.

"It was pretty much a 'no comment' office," Walter N. Elder, executive assistant to Allen Dulles, John McCone, and Adm. William Raborn, said. "People badgered the agency, and most of the time, the assistant had nothing to say."[234]

Walter Bedell Smith appointed the first person to the job in May 1951. He was Col. Chester B. Hansen, a former public relations aide to Gen. Omar Bradley. He was followed in October 1952 by Col. Stanley Grogan, an Army public affairs specialist. Then came Joseph A. Goodwin, a former operations officer and Associated Press editor; Angus Thuermer, a former intelligence officer and AP correspondent; and Andrew T. Falkiewicz, a career U.S. Information Agency officer.[235]

If these assistants had anything to say to the press, it was very specific, very circumscribed, and only on orders of the DCI. For example, when Francis Gary Powers was scheduled to testify before congressional committees about the U-2 incident, then CIA director John McCone directed Grogan to call a dozen members of the press—from Ben Bradlee of *Newsweek* to John Scali of ABC. Contrary to press reports, Grogan told them, McCone would not be appearing before congressional committees that week to testify on the incident himself.

"He has notified the committees that are concerned," Grogan told the press, "and they, with him, will set dates . . . when he will appear before Congress."[236]

In addition to conveying such messages, CIA directors such as John McCone and Richard Helms talked with particular reporters or columnists who tended to be favorably disposed to the agency.

"Arthur Krock and Scotty Reston [the *New York Times* columnists] were friends of McCone," Elder said. "He talked with them on a background basis."

But mostly, reporters who called the CIA for comment on allegations about the agency encountered silence on the other end of the line.

"The necessity of procuring good intelligence is apparent," George Washington said in a letter to one of his officers during the American Revolution, "and need not be further urged. All that remains for me to add is that you keep the whole matter as secret as possible."[237]

With that in mind, the CIA for most of its existence has treated the American press as an adversary—a target that was to be manipulated at times but never confided in or trusted. If the CIA thought it could use the press to its advantage, it did.

Over the years, the agency put dozens of American journalists or foreign journalists working for American media on its payroll, tasking them to obtain secrets. The Church Committee and William Colby put an end to the practice, recog-

nizing that to use the press for clandestine purposes impaired
its credibility and hampered its effectiveness. When he became director, George Bush further tightened the restrictions.
But as the Church Committee conducted its hearings and the
media played up the abuses engaged in over the years by the
CIA, the agency's disdain for the press intensified.[238]

The CIA had an Alice in Wonderland approach: If the
agency were to deny a charge, the reasoning went, then the
CIA's decision not to comment on other charges would be
interpreted as meaning those charges were true. If other intelligence services knew that the CIA talked to the press, they
would never deal with the agency. Sources and methods must
be protected, the CIA said, refusing to acknowledge that there
were shadings of secrets, that the fact that the CIA has a
headquarters building in Langley could be considered a
method, and that everything about the CIA is classified. Yet
it was unrealistic and self-defeating for the agency to withdraw
from American society.

America was not like other countries, where secrecy was
often considered a virtue. America had been founded by men
who considered the press to be an essential partner to government. They had won their freedom from the British Crown
in part because of the ability of an unfettered press to publish
tracts questioning established authority. The experiment had
worked well. A free press stimulated the country's robust
economy and competitive spirit. In the end, the CIA, like
any other American institution, needed the support of the
American people, who formed their views in part from what
they read in the press.

Other more established government agencies such as the
FBI were more sophisticated at dealing with the press. They
knew how to tell their stories, how to head off bad raps, and
how to balance criticism without giving away all their secrets
or appearing to sources to be untrustworthy. At any given
moment, the FBI is pursuing thousands of criminal investigations, each one of which must be kept secret. The FBI, like
the CIA, could pay someone to say "no comment" each time
a question came in about its work. But the FBI realized there
were ways to help the press around these sensitive areas, to

deal with allegations without giving away everything the FBI does—ways the CIA had yet to understand.

The CIA could be so good at influencing other governments, yet it seemed naive, almost obtuse, in dealing with the American press. It was one of the CIA's greatest failings. Often, it was simply a disinclination to focus on the problem.

"I don't know if the CIA should explain itself better. I suppose it could, but I have to admit, I don't know how it would go about that," said Richard M. Bissell, Jr., deputy director for operations from 1958 to 1962.[239]

"I don't think we could do a better PR job. Not in a democratic society," said John McMahon, deputy director of Central Intelligence under William Casey. "You have to live with the fact that when it screws up, it's going to get a lot of publicity, and when it does good, you're not going to see it. That's the life of an intelligence officer. If the people [in the agency] can't deal with that, they ought to be Fuller brush salesmen. That's the nature of the work."[240]

William Colby understood the need to let the American public know what the CIA does. "A public informed of the CIA's accomplishments and capabilities will support it," he wrote in his book *Honorable Men*.[241] Yet even Colby, who helped bring the agency into the modern world, considered the duties of his press assistant primarily to be to keep the CIA informed about what was being said about the agency.

"Your comment is usually 'no comment,' " Colby told his press assistant.[242]

That bunker mentality began to change when Stansfield Turner became DCI on March 9, 1977. Two months later, Turner appointed Herbert E. Hetu, a former career Navy public affairs officer, to open the CIA's first office of public affairs. The idea was that the office would function more or less like the public affairs offices of other government agencies. Like the assistants who previously dealt with the press, the office also clipped articles so the CIA knew what the press was saying about the agency.

Both Turner and Hetu believed that to the extent practical, an agency funded with tax dollars ought to let the public know what it is doing. They got a boost from Executive Order 12036, signed by President Carter on January 24, 1978, which authorized the director of Central Intelligence to "act, in appropriate consultation with the departments and agencies, as the intelligence community's principal spokesperson to Congress, the news media, and the public."

The idea was heresy at the CIA, particularly in the Directorate of Operations, which looked upon Hetu as something approaching a traitor.

"I am not here to give away secrets," Hetu told operations officers in meetings. "I am trying to be the lightning rod to make your jobs easier."[243] But Hetu came away feeling he was hated by the clandestine service.

At one staff meeting, an officer said, "You are hurting us when potential agents read we have a PR office. They could get killed."

Hetu wondered if they were right. During his tenure at the CIA, Hetu had come to be impressed by CIA employees. In his twenty-five years in the government, he had never encountered such honest, smart people. Hetu did not know anything about intelligence. He simply had a gut feeling that the CIA could be doing a better job in the press area. In the end, Hetu did not decide on his own what would be released. He attended staff meetings with the DCI so he was fully informed on major issues. Then Turner and his deputies decided what to release.

Almost immediately after taking the job, Hetu was faced with a controversy over the publication of *Decent Interval* by Frank Snepp. A former CIA officer, Snepp had written about his experiences in Vietnam without clearing the manuscript with the CIA, as required by his preemployment agreement. The contracts state that anything CIA employees write must be cleared to make sure the material does not contain classified information. In the past, the clearance process had been handled haphazardly by the Office of Security and the general counsel. Former employees were discouraged from writing books because they feared that the long process would gut their work.

Indeed, over the years, the CIA had been engaged in the business of trying to suppress books rather than encouraging them. In 1964, for example, John A. Bross, then the CIA's comptroller, got the bound galley proofs of David Wise and Thomas B. Ross's book *The Invisible Government.* The book was an exposé of the CIA, FBI, and other agencies that had engaged in illegal activities. Bross obtained the galleys through a friend of a family member who was then working for Random House.[244] With the authorization of John McCone, then DCI, the CIA asked Bennett Cerf, president of Random House, if the agency could buy up the first printing.

"Cerf responded that he would be delighted to sell the first printing to the CIA, but then immediately added that he would then order another printing for the public, and another, and another," according to Wise's subsequent book, *The American Police State.*[245] The agency dropped the idea.

While the CIA would have liked to have brought legal action against the authors, they were journalists, not former employees. The CIA has gone to court only to enforce contracts signed by CIA employees when they enter and leave employment.

The first test of this restriction came in 1974, when Knopf published *The CIA and the Cult of Intelligence* by Victor Marchetti and John D. Marks. Marchetti had been executive assistant to the deputy director of Central Intelligence. As a CIA employee, Marchetti had signed the preemployment contract, giving the CIA a legal basis for moving against him. Acting on behalf of the CIA, the Justice Department first sued Marchetti to prevent him from publishing a magazine article about the agency. Then Marchetti and his publisher sued the CIA over the deletions the CIA insisted upon in the book. The CIA won in both cases, and the Supreme Court declined to hear the appeals.[246]

Eventually, Knopf published the book with 168 blank spaces to show where the CIA had required deletions. Over the years, the CIA approved new material for publication, filling in some of the blanks. The publisher included it in subsequent editions in different typefaces. By highlighting the secret nature of the material, the publisher made the book appear even more desirable.

William Colby would later admit he should have taken the advice of John S. Warner, then the CIA's deputy general counsel, who said the CIA should demand deletion only of classified material that had not appeared publicly. As a negotiating ploy, Colby had ordered Warner to demand deletion of all the classified material. Later, Colby said, the CIA could back down on many of the items that had already appeared publicly. The strategy backfired, and the book has continued to sell well ever since.[247]

Like Marchetti, Snepp had not cleared his book with the agency. Because Snepp had violated his employment agreement, the agency took him to court and won. Snepp had to turn over all his royalties to the government.[248]

On the other hand, when Philip Agee resigned from the CIA and wrote his 1975 book, *Inside the Company: CIA Diary,* there was nothing the CIA could do because the book was published overseas.

With the Snepp experience fresh in his mind, Hetu decided the CIA needed a more systematic approach to clearing books. It was obvious employees such as Snepp would rather risk legal action by bypassing the clearance process than submit their manuscripts to possibly arbitrary censorship. Indeed, after looking over the Snepp book, the CIA decided only a few sentences would have been deleted if it had been submitted for review prior to publication.

Hetu set up a Publications Review Board within the Office of Public Affairs to review books and other manuscripts. With Hetu as its chairman, the board included a lawyer from the office of general counsel. The review board drew up strict standards. To show that material should be deleted, the board had to demonstrate that the item was classified. Even then, if the material had already appeared publicly, the board sometimes let it pass. But when William Casey became CIA director, the board stuck it to Stansfield Turner when he submitted his book for review. It demanded more than one hundred deletions in *Secrecy and Democracy: The CIA in Transition.*[249]

Another area that needed improving was the agency's relations with the academic world. Like any large technologically oriented company, the CIA needed a wide range of contacts with universities, both to recruit new employees and to sponsor research and obtain fresh insights. Recognizing that, William J. Donovan had persuaded President Roosevelt of the need for a coordinated intelligence service that would "draw on the universities for experts with long foreign experience and specialized knowledge of the history, languages, and general conditions of various countries."[250]

Over the years, the CIA had sponsored classified and unclassified research, conferences, and special projects on everything from new security devices, technology transfer, terrorism, and the illicit arms market to the future of Japan, human rights, population trends, and changing commodity markets.

But any CIA contact with the academic world tends to be regarded with suspicion by some students and faculty members. Because of that reflex response, faculty members and universities involved in CIA projects often want to keep their involvement secret. That only exacerbates the problem. By CIA policy, a senior officer of a university must give his approval before a CIA contract can be awarded. When he was DCI, George Bush told the American Association of University Professors that the only ties the CIA sought with campuses were those made with the "voluntary and witting cooperation of individuals who can help the foreign policy processes of the United States."[251]

Because of fear of protests, the university officer who knows of a CIA relationship—in many cases the president of the university—keeps the matter to himself. When it comes out, it appears that the CIA—rather than the university—was trying to hide something. For example, in June 1991, a major controversy erupted over the fact that M. Richard Rose, the president of the Rochester Institute of Technology, had taken a sabbatical to work for the CIA without informing the university where he would be working. The fact that the university had received contracts amounting to $5 million over five years then became an issue.

Rose later admitted that he had made a mistake by failing to inform the trustees that he would be working at the CIA.

He also admitted he should have let others at the university know of the CIA contracts.[252]

In the end, there was nothing wrong with the relationship —only that Rose had chosen to keep it secret.

Still another kind of controversy erupted in the fall of 1990 at the University of Connecticut, where a CIA officer from the Foreign Resources Branch had asked for information on foreign students enrolled there.[253] Under Executive Order 12333, which governs the agency's domestic activities, this was perfectly permissible. So long as the target is foreign, the CIA can obtain information on students and attempt to recruit them for later spying once they return to their countries. But by asking for lists of foreign students, the FR officer had used an unnecessarily intrusive and clumsy approach. It would have been far better for him to ask contacts he had developed for names of possible candidates for recruitment.

To try to demonstrate that the CIA is not a bogeyman, Turner and Hetu began inviting presidents of universities to the CIA for all-day programs designed to acquaint them with the agency and what it does. Later, under Casey, the CIA started an officer-in-residence program, paying CIA officers —eleven at last count—to teach at universities for two-year stints. In that way, the CIA hoped to show students that agency officers are human beings. Finally, under Turner and Hetu, the agency began selling maps and analytical studies to the public.[254]

Besides coordinating academic exchanges, clearing manuscripts, and responding to press inquiries, Hetu arranged during his four-year tenure for hundreds of background briefings for reporters interested in particular issues being pursued by the agency's analysts. For example, a newsmagazine interested in the Soviet economy might obtain a briefing from CIA analysts working on the issue. It was never startling stuff, but reporters found the briefings helped to fill in gaps. By enhancing the CIA's credibility and building bridges to reporters, the practice helped the agency as well.

By executive order, the CIA may not disseminate propaganda, whether true or false, in the U.S. If there is any possibility that information disseminated abroad might unintentionally wind up influencing the U.S., the activity must be approved by the DCI. But in the case of briefings to reporters, the source—the CIA—is known and openly acknowledged to reporters. The practice of giving briefings therefore does not violate any U.S. government policies.

When Casey became DCI, he abruptly ordered Hetu to stop the briefings. Hetu wrote him a one-page memo explaining that the practice helped the CIA's credibility with the media.

"We have never been burned," Hetu wrote.[255]

The next morning, Casey asked Hetu, "Have you stopped the briefings?"

"I wrote you a memo on it," Hetu replied.

"I didn't ask you to debate it," Casey said. "I asked you to stop it. Now I'm ordering you to stop it. Stop it today. If you have any scheduled today, cancel them."

Later that day, Casey called Hetu.

"You can let them come in if they will do some work for us overseas and report to us when they get back," Casey said.[256]

Hetu realized Casey was asking him to break the CIA's policies against using the press in operations, policies that went back even before the Church Committee hearings.

"It's against our policies. We're not allowed to task them," Hetu said. "We would get nailed."

Soon, Casey replaced Hetu with George V. Lauder, a former CIA operations officer. Ironically, Lauder reinstituted the briefings, but on a much more limited basis. With the stated objective of lowering the agency's profile, Casey on June 4, 1981, reorganized the office of public affairs as a branch within a larger office. As in the agency's relations with Congress, the CIA's relations with the press quickly began to deteriorate.

Stephen Engelberg had just begun covering the intelligence beat for the *New York Times* when he wrote a story saying Vitaly S. Yurchenko, the high-ranking KGB officer who had defected to the U.S. in August 1985, had "identified several employees of the Central Intelligence Agency as Soviet agents." According to the September 27, 1985, story, it was not clear "whether those reportedly involved were contract employees or full-fledged CIA officers."

The night before the story ran, Engelberg called Lauder at home and read it to him over the phone. In journalism, one cannot be more fair than that. By reading the story to him, Engelberg had provided the agency with every opportunity to deny the story, or to offer reasons why it should not run.

Based on Lauder's response, the story that ran the next day said, "George Lauder, a CIA spokesman, said he would have no comment on any defections or on suggestions that double agents had been discovered."[257]

Nevertheless, later that day, the CIA issued a statement denying the *Times'* story.

"An agency spokeswoman, without identifying the defector, said only that a story in Friday's edition of the *New York Times* on CIA turncoats 'is untrue,' " United Press International reported.[258]

Engelberg felt he had been stabbed in the back. He had gone to the trouble of reading the story to Lauder before it ran, laying all his cards on the table. If Lauder had issued a denial then, the denial would have appeared in the story. If Lauder had questioned a particular fact, Engelberg would have had an opportunity to go back to his sources and question them further.

As it was, the agency had lied. Yurchenko had identified Edward Lee Howard, a former CIA officer, as an agent for the KGB. Technically, the CIA could argue that Howard was a single employee and was no longer working for the agency. The *Times,* on the other hand, had referred to "CIA employees," implying that there was more than one and that they were still employed by the CIA. But that was nit-picking and possibly not correct either. In addition to Howard, Yurchenko provided clues that are still being pursued about others who worked for the KGB. When Engelberg's story appeared, they may still have been detailed to the CIA or may still have been working for the agency as contract employees.

Thus the thrust of Engelberg's story was correct. The CIA had publicly called into question the accuracy of his work after he had taken unusual pains to make sure it was accurate.

Understandably, Engelberg was furious. He called Lauder and ripped into him.

"This is dirty pool," he told him. "You had your shot last night, you waited until the story appeared, now you issue your statement. You're calling me a liar in public, and I resent it."[259]

"My absolute bottom line was we weren't going to tell anybody any lies," Lauder would later say. "To the best of my knowledge, we never did." But he said he has no recollection of the details of the story.[260]

After that experience, Engelberg operated differently. He wrote a subsequent story saying that Yurchenko had identified a former National Security Agency employee as working for the Soviets. At the time, the FBI was keeping the former employee, Ronald W. Pelton, under constant surveillance while the bureau tried to develop more information on him. The *Times* story could have warned Pelton that he was under suspicion, prompting him to try to hide his tracks or try to flee. So far as anyone at the FBI knows, Pelton did not learn about the story. But this time Engelberg was not going to give the CIA the opportunity to pass on his story. He simply ran it without calling Lauder for comment. If the CIA had approached Engelberg to hold off on the story, the reporter would most likely have told the agency to bug off.

"At that point, I was so angry at George Lauder and the CIA that it would have taken a lot for me to hold anything back," Engelberg would later say. "I was not going to call George Lauder and say, 'George, this is what I got,' " Engelberg said. "He had lost that right."[261]

When William Webster became director of Central Intelligence, those kinds of encounters became a thing of the past. Besides the president, Webster saw the press and Congress as his two most important constituencies. As Webster would often state, it was all part of keeping the agency accountable and remembering that it was there to serve the American people. He had learned a few things about handling the press from the FBI, which was highly sophisticated at feeding reporters just enough to keep them happy without blowing cases.

Webster wanted a change in the way the CIA dealt with the press, and he gave considerable thought to whom he should appoint as his director of public affairs.

"The PR person is one of the most important choices you make over time, because you can't see the press as much as you'd like to," Webster explained later in his office at the CIA. "They [the press] figure that if the PR person is trustworthy and helpful and honest, that must be the kind of person I [as director] want. If they are not, they figure I [the director] put them there.[262]

"I didn't think I could find anyone in this organization, given their training, who could be open with the press," Webster said. For that reason, he chose as his first director of public affairs William M. Baker, who was assistant FBI director for public and congressional affairs when Webster was at the bureau.

Baker, then forty-seven, had movie star good looks, with a tanned, youthful-looking face and innocent-looking blue eyes. He had remarkable antennae that could sense exactly what people wanted before they expressed it, and he had a direct approach that made people want to cooperate with him.

Baker's appointment generated the usual false reports about Webster's motives in choosing him. According to these rumors, the two were close friends who played tennis together. In fact, Baker had first come to Webster's attention when Baker was in charge of a unit in the FBI's personnel office that deals with transfers.

Baker had denied a request by a female agent for a transfer from one FBI office to another. Her husband had been transferred by his work, and she wanted to move with him to the new location. Both offices were within commuting distance, so the agent would not have been greatly inconvenienced in either case. Webster asked Baker to reconsider, saying it was a hardship case. Baker held his ground, and Webster called him to his office.[263]

Baker outlined his reasons: he said twenty-seven other agents had previously asked to transfer to the same office, and it would not be fair to them to put the female agent ahead of them.

"We have to have fairness in our transfer policy," Baker said. "If a female is involved because of her husband's occupation, certainly we should consider that. But there are agents with more seniority who wanted the same office, and in my opinion, some have a tougher hardship."

Webster agreed with Baker and denied the transfer. If a subordinate could defend a position with a good factual argument, Webster would go with it.

Later, Baker was in charge of the FBI's Portland, Oregon, field office in 1983 when a Northwest Airlines jet was skyjacked. Webster was impressed by Baker's cool demeanor and forthright answers when he was interviewed about the crime on the evening news.

Based on several recommendations, Webster appointed Baker to take charge of the FBI's public relations in 1984. In that job, Baker got to travel with Webster when he gave speeches, and he became one of Webster's most trusted advisers.

One of Baker's friends said he must have gotten the job because he played tennis and had gone to a good college— the University of Virginia. The truth was the opposite. Not only had Baker never played tennis with Webster, Baker made sure he never did. Webster had heard that Baker played, and before one of their out-of-town trips, he asked him to bring along his tennis racket. Baker said he no longer played.

Baker did not want to be known as a crony who had gotten his job because of friendship. He would help find other tennis partners for Webster during their trips. But when Webster was playing tennis, Baker took advantage of the time off to relax and jog.

Baker also avoided visiting Webster's farm near St. Louis. One of Webster's St. Louis friends had told him the farm was "as rough as a cob," and Baker vowed he would never go there. People who did not know the true reason thought he never visited the farm because he was afraid of horses. They were not far from the truth, since he detested horses.

When Webster asked Baker to take charge of public affairs at the CIA, Webster asked Baker if he wanted to be detailed from the FBI. After they discussed it, they agreed that would send the wrong message, so Baker resigned from the FBI and joined the CIA.

Like everyone else, Baker had to undergo a polygraph examination and a background check by the CIA's Office of Security. One day, Baker's wife, Robin, was taking their trash to the incinerator in their apartment complex in Maryland. A man identified himself as being from the Defense Department. In fact, he was from the CIA's Office of Security.

"Do you know Bill Baker?" the man asked her.

"He is my husband," she said.

Flustered, the man explained that he was supposed to do a background check on Baker. He quickly retreated.

When Baker took over the CIA's public affairs in June 1987, he found that much of the good work Herb Hetu had accomplished under Turner had been torpedoed by Casey. Baker had to begin the job all over again of explaining to the agency why it was important to let the public know in a general way what the CIA was doing.

Clair George, then deputy director for operations, agreed to let Baker talk to each of his division and branch chiefs and later to all of the operations employees at headquarters in separate groups. In the talks, Baker would explain his own background. He would point out that, including a stint with the Air Force Office of Special Investigations, he had dealt with classified material for over two decades. He understood the need to keep secrets. Then he would get their attention.

"Why is it," he would ask, "that when you people are dispatched all over the world, you deal with the foreign press, distill intelligence, send back your observations, and then when you are posted back to this country, you seem to want to refuse to recognize the two entities that probably have more impact on the agency's future than anything else: the Congress and the press? Both were around before the agency began, and both will be around a long time after the agency is gone."

Baker would tell the operations people he could do the agency some good. In some cases, he said, he could let operations people know of forthcoming stories so they could withdraw agents who might be in danger.

"There is a lot you do that we *can* talk about," Baker would say. "The image that many Americans have of you, particularly after Iran-contra, is not positive. There are ways we can work on that and improve public opinion and still be credible."

Baker came to be impressed by the CIA and the dedication and competence of its employees. Yet smart as they were, they seemed to have difficulty understanding why so many people had a negative impression of what they do.

"Over the years, public views of the Central Intelligence Agency and its role in American foreign policy have been shaped primarily by movies, television, novels, newspapers, books by journalists, headlines growing out of congressional inquiries, exposés by former intelligence officers, and essays by 'experts' who have never served in American intelligence, or have served and still not understood its role," Robert Gates has said. "While the CIA sometimes is able to refute publicly allegations and criticism, usually it must remain silent. The result is a contradictory mélange of images of the CIA and very little understanding of its real role in American government."

If possible, most CIA people would like to keep it that way. Early on, one high-ranking operations official told Baker the ideal CIA spokesman always said "no comment," never volunteered anything, and minded his or her own business.[264] Then some of those same people wondered why the public had such a negative impression of them.

In effect, Baker was there to market the agency, to let the public know that it *does* do good things. He had found in private surveys that the more people knew about the CIA, the more they trusted it. To be sure, the CIA's mission was not like the FBI's. At the bureau, Baker could take advantage of a window—often when an indictment was announced—to trumpet the FBI's success. At the CIA, the greatest successes were the ones that the agency never wanted anyone to know about. But there were still ways to work things to everyone's mutual benefit.

Baker would disarm reporters by asking if he could talk with them on a background basis, then engage them in give-

and-take discussions. After all, the CIA was not like the Labor Department. Every responsible journalist realized that with the job of writing about the CIA went certain self-imposed restrictions. Most would not want to jeopardize a current operation if it did not entail an abuse. Nor would most blow the cover of a CIA officer unless he or she had been involved in wrongdoing that had larger implications for the agency or country as a whole. Since the passage of the Intelligence Identities Protection Act of 1982, which makes disclosing identities of "covert agents" a crime, journalists had to tread carefully in that arena in any case.[265]

"Can you still have your integrity and still have your story and not say that?" Baker would ask.

Sometimes the answer was yes, sometimes no. Baker was doing damage control, and he was effective at it. For example, a year after Baker took over, Jeff Gerth of the *New York Times* picked up a story that led to the disclosure that Clyde L. Conrad, a retired Army sergeant, was being investigated for transmitting classified documents to the Hungarian intelligence service. At the time, American and West German intelligence agencies were still pursuing sensitive leads in an effort to nail him.

When Gerth called Baker about the story, Baker told him that running the story then could well mean that it would be blown. The *Times* did not believe that the public's right to know necessarily included publishing stories that would jeopardize legitimate espionage investigations. It all depended on the facts and the timing. Baker did not actually ask Gerth to hold off on the story. But he let Gerth know that he would help him with the story if he could hold off.

Gerth knew from having dealt with him at the FBI that Baker could be trusted. When he said the case could be blown, Gerth believed him. This was a different shop from the one run by William Casey, who had approached news organizations asking them not to print stories about what former NSA employee Ronald Pelton had told the Soviets—even though the Soviets already knew all about it, and Pelton had already been arrested for espionage.

Gerth agreed to hold off on the story. What Baker did not

know was that at the time, Gerth did not have enough to go on anyway. The person who had tipped him to the story was not in the government. He had mentioned the report off-handedly at lunch. The man did not know the name of the suspect, and as it turned out later, he had told Gerth the wrong country involved in the espionage operation.[266]

But Gerth could most likely have pieced the story together. Helped by Baker's tips, Gerth unearthed the correct facts. Three months later, Gerth scooped the rest of the media with one of the biggest spy cases in U.S. history. For nearly a decade, Conrad had copied and transmitted classified documents about U.S. missile bases and facilities and NATO's fuel system for resupplying tanks to two Hungarian couriers. For the secrets, the Hungarian intelligence service paid Conrad $1 million.[267]

Gerth's story led the August 26, 1988, editions of the *New York Times*. Conrad was later convicted of espionage. In June 1990, he was sentenced in Germany to life in prison.[268]

Baker had performed a service by making sure the story did not appear at a point when the investigation might have been damaged. Gerth, in turn, had gotten a better story than he otherwise would have. It was a symbiotic relationship that would have boggled the minds of most of the earlier CIA spokesmen.

Baker would deal with any reporter so long as the reporter was a professional and demonstrated that he or she would be fair. Like an advertising executive, he would refer to the "*Times* account" or the "*Post* account." These and other major accounts he handled himself, delegating lesser lights in the journalistic world to his assistants.

If a reporter was interested in a subject that the CIA could be helpful on—say Mikhail Gorbachev's perestroika, or restructuring, plan—Baker arranged a briefing by the CIA's analysts. The CIA gave 122 briefings to the press in 1988, compared with 32 in 1986, the year before Baker took over.

By earning the trust of reporters, Baker could do a better job of alerting Webster and other CIA officials to impending stories so they could prepare for them. If a story was untrue, Baker either issued a "no comment" or expanded on the matter on a background or not-for-attribution basis. In addition, Baker might suggest that the reporter talk to another source to get more information, such as the Association of Former Intelligence Officers. In turn, Baker kept AFIO abreast of important issues without revealing classified information.

David Atlee Phillips, a former chief of the CIA's Latin America and Caribbean operations, and six former colleagues, founded AFIO in 1975 to help explain the importance and meaning of intelligence to the American people.

"There wasn't a magazine or newspaper in the country or radio or TV that wasn't peeing from a great height on the CIA and the intelligence community as a whole," Samuel Halpern, one of AFIO's founders, said in explaining its purpose.

Based in McLean, Virginia, AFIO has about 3,300 members from the entire intelligence community. About 10 percent are associate members who are interested in intelligence but not former intelligence agency employees. Besides answering questions from the press, AFIO sponsors luncheon addresses by intelligence officials and holds an annual meeting that features panels by people from the intelligence community.

During one four-month period in 1990, David D. Whipple, the retired CIA operations officer who is AFIO's executive director, calculated that he did ninety-six press interviews, either in person or on the phone, on such subjects as the Iraqi invasion of Kuwait and allegations that the CIA assassinated Swedish prime minister Olaf Palme.[269]

There are a number of other associations of retired intelligence officers, and all of them exchange information through an informal organization known only as the Common Interest Network Luncheon. Representatives meet periodically at the Army Navy Country Club in Arlington, Virginia. But while their agenda is to boost intelligence, organizations such as AFIO are not funded or controlled by the CIA or any other intelligence agency. By CIA policy, the agency may not fund or own an organization within the U.S. unless the organization discloses that it is funded by the U.S. government.

Webster took the attitude that when an allegation is so outrageous or controversial that it hurts the reputation of the agency, or accuses the agency of wrongdoing where there was none, Baker should respond. Over the years, thousands of stories had appeared charging the CIA with everything from murder to drug running. In the CIA's early days, the agency had engaged in abuses ranging from illegal wiretapping to breaking and entering. It was exposure by the press, more than anything else, that led to the Church Committee hearings and the subsequent reforms.

Occasionally, CIA officers learned about abuses from the press and took action as a result. For example, in his book, Colby recounted that he had first learned that the CIA might have attempted assassinations from "a Jack Anderson column of a few years past making some allegations about a plot against [Fidel] Castro." After finding out that there was some basis for the Anderson story, Colby, as the CIA's deputy director for operations, got Richard Helms, then the DCI, to sign a directive prohibiting the CIA from engaging in, stimulating, or supporting assassinations.[270]

But because of the CIA's earlier record, its refusal to confirm or deny stories, and some overactive imaginations, the stories continued even when the agency had reformed itself. Some reporters as well as some underground publications created cottage industries churning out stories of CIA treachery. Usually, the stories started with a few grains of truth—grains that could easily be planted to grow tales of high intrigue.

For example, on a lonely stretch of road ninety miles from Sydney, Australia, two police officers came across a Mercedes with its parking lights on at four A.M. on January 27, 1980. Inside was a grisly sight: under the steering wheel slumped the body of a man swimming in a pool of blood, a rifle in his hands. They searched the man's pockets and found the business card of William Colby, the former director of U.S. intelligence. On the back of the card was the itinerary of a trip Colby planned to take to Asia the next month. On the seat was a Bible with a meat-pie wrapper between the pages. On the wrapper were the names of Colby and U.S. Rep. Bob

Wilson of California, then the ranking Republican on the House Armed Services Committee.

The body was quickly identified as that of Francis J. Nugan, a cofounder of the Nugan Hand Bank, a merchant banking firm with offices in twenty-four countries.

Within hours, telephones began ringing in the homes and offices of a spooky cast of characters who were some of the bank's directors, employees, or consultants: three-star U.S. Gen. LeRoy J. Manor, who had recently retired as chief of staff for all U.S. forces in Asia and the Pacific and who was still on secret duty for the Air Force; Gen. Edwin F. Black, who had worked for the Office of Strategic Services, which later became the CIA, and had been chief administrative aide to Allen Dulles; Walter McDonald, a career CIA employee since 1975 and former deputy director in charge of economic research at the agency; Robert "Red" Jantzen, a former CIA station chief in Bangkok; and Rear Adm. Earl "Buddy" Yates, whose CIA work went back to the U-2 spy missions over Russia and who had recently retired as chief of strategic planning for U.S. forces in Asia and the Pacific.

The bank's apparent intelligence connections, together with the suspicious circumstances of Francis Nugan's death, quickly led to allegations that the CIA had been using the bank to help topple Australia's Labor government, that the bank had been engaged in drug running for the CIA, and that the bank was a CIA front.

As it turned out, the Nugan Hand Bank was engaged in plots of a different sort. It was a pyramid scheme that bilked thousands of investors of their money. As front men, the founders, Nugan and Michael J. Hand, a highly decorated Green Beret, had enlisted a number of unwitting former intelligence officers to lend respectability to the bank's board. Hand, in turn, got Colby involved as a lawyer for the bank. When the scheme began to unravel, Nugan took his own life, leading to investigations all over the world.[271]

What the investigations uncovered was that the CIA had used the Nugan Hand Bank for money laundering—a perfectly legitimate CIA activity that the CIA engages in to conceal its covert operations. The CIA uses a number of banks worldwide for the purpose.

"You have to launder your money someplace," a former CIA operations officer said dryly.

According to a former staff member involved in the Senate Select Committee on Intelligence's investigation of the CIA's use of the bank, "They [the Nugan Hand Bank] performed certain services. If you want to move a little money around, or get some checks certified, you go to a bank to do it. Nugan Hand had a reputation for being very aggressive. They would take your money and wouldn't ask any questions. What they [the CIA] was taking advantage of was a bank whose employees were willing to extend the full range of services, no questions asked. It was for laundering and concealing money."

The fact that the CIA uses a bank for its transactions does not mean that it is a CIA front. Nor did any of the front men know that the CIA was a customer of the bank. In the same way, the CIA used the Bank of Credit and Commerce International, the notorious international bank that regulators closed down in July 1991, to move money for the agency's clandestine operations. At the same time, as far back as 1986, the CIA began to report to other government agencies on the bank's criminal activities and secret control of First American Bank of Washington—reports that were ignored. Because the CIA decided the bank was dirty, it had closed all its accounts with BCCI by 1989.[272]

The claim that the CIA engages in drug running as a way of generating income goes back to the Vietnam days, when some individual operatives, working with or for the CIA, sold and transported drugs. But that did not mean the agency itself engaged in drug running.

"The allegation that the CIA engages, as a matter of policy, in drug smuggling is absolute nonsense," Herbert Saunders, a former CIA officer, said. "This is not to say that a Laotian kicker, employed to kick supplies out of airplanes, working for Air America, a CIA proprietary during the Vietnam era, wasn't peddling. There may have been bush pilots as well. But we didn't brand Eastern Airlines a professional drug smuggler every time a passenger or crew member was caught with some drugs in Miami. It's possible a CIA staffer went wrong along the way as well. It happens occasionally to the police and DEA."

The Christic Institute, meanwhile, generated a stream of donations by undertaking litigation claiming that former CIA officers who called themselves the Enterprise had for years operated an assortment of nefarious plots that the CIA could not itself undertake, including a guns-for-drugs scheme to aid the Nicaraguan rebels.[273] The institute is a nonprofit, liberal public-interest organization.

As usual, there was a grain of truth to the allegation. The Enterprise did exist. It was the self-financed clandestine operation developed by White House aide Oliver L. North during the Iran-contra affair. Using its own airplanes, pilots, operatives, airfields, and Swiss bank accounts, the Enterprise helped funnel arms to the Nicaraguan rebels.

North called the operation Project Democracy. Richard V. Secord, a retired Air Force major general who was one of the participants, and his partner Albert Hakim, dubbed it the Enterprise.[274]

But there is no evidence that such an operation began before North came on the scene. U.S. District Court judge Lawrence King in Miami threw out the Christic lawsuit in February 1989. Saying the lawsuit filed on behalf of journalists Tony Avirgan and Martha Honey was based on "unsubstantiated rumor and speculation from unidentified sources with no firsthand knowledge," the judge ordered the institute to pay the defendants—including Secord and Hakim—$955,000 in legal fees plus $79,500 in court costs.[275]

Another well-publicized myth was that the KGB assassinated John A. Paisley, a former officer in the Directorate of Intelligence, and that his body was never found. The fact is the FBI matched Paisley's fingerprints with those on a body found floating in the Chesapeake Bay on September 25, 1978.[276] But that did not prevent some journalists from weaving fantastic tales about the case. Those who knew Paisley said he was depressed about financial problems and undoubtedly committed suicide.

Often, conspiracy theories are generated by disgruntled former CIA employees, by people who claim to have been employees but never were, or by people who are literally crazy. At any given time, U.S. District Court in Washington has a handful of lawsuits pending against the CIA by people who claim the CIA has bugged their teeth or is following them.

Journalists tend to form an unfavorable impression of CIA operatives because they never meet real CIA officers. Generally, the people they meet had only tangential involvement with the agency as contract employees. In some cases, they are pathological liars and never worked for the agency at all.

Sometimes, the stories on their face don't make sense. The *Houston Post* ran a series in 1990 claiming a "possible link between the CIA and organized crime in the failure of at least 22 thrifts, including 16 in Texas." The rest of the press dismissed the Houston stories because they lacked documentation and were so murky that it was difficult to understand what they were saying.[277] After an investigation, the House Permanent Select Committee on Intelligence concluded that the CIA had briefly used the services of four of the institutions mentioned by the newspaper, but "those relationships were consistent with routine agency financial practices."[278]

Other stories are so lacking in credibility that one wonders why any paper would run them. For example, an unemployed oil-equipment salesman held a press conference in Dallas in August 1990 to say his father, Roscoe White, joined the Dallas Police Department on orders of the CIA so he could shoot John F. Kennedy. His son, Ricky White, said he based this on his father's diary, which disappeared after he told the FBI the story in 1988.[279]

If they can show any tangential connection to the CIA, accused criminals often use the "CIA defense" to try to get off. When Ronald Rewald was accused of bilking investors out of millions of dollars through a pyramid scheme in Honolulu, he claimed he was only following CIA instructions. In fact, the CIA admitted that it had used the firm as a "drop" for mail and phone calls. Rewald was convicted and is serving time. But stories persist that the CIA was more involved in the Rewald scheme than it admitted.[280]

Finally, the fact that the CIA has done something right is sometimes turned around to show that it has done something wrong. For example, Mark Hosenball, a producer with NBC-TV's "Exposé," claimed in the Outlook section of the *Washington Post* that the CIA had launched a public relations campaign to put its own "spin" on the scandal involving the Bank of Credit and Commerce International.

"Through a campaign of hints, leaks, and unusual public pronouncements, the agency appears to be trying to keep ahead of the scandal by admitting a certain range of knowledge and involvement [in BCCI]," according to the article, headlined "The CIA's BCCI Laundry."

"The agency's tactic has been to admit that it was aware of the bank's involvement with criminals, and that it used the bank to move money around the world. But the agency has insisted that its own involvement with the bank was entirely legal," the article said.[281]

Thus by acknowledging that it warned other government agencies as early as 1986 that BCCI was crooked, the CIA was engaging in some kind of cover-up of its involvement with the bank, or so Hosenball seemed to be saying. When the agency declines to comment, it gets criticized, and when it comments, it gets criticized for commenting.

The Outlook article went on to assert that the CIA did not provide enough support to back up its early warnings to the U.S. government's law enforcement agencies that the bank was crooked—as if the CIA's job was to regulate banks and prosecute criminals rather than to gather intelligence overseas.

In what sounds like a *Harvard Lampoon* satire on media treatment of the CIA, the article said of one CIA warning about BCCI, "In reality, apart from references to 'unorthodox and unconventional practices,' 'money laundering,' and 'narcofinance' . . . the five-page document is matter-of-fact in tone and hardly a call to action for American law enforcement agencies."

Over the years, the CIA has learned to take it, just as CIA officers have learned to lie as part of their cover.

"It's no fun to see things in the papers that are not right," retired CIA officer David Whipple said. "But the policy has been take it on the chin. If you are criticized for something unfairly, shut up, take it. Part of the penalty for being in the intelligence service is to take the fall. We're the scapegoats. This is something others in the Foreign Service applaud us for. We often take the blame when we are not responsible. We don't comment on our successes or our failures. When failures are ascribed to us unfairly, we don't comment on that. When we succeed, we never take credit, lest we give away how we accomplished the success."

Even those who know from the inside that the modern CIA does not engage in illegal activities sometimes find it hard to keep from believing some of the stories.

"I am amazed that sometimes I fall into the trap myself," said Russell Bruemmer, Webster's former general counsel, who is now a partner with Wilmer, Cutler & Pickering in Washington. "I know mistakes get made, and I read things I don't know about, and I say, 'My God! How could they have done this?' Then I catch myself and say, 'There must be another side to this.' "[282]

To be sure, the CIA has had its share of rogues. Edwin Wilson, an officer assigned to special operations within the Directorate of Operations, is a prime example. After leaving the CIA, he became involved in smuggling weapons and explosives to Libya. He was then convicted of plotting to murder the government prosecutors who had brought a case against him. Wilson is serving a twenty-six-year prison term.[283]

But for all the aberrations, CIA officers tend to be at least as law-abiding as any other citizens. Baker, who came from an agency that had traditionally been rivals with the CIA, came to be impressed by its employees. Because their mission was not as well defined as the FBI's, they sometimes got themselves into more difficulties. But the CIA was not doing crazy things; it was performing a vital mission.

Webster took the allegations personally. If the CIA was covering up or engaging in illegalities, then that meant he

was, and he could not stand the thought. Overall, he admired
the press, but some reporters simply were not fair. He particularly resented the items about the agency that appeared
in newsmagazine gossip columns; it seemed to him that by
and large, they were pure fiction.

It was Webster's policy to try to deal with the unfair stories
head-on—to issue denials where possible, and in other cases
to present the facts on a background basis. Only once did a
CIA official ask Baker to issue a denial that was deceptive.
Baker refused, explaining that the effectiveness of the press
office depended on his maintaining his credibility.

Early on, Webster asked for a check of CIA indexes to see
if the agency had any record of dealings with a Greek banker
said by some press stories to be a CIA agent. Based on the
negative response, Baker issued a denial that the man had
ever been a CIA agent. But later, another index was checked,
and Webster found out that the man did show up in CIA
files—not as an agent but as someone who had had covert
dealings with the agency.

Webster was furious. Even though the denial was technically accurate, he did not want ever to be in the position of
making a public statement and then having to retract it because he had not been apprised of the facts.

"I don't understand how this could happen," he said.

Both Webster and Baker were used to the FBI's system,
where matters as disparate as a letter from the director to an
investigation into drug dealing all appeared in the FBI's files
under an individual's name. Because of the need to com-
partment information, the CIA has many indexes.

Webster issued orders to engage in more extensive checking
before such statements were made in the future. He wanted
to be right the first time. As Baker would later crack, "I want
to have full information so that when I say 'no comment,' I
can say it with authority."

Ironically, while Casey tightened access to the CIA through
his press office and fulminated about supposed leaks by
congressional committees, most reporters who covered intelligence found the executive branch was the greatest source of
leaks. Indeed, it was Casey's reckless boasting about Vitaly

Yurchenko's defection from the USSR that spawned so many stories about his case, leading in part to Yurchenko's decision to redefect.

"I always thought the allegation that the Hill leaks was a lot of bullshit," Engelberg of the *New York Times* said. "If you go and look at the universe of secrets that the Hill is told about, and you look at the percentage that gets into print—which is a very low percentage—then I think you have to come to the conclusion that finding out intelligence secrets is not as simple as calling the head of the intelligence committees and stopping in for lunch."

According to Engelberg, Casey and his aides often leaked material about Central America to bolster their case for whatever policy agenda they were pushing.[284]

Even when stories had already run on a particular case—such as the fact that Edward Lee Howard had begun working for the Soviets—the congressional committees were often close-lipped, Engelberg said.

"You'd bump into a member of the committee on the Hill the next day [after the story ran], and he would say, 'That was a really good story.' " Engelberg said.

"What else can you tell me about it?" Engelberg would ask.

"Well, I can't say anything, but if I were you, I would keep on going. I'd really keep on going."

"Well, like what?"

"Well, I would just look at the CIA if I were you."

"Well, what else?"

"I can't say."

"The majority of leaks came from the administration," Engelberg said. "But I don't think there are too many to begin with, in the sense that someone sits down and says, 'We're going to give the *New York Times* a piece of intelligence information.' It's much more likely to be the case that on any given day, you have a lot of reporters working hard. They'll hear something from someone who doesn't understand what it is—a piece of information that is only valuable and comprehensible to people who understand the business. You go around, you check it out."[285]

John McMahon, the former deputy director of Central Intelligence under Casey, said, "I witnessed more leaks coming out of the administration than out of Congress. I felt Congress was always fairly responsible.

"The only time in my experience when they really began to leak was when the Nicaragua program became so controversial," McMahon said. "Literally, we would give a presentation to Congress, and before we could get downstairs, there was a press conference where it was being passed out what we were doing."[286]

Baker would later say that while he was director of public affairs, no U.S. reporter double-crossed or misquoted him. Often, he found, it was the CIA's own carelessness with information that led to the stories that CIA people so detested. Or the administration had leaked a story in order to push its own agenda.

"Baker's approach was to get out in front of the news, to know the reporters, to have some idea of what they were working on, and to be helpful when possible," Engelberg of the *New York Times* said. "On several occasions, he said we would rather you thought hard before you printed that. It was a very different kind of relationship [than with Casey's public affairs office]."

As a result, Engelberg said, "There were stories where we treaded initially more softly than we otherwise would have because we were presented with what we considered to be reasonable objections. I would have to say that because of the way Webster dealt with the press—which is with a more open manner—we were more likely to give them the benefit of the doubt."[287]

Eventually, FBI director William S. Sessions offered Baker the job of assistant FBI director for criminal investigations. For an FBI agent, this was like offering a Supreme Court judgeship to a lawyer. Baker left the CIA and rejoined the FBI in May 1989.

Still not sure he could be comfortable with a CIA officer in the job, Webster replaced Baker with James W. Greenleaf, another FBI executive. Greenleaf had been assistant FBI director for training, which meant he headed the FBI's training center at Quantico, Virginia. Before that, he had headed the laboratory division.

Like Baker, Greenleaf had a hard time adjusting to the special characteristics of the CIA. Each year, the agency holds a family day to commemorate the September 18 founding of the agency, a day when husbands, wives, and children can come to see where their parents or spouses work. Greenleaf got the idea that the agency could pass out CIA T-shirts, shorts, and caps. At Quantico, anyone could buy FBI shirts, shorts, or running outfits. But the Office of Security vetoed the idea. It was the same old problem that later led to Webster's rejection of the CIA employee association's plan to sell CIA mugs. What if the children of covert employees call attention to their parents' employment by wearing the garb?[288]

Unlike Baker, Greenleaf had no qualms about playing tennis with the boss. After Webster's first wife died and George Bush invited him to his Kennebunkport home, Greenleaf went along and played doubles with the then vice president, Webster, and a neighbor.

Greenleaf, like Baker, came away impressed by the CIA. He felt the agency was one of the most misunderstood agencies in the government.

When Greenleaf left in May 1990 to become the FBI's associate deputy director for administration, Webster felt comfortable enough with the CIA and its people to give the job to a CIA officer. He chose Joseph R. DeTrani, who had headed the CIA's Office of Technical Service, the unit that makes the tools of the spy trade. DeTrani was smart, witty, and direct. Before he left, Baker had recommended him as his replacement.

"They all seem to have the same style: smooth in the good sense of the word, quick-witted, able to take a jab and keep rolling," Russell Bruemmer said of Webster's choices as public affairs directors.

DeTrani came into the job joking that public relations within the CIA is an oxymoron. After a year, he was saying that he had been wrong: the concept of public relations did not conflict with the CIA's mission.

Today, the Office of Public Affairs has twenty-eight employees, including secretaries. Besides two people who handle media inquiries and four others who clip papers and help in the media area, the staff includes members of the Publication Review Board, which reviews manuscripts, the director's speechwriters, and an academic coordinator.

Some critics said that in emphasizing public relations, Webster was promoting himself at the expense of the agency. It was a shortsighted view. The truth is that one hand washed the other.

"That is like saying capitalists are mainly interested in making a profit," Engelberg of the *New York Times* observed. "That's true, but in doing that, they make the economy work better. I think Webster was terrified that something the agency does is going to end up on the front page of the *New York Times* or *Washington Post.* He would look like an idiot, the president would be angry at him, and his reputation would be ruined. That's true. So?"

The other side was that by being more open with the press, Webster was taking a risk. What if his policy backfired? What if the agency helped a reporter who wrote a story that damaged an operation? What if the agency turned against him, and the president became displeased with him?

It was so much easier and safer to sit back, as in the old days, and say "no comment." But to Webster, this was the only way an intelligence agency could function effectively in a democracy.

As a lawyer and former judge, Webster felt just as strongly about the need for an aggressive office of general counsel as he did about an active press office. He wanted a first-rate legal department, one whose advice would be actively sought by CIA executives. But to many, an office of general counsel seemed even more out of place at the CIA than an office of public affairs.

26 | *The Lawyers*

FOR MUCH OF THE CIA'S EXISTENCE, THE OFFICE OF General Counsel occupied a tenuous position within the CIA, and with good reason. It was the CIA's job to break laws, not to follow them. While the laws that the CIA broke were those of other countries, it was easy for the distinction between foreign laws and American laws to be lost. In establishing the agency, Congress seemed to lend support to the notion that the CIA was a law unto itself by outlining in only the skimpiest detail what it was supposed to do. Beyond centralizing the collection of intelligence, it was supposed to advise the National Security Council on intelligence matters, protect intelligence sources and methods, never exercise police or internal security functions, and "perform such other functions and duties related to intelligence affecting the national security as the NSC may from time to time direct."[289]

By reviewing the legislative history of the 1947 act, one could divine that Congress also intended the CIA to collect intelligence by engaging in espionage overseas. But nowhere in the law was covert action mentioned, and no other restrictions were placed on the new agency's activities.[290]

Lawrence R. Houston, the agency's first general counsel, helped draft the law establishing the agency. According to him, the clause permitting the agency to engage in "such other functions" as the NSC directed referred only to intelligence collection, not to covert action. An avuncular graduate of Harvard College and the University of Virginia School of Law, Houston was the first to admit that, by later using the clause to justify covert action, the agency was probably stretching the original intent.

"All during this drafting of the act, all during the presentations to congressional committees and debates, and all during the consideration in Congress, there was no mention of covert action," Houston said. "It was entirely intelligence. The CIA's function was to do the best collection and coordination of intelligence information and to produce intelligence assessments and estimates. That was [to be] the sole product."[291]

It was only after the law was passed, at the direction of Truman administration officials, that Houston wrote an opinion saying that covert action could be carried out by the CIA if the president gave it a directive and if Congress gave it the money to carry it out.

"I was not particularly happy about this, but you have to remember the great pressure to do something [about the communist menace]," Houston said.

With few other legal restrictions and little oversight, the CIA was soon plotting assassination attempts and even violating existing laws on the grounds the national security required it. Only rarely did the CIA consult the general counsel on activities later determined by the Church Committee and the Rockefeller Commission to be abuses. For example, the general counsel knew nothing of the CIA's plans to assassinate Fidel Castro. In those few instances when the general counsel was informed, the lawyers objected, and the practices were stopped.

In an effort to identify narcotics traffickers, the CIA in the fall of 1973 began intercepting telephone calls made between the U.S. and Latin America. John S. Warner, then Houston's deputy, pointed out that it was against the law to eavesdrop on American citizens, and the CIA stopped the practice. Earlier, Warner objected when he learned that Richard Helms had approved the imprisonment of Yuri I. Nosenko, the KGB major who had defected to the U.S. in 1964. Because of objections from Warner and others, Helms ordered a review of the case. Eventually, the CIA released Nosenko.[292]

In view of the general counsel's status, it was not surprising that the office was considered a backwater. While it had lured some good lawyers from respected law firms because of the interesting work, others who were not as sharp far outnumbered them. Other government lawyers who dealt with the office found it to be sleepy, particularly before the Church Committee hearings. William Casey symbolically downgraded the office even further by banishing it from the CIA's compound to rented buildings in McLean.

That began to change under William Webster. As a lawyer and former judge, Webster wanted a first-rate legal department. His entire approach to government emphasized adherence to the Constitution, and he was not going to tolerate any winking at the law. Webster began in September 1987 by appointing Russell J. Bruemmer, his thirty-five-year-old former special assistant at the FBI, as special counsel to investigate the agency's involvement in the Iran-contra affair.

Bruemmer had left the FBI to join Wilmer, Cutler & Pickering. Webster admired Bruemmer's sharp legal mind, his ability to absorb vast quantities of information and make sense of it, and his low-key approach. Six feet two inches tall, with blond hair and a mustache, Bruemmer had grown up in Iowa, where his father was a college financial administrator. He had graduated magna cum laude from the University of Michigan's law school and had been editor in chief of the *University of Michigan Journal of Law Reform*.

Bruemmer became close to Webster when Webster first moved to Washington to become FBI director. Webster's first wife, Drusilla, had stayed behind so their daughter could finish the school year at her high school. After Webster left the

FBI, Bruemmer maintained a social relationship with Webster. Many thought the two had a father-son relationship.

At the CIA, it became Bruemmer's job to find out what the role of agency employees had been in the Iran-contra affair and to recommend disciplinary action if warranted. The Iran-contra scandal broke in November 1986 with disclosures that the Reagan administration had secretly sold arms to Iran in exchange for help in obtaining the release of U.S. hostages in Lebanon and at the same time, had used profits from the sales to pay for covert military assistance to the Nicaraguan contras.

Webster could have swept the CIA's involvement under the rug by saying—as Police Chief Daryl F. Gates said of the beating of a black motorist by Los Angeles police officers—that the abuses that occurred during the Iran-contra affair were an aberration.

Every year, the CIA quietly terminated five to ten employees for embezzlement or security questions. But the concept of meting out punishment for misjudgment, failure to follow established procedure, or not being truthful with appropriate authorities was alien. Those CIA employees who administered LSD to unsuspecting Americans—an act considered by most CIA officers to be the most unforgivable offense in the CIA's history of abuses—received only a letter of reprimand from Allen Dulles. The letters were not placed in their personnel files.[293]

Webster's life at the CIA would have been far easier if he had forgotten about Iran-contra. But that was not Webster's way. He chose his battles carefully. Allowing CIA mugs to be sold by the agency's employee activity association was not an issue worth alienating employees over. Misusing the CIA in violation of the law was.

As a result of Bruemmer's investigation, Webster dismissed two CIA employees who had not been candid with the inspector general. They had not lied, but they had not told the whole story. The CIA issued letters of reprimand to four others, and one employee was demoted.[294]

Bruemmer found that several other key officials—Thomas A. Twetten, then assistant deputy director for operations, and

Robert Gates, then deputy director of Central Intelligence—had received bits and pieces of information about Iran-contra, but did not realize at the time what was happening. On the other hand, Twetten, who would later succeed Richard Stolz as deputy director for operations, had taken positive steps to protect the agency: he warned that Manucher Ghorbanifar, one of the middlemen in the shipment of arms to Iran, should not be trusted. He advised White House aide Oliver L. North that it was not a good idea to use nongovernment people in his clandestine operation. While Twetten became involved in overseeing the distribution of funds for some of the operation, he made sure that what he did was authorized and within the law. Moreover, every penny had been properly accounted for.

It was clear to Bruemmer that CIA officers had been influenced by Casey's attitude. Casey didn't like congressional oversight. He was selective himself in what he said, giving answers that were technically correct but factually misleading. It was not surprising to Bruemmer that officers under the director wound up emulating him.

As for Casey's involvement, Bruemmer came away as mystified as everyone else. On the one hand, there was the testimony of Oliver North, who had directed the shipment of arms to Iran and the diversion of excess payments from some of the arms sales to the contra rebels fighting the Sandinista regime in Nicaragua in violation of a congressional prohibition known as the Boland Amendment. North said Casey had masterminded the operation. On the other hand, CIA officials whom Bruemmer trusted and who had some involvement in the matter insisted that North had exaggerated Casey's role. What was clear was that Casey tried to insulate the CIA's employees from his activities, a tip-off that Casey realized it would not be easy to involve the CIA in illegal activities.

In the end, only a handful of CIA employees were found to have detailed knowledge of aspects of the affair.[295] One of them, Alan D. Fiers, Jr., who directed the CIA's covert operations in Central America from 1984 to 1986, later pled guilty to two misdemeanor counts of withholding information from Congress. In doing so, he said in federal court in Washington that Clair E. George, then deputy director for operations, and other CIA superiors told him not to tell Congress about the CIA's early knowledge of the diversion of funds from the sale of arms to Iran to support the Nicaraguan rebels.[296]

After Bruemmer finished his report on Iran-contra, Webster asked him in 1988 to become the agency's general counsel. When he first came to the agency as special counsel in 1987, Bruemmer had laid down one condition: that his office would be in the main building, not in rented buildings in McLean. As a result, Bruemmer had an office on the seventh floor. A few doors from Webster's office, it was on the same hallway as the offices of the deputy director for operations and the deputy director for intelligence.

When Webster asked him to become general counsel a year later, Bruemmer jokingly laid down a new condition: that he would have nothing to do with Freedom of Information Act requests. In fact, the function was handled by the Office of Information Technology within the Directorate of Administration. But when the requests generated lawsuits, the general counsel became involved. As far as Bruemmer was concerned, handling the requests was a thankless job, one that only earned the enmity of agency employees for giving out information and the enmity of requesters because the process always took so long, and so much of the information was blacked out.*

At the time, the general counsel's office was still off campus. Bruemmer continued to work at headquarters until the rest of his staff moved to the new building in January 1989.

---

* On August 16, 1976, the author requested from the CIA's Freedom of Information Office material relating to John (Johnny) Roselli, who had been an intermediary in the CIA's attempts to enlist the Mafia to assassinate Fidel Castro. When the material was not forthcoming after several months had elapsed, the author appealed. The material—primarily the CIA inspector general's report on the agency's attempts to kill or embarrass Fidel Castro—finally arrived on December 27, 1990, more than fourteen years later. It contained some additional details on the CIA's fruitless attempts to do in Castro, but nothing earth-shattering.

Both Webster and Bruemmer wanted to upgrade the importance of the office. It was not an effective part of the decision-making process; lawyers were often consulted after the fact. In part, that was because of the slowness of the office. CIA officers became frustrated because it took so long for the general counsel's office to get back to them when they did ask its opinion.

"The general attitude [of the general counsel's office] was to say no and to take a long time in saying it," a former operations officer said.

On the other hand, the lawyers sometimes were not consulted because of a disinclination to take their advice. It was not until John N. McMahon, then deputy director of Central Intelligence, learned about the CIA's involvement in the effort to trade arms for hostages in Iran that Stanley Sporkin, the CIA's general counsel under William Casey, was asked about the issue. Sporkin said that for the effort to continue, a presidential finding should be issued. But no one asked the general counsel's office about diverting money from the arms sales to the effort to support the contras in Nicaragua: the answer almost certainly would have been that it would have been illegal.[297]

"What we set out to do was get the lawyers involved in the decision-making process early," Bruemmer said. "Not to make the decisions but to point out the legal pitfalls and help structure proposals to address them. Over and over again we told my office—and Webster said this as well—that the job of a lawyer is not to say *no,* but to say *yes if* or *no but* and help people do what they want to do within the structure of the law."[298]

Bruemmer began sitting in at the Tuesday breakfast that Webster had with eight of his senior staff. Then Bruemmer became a regular at Wednesday-morning meetings held by the deputy director of Central Intelligence with the agency's deputy directors. He also sat in on Friday-morning meetings held by the deputy directors.

Bruemmer served on a task force that developed a new structure to improve the operations of the inspector general's office, and on another task force that led to establishment of the counternarcotics center.

Later, Bruemmer became involved in the decision made by Webster to withhold from public disclosure by the courts classified information relating to Joseph F. Fernandez, a twenty-two-year veteran of the agency who was CIA station chief in Costa Rica from 1984 to 1986. In that role, Fernandez aided North in secretly resupplying the contras at a time when Congress had prohibited all U.S. military aid to the Nicaraguan rebels. In April 1989, Fernandez was indicted for making false statements about his involvement in the Iran-contra affair to the CIA inspector general and to the Presidential Review Board headed by the late Sen. John G. Tower.

Fernandez claimed the material withheld by the CIA would show that CIA officials knew of his activities and that therefore he had no need to lie about them. Attorney General Richard Thornburgh backed Webster's decision to withhold the documents, saying use of the classified material in the trial would cause "serious damage to the national security."

The Classified Information Procedures Act of 1980 provides ways for classified information to be handled by a court without making it public. For example, after classified information has been seen by the judge, the defense, and the prosecution, the information can be disclosed in a trial in summary form. Instead of naming a country, the summary might refer to it as a "Latin American country."

None of the information Webster wanted to withhold from public disclosure was really new. Most of it had already appeared in the press. But Webster accepted the position of Stolz, then the deputy director for operations, and others, who said that for the CIA to confirm—even in a judge's chambers—that a company was used as a CIA front, or that a country helped the CIA, would breach the trust that others place in the agency and would embarrass the countries involved.

Both Bruemmer and Webster felt that the kind of information they withheld in the Fernandez case was similar to the information withheld by the CIA at Webster's direction in the trial of Oliver North. In the North case, U.S. District Court judge Gerhard A. Gesell in Washington had allowed the trial to proceed. However, U.S. District Court judge Claude M. Hilton in Alexandria threw out the charges against Fernandez, saying the former CIA officer could not receive a fair trial without the ability to use the documents. Webster and Bruemmer believed that if Gesell had been the judge on the case, the trial would have been allowed to proceed.[299]

Bruemmer made it a point to drop in every day on Webster and the deputy directors. They were his clients, and he wanted them to feel he was accessible. He established a particularly close relationship with Stolz, who relied on him more and more for his advice. Even if an operation was taking place overseas, there were all kinds of tricky legal questions. For example, a proposed action might fall somewhere between a covert action and an intelligence operation. Should Congress be told under the law that requires notification of covert actions? Much of the agency's day-to-day activity was governed by Executive Order 12333, which even the lawyers found confusing.

Meanwhile, in the fall of 1988, Bruemmer settled a lawsuit filed against the CIA by people who had unknowingly been subjected to mind-control drug testing by Dr. D. Ewen Cameron of the Allan Memorial Institute of McGill University in Montreal. To try to alter human behavior, Cameron subjected patients who had come to him for help with psychiatric problems to LSD, electroshock treatment up to seventy-five times the normal level, and drug-induced sleep that lasted for weeks—all without their consent.

After learning of the experiments, the CIA had used a front organization to provide funding for Dr. Cameron in exchange for access to his results. While Bruemmer thought the government would have won the case, he decided the bad publicity from a trial would not be worth it. Under the settlement, the seven defendants received a total of about $750,000.[300]

Bruemmer left in 1990 to return to his partnership at Wilmer, Cutler & Pickering. To replace Bruemmer, Webster appointed Elizabeth Rindskopf. A former general counsel at the National Security Agency who had previously worked as a civil rights lawyer, Rindskopf had dealt with Webster and Bruemmer on a variety of cases while at NSA.

Rindskopf had raised the hackles of independent counsel Lawrence E. Walsh because of the way she refused to provide him with NSA information relating to the Iran-contra affair. On the other hand, while at NSA, she had sided with agency employees who had had difficulty getting their writing cleared for publication. Often, it took a year to obtain clearance, and Rindskopf took on the NSA offices that resisted changes she wanted to speed the review process.

Today the office of general counsel has 125 employees, including 60 lawyers, compared with 14 lawyers before the Church Committee hearings. The office now details attorneys to most of the directorates, including the directorate of operations. There, eight lawyers sit in on many of the meetings held by the agency's top spy—something that would have been bitterly resisted in earlier years.

27 | *The Future*

AS THE COLD WAR ENDED, NEWSPAPERS AND MAGAZINES carried stories questioning the role of the CIA. Now that the Soviet threat had diminished, was it relevant? Should the agency turn its attention to economic matters? Should it emphasize analysis more than human spying? Should it emphasize human spying more than technical surveillance? Should its staff be cut? Should it be abolished?

As with almost everything else concerning the CIA, there was a gap between the public perception and the reality. Even at the height of the Cold War, the CIA had allocated no more than 12 percent of its budget to spying on the Soviets, excluding the costs of major technical collection systems. With the exception of Great Britain, Canada, and Australia, the CIA had always spied on every country in the world. The reason was that no one knew when a country such as Iraq, which the U.S. had supported during its war with Iran, might decide to threaten U.S. interests.

Well before the media questioning began, the CIA had started shifting its resources. Soviets were no longer the first-priority target in many stations around the world. Counter-terrorism, counternarcotics, nuclear proliferation, and economic issues assumed greater importance. When the Persian Gulf War began, the CIA reallocated money from the rest of its divisions to the Near East Division to cope with that crisis. As the Soviets released their grip on Eastern Europe, the CIA prepared to deal with friendly governments there. In one year alone, two thousand new publications sprang up in Eastern Europe, and each had to be reviewed as well. Covert action had already been cut to no more than a dozen programs a year, compared with hundreds in the 1950s and early 1960s.

Meanwhile, the CIA began planning reductions in staff. For the past ten years, the CIA's staff had been increasing by an average of five hundred a year. But over the next six years, Congress had mandated a 15 percent cut in personnel. Within the Directorate of Operations, this would mean a reduction of 890 positions.

"Twenty years ago, we watched the Soviet Union," William Webster said just before he retired in 1991 as director of Central Intelligence. "We listened for hiccups. Today, we have an entirely different picture. The Soviet hegemony over Eastern Europe is gone. We have new countries seeking relationships with us. We have the Soviet Union in turmoil. It's a different kind of instability. It [the end of the Cold War] also unlocked a lot of old rivalries and hatreds. Yugoslavia is breaking up. You have regional conflicts everywhere. We were not poised to deal with every kind of regional conflict."[301]

To deal with the future, Webster took a slot for the CIA's executive director, a largely irrelevant position used primarily to sign off on financial matters, and used it in the fall of 1990 to create a new position—deputy director for planning and coordination. The first official in the job was Gary E. Foster, a former director of the Office of Medical Service within the CIA.

Unlike the other deputy directors, Foster had no directorate under him. With offices on the seventh floor of the CIA's old building, Foster had a staff of just twenty. It was his job to be a catalyst—to bring together CIA officers from each of the directorates to help chart the agency's future.

A short man with a salt-and-pepper beard, Foster set up twenty-four teams of officers from the relevant directorates to look into a range of issues, from counterintelligence, economics, and weapons proliferation to training, the agency's work force, and how the CIA deals with its assets or agents. Each of the task forces produced working papers to take the CIA into the next century.

"The key is flexibility," Foster would say. "Each plan must be reevaluated every year."

Meanwhile, the CIA was buffeted by a range of criticism, much of it uninformed. Some said the agency had failed to predict the Iraqi invasion of Kuwait, which was not true, or that it had failed to predict that hardliners would seek to topple the government of Soviet President Mikhail Gorbachev, as they did in August 1991. That also was not true. As Sen. David L. Boren, the Oklahoma Democrat who headed the Senate Select Committee on Intelligence, said just after the coup failed, "For several months now, the President and those of us in the congressional leadership have been told by the intelligence community that we had to take very, very seriously the possibility of this kind of coup."

The criticism underscored the need to continue to spy on the former Soviet Union even after the cataclysmic changes that rocked that country in 1991. For regardless of whether the former Soviets are considered enemies or friends, the U.S. needs to know what is happening within a government that controls thousands of nuclear weapons. For its part, the KGB continued to spy on the U.S. after the coup much as it always had. And Iraq's invasion of Kuwait demonstrated why the CIA is needed regardless of whether the Soviets pose a threat.

Nevertheless, some members of Congress called for a reorganization of the intelligence community. Saying one man could not do both jobs, Sen. Arlen Specter, a Republican from Pennsylvania, introduced a bill that would take away the role of the CIA director as overseer of the intelligence community. Instead, a new official would perform that function. This was a step backward from Congress's original intent of establishing an organization that would centralize all intelligence to prevent surprises such as the one at Pearl Harbor.

Sen. Daniel Patrick Moynihan, the New York Democrat, introduced a bill that would abolish the CIA and transfer its duties to the State Department. According to Moynihan, this would "purge the vestiges of this struggle [the Cold War] and would establish the principle that the executive branch may not resort to illegal means in the pursuit of national security, as it did in the Iran-contra affair."

Meanwhile, the Senate and House intelligence committees began drafting legislation that would streamline the organization of the intelligence community. As part of that review, the committees began considering whether to make public the intelligence community budget.

At about the same time, the Senate Intelligence Committee put Robert Gates, the former deputy director of Central Intelligence under Webster, through a grueling confirmation process to succeed Webster as DCI. Former CIA employees whose views had not been accepted by Gates, or who would have done his job differently if they had had it, came forward to testify that Gates had "politicized" the analytical process. In fact, Gates had frequently presided over analyses and estimates that ran directly afoul of the policies of the Reagan administration. While it was difficult to accept Gates's claim that he knew nothing of the diversion of funds from the sale of arms to Iran to the contra rebels in Nicaragua, no clear evidence was ever presented that he did know of the diversion. While the hearings disclosed massive amounts of information about the CIA's Directorate of Intelligence, in fact they produced little that would enlighten the public about the way the CIA worked or what its problems really were.

Despite Webster's best efforts, the Office of Security is still in the Dark Ages, still prone to overlook legal niceties and to act in heavy-handed fashion. While defector handling has been improved, the CIA still has an institutional bias against defectors, considering them difficult to deal with. In contrast to the FBI, whose agents are encouraged to become friends with them, the CIA builds a wall between defectors and their handlers, using aliases to make sure defectors never bother CIA officers at night. These negative attitudes become self-fulfilling: people who sense they are looked upon as difficult become difficult. In part, the CIA's cold approach led to the 1985 redefection of KGB officer Vitaly Yurchenko.

The agency as a whole still has difficulty separating what should legitimately be kept secret and what can be disclosed without causing damage.

"Articles from the *Times* are classified all the time," a former operations officer said. "It's just bureaucrats at work."

The individual directorates still tend to go their own way sometimes and still tend to be parochial in their outlook.

"We have institutional biases that act as a wet blanket on judgment," Thomas Polgar, a former CIA station chief, said. "If you say there is no more threat from Eastern Europe, that means somebody's budget is going to be reduced. Self-interest enters into it."

The CIA still reflexively thinks of the media as the enemy.

"It [the CIA] doesn't understand Congress as well as it should; it doesn't understand the press as well as it should," Russell Bruemmer, the CIA's general counsel under Webster, said. "These are the constituent agencies. To many people in the agency, even to a lot of senior managers, they are necessary evils, not something that can have positive impact.

"I believe it goes back to values that reflect what many people perceived to be the tenuousness of democracy's hold on the world," Bruemmer said. "The people who created the culture, the Dick Helmses of this world, they are all people for whom this really was a life-and-death struggle between democracy and communism. That kept them in the game, that kept them playing."[302]

To face the latest challenges, the CIA needs to beef up human intelligence. It needs to emphasize quality over quantity. It needs to highlight regional issues more than before. And it needs to improve the way it presents information. "We publish too much intelligence of questionable relevance to policymakers," Robert Gates said just before he became the 15th DCI. "Less and better should be the rule."

Because the CIA's role is so tied to changing world conditions, its coverage must constantly be reshaped. Nor can the CIA change course overnight. Like a supertanker, the CIA is not always nimble but gets the job done. Over the years, the CIA has predicted nearly everything that it should have predicted, foreseen every weapons system that it should have foreseen, and found out most of the things that it should have found out. While it occasionally strayed into illegalities and foolish operations, it did so in virtually every case with the approval of presidents or cabinet officers.

"We've had our problems, disasters, horror shows. But on a day-to-day basis, we've been able to get the information, process it, and deliver it," said Robert R. Simmons, a former CIA officer who later became staff director of the Senate Select Committee on Intelligence. "We tend to see the failures in print, not the successes. In the aggregate, I felt the CIA was successful eighty-five percent to ninety percent of the time. That ten percent to fifteen percent were big failures."

"The mistakes get publicized. There is no Pulitzer for the guy who does excellent reports," a former CIA operations officer said.

"I think the key thing to remember about this place is that it has constantly evolved," Gates said in an interview after he became DCI. "There has been this preoccupation with the idea that we were stuck on the Cold War and the question of whether we could make the change at the end of the Cold War. People didn't really realize that as part of this evolutionary process, for years we have taken on roles other than just looking at the Soviet Union and the Warsaw Pact countries. We have been doing a lot of things on a lot of subjects on the Third World, regional disputes, economic intelligence, proliferation."

There was a certain safety in the Cold War. Each side knew its part and played it more or less consistently. Now the CIA was faced with more uncertainty.

"With the collapse of the Soviet Union and the end of the Cold War, the danger of nuclear war or of a war in Europe has receded at least for the foreseeable future nearly to the vanishing point," Gates said. "So the world in the sense of cosmic destruction is an extraordinarily safer place than it was a year ago. That said, on a day-to-day basis, the world is as dangerous and perhaps a little more so because some of the restraints imposed by the Cold War, particularly in regional conflicts, have been lifted."

The evolution of the former Soviet Union toward a market economy and democratic politics "is probably going to take two generations," Gates said. "During that period, I think there will be a lot of setbacks, a lot of detours, perhaps a fair amount of violence. We will still have for another decade or more tens of thousands of nuclear weapons that we are going to have to track and somebody has to monitor. We still are going to have to see if they are implementing arms control agreements. Now we have fifteen republics and their political, economic, and social development to monitor, not just one country. We have to operate not just out of Moscow but in fifteen republics.

"We will have to devote, ironically, more attention to monitoring regional disputes," Gates said. "Some big ones, like Afghanistan, Cambodia, Angola, and Central America, have all gone away, but India, Pakistan, the Middle East still are problems. What is happening on the Korean peninsula is not entirely clear . . . So there are a lot of regional problem areas that we have watched in the past but that are going to become even more dangerous or where the political circumstances are reaching a new critical phase."

Meanwhile, Gates said, the CIA is intensifying its efforts to track nuclear proliferation, narcotics, and terrorism.

Almost immediately upon taking over, Gates set up internal task forces to recommend change. Based on the reports of the task forces, Gates approved plans to develop an intelligence community television channel that would beam classified news to policymakers six days a week. In response to the scandal involving the Bank of Credit and Commerce International (BCCI), Gates encouraged CIA employees to be on the lookout for criminal activities and to make sure that other agencies that receive CIA reports of such activities follow up on them.

Gates approved a more open policy in dealing with the press, allowing on the record interviews with officials below the level of deputy director of Central Intelligence and expanding background briefings. He also took a number of steps that will result in declassification of agency files on older operations like the Bay of Pigs.

In a symbolic gesture, Gates said in the interview after he took over that he saw no reason why the CIA employee association should not be allowed to sell CIA mugs, a request that had stirred opposition from senior CIA officials reporting to Webster.

"If they want to sell CIA mugs, I couldn't be more pleased," Gates said. "They can even sell T-shirts for all I care: The mug gap."

Today, the CIA is a very different agency from the one that created sensational headlines in the early 1970s about drug testing and domestic surveillance.

"We are in a wilderness without a single footstep to guide us. Our successors will have an easier task," Rep. James Madison, a member of the first federal Congress, wrote to Thomas Jefferson on June 30, 1789. So it was in the CIA's early days.

In most respects, the modern CIA is meticulous about obeying the law. Under William Webster, having a lawyer detailed to one's program became a status symbol at the agency, demonstrating that whatever one was doing was complicated and important enough to warrant the attention of an attorney. Besides his deputy, the first slot Howard P. Hart asked for when he started the CIA's counternarcotics center within the Directorate of Operations was a lawyer.

"Intelligence excesses are largely behind us," Sen. Boren, chairman of the Senate Select Committee on Intelligence, has said. "We now have a body of laws and a process of congressional intelligence oversight that aggressively seeks to insure that the CIA operates in a manner consistent with the fundamental values of the American people."[303]

The CIA now looks upon Congress more as an ally than an enemy.

"When the shit hits the fan, I want to have Congress with me when people say, 'What the hell did you do that for?' " John N. McMahon, deputy director of Central Intelligence under William Casey, said. "It's a way to cover your ass. But to me, it's part of being in the United States and in a democratic society. I never want to have a handful of people deciding what is good for the United States. That's why I want Congress involved."[304]

Much of the criticism of the CIA stems from the fact that its activities are secret. The public—and particularly the media—resent being told they cannot know something. Silence is interpreted as arrogance. Moreover, when people do not know what an agency is doing, they assume that it is either doing nothing and not changing with the times, or that it is doing something wrong. In the absence of concrete information, it is human nature to accept rumor as fact. If the identity of the perceived enemy is in flux, it is assumed that the CIA officers are dinosaurs still fighting the Cold War.

Compounding the problem is widespread misunderstanding of the CIA's role. The assumption is that with its massive resources, the agency must know everything. But the CIA has no crystal ball; it is not omniscient. Every day, the media publish or broadcast stories that are incorrect. Beyond the correction column in most newspapers, no one goes back a year later and points out that a publication incorrectly predicted an election or erroneously said that the CIA established a task force to target Saddam Hussein for assassination. But no one forgets the CIA's mistakes.

For all the misperceptions, former U.S. government executives rate the CIA as one of the "most respected" government agencies. In a 1990 opinion poll of these executives, the agency was ranked ninth between the FBI, which came out slightly higher, and the SEC.[305]

The CIA today is the most powerful and effective intelligence agency in the world. While the KGB has had many successes, it never had the technical or analytical capabilities of the CIA. It never had the broad kind of intelligence coverage that the CIA enjoys. And it never was as honest in its reporting to headquarters as the CIA is.

"[The CIA], like the country it serves, has the broadest interests throughout the world, and that is reflected by this institution," Richard J. Kerr, deputy director of Central Intelligence under Webster, said. "There aren't many countries whose interests are truly worldwide."[306]

The CIA is one of the most important institutions in American society, one that Americans are fortunate to have. The agency has seen the country through some of the most difficult times in the nation's history, providing information that has kept the country out of a major war with the Soviet Union and helped the U.S. to win smaller ones, including the war in the Persian Gulf. Like the FBI or the military, the CIA is an agency that is desperately needed and appreciated in times of crisis: When a child is kidnapped, the family looks to the FBI for help. When dictators such as Saddam Hussein threaten the world, it is the CIA that the U.S. government turns to for the information necessary to meet and counter the threat.

But the CIA occupies a fragile place in American society. Its role is difficult to define and even more difficult to carry out. The secrecy that envelops it conflicts with inherent American values and leads to mistrust. Too many times in the past, that mistrust has been warranted. And the CIA is often guilty of arrogance.

No longer should Americans "to a degree take it on faith," as Richard Helms proposed to a meeting of the American Society of Newspaper Editors in 1971, "that we, too, are honorable men, devoted to her [the nation's] service."

While the laws and executive orders in place are sufficient, the CIA's power can easily be misused by unscrupulous directors or presidents. This happened when President Johnson ordered the CIA to investigate the movement against the Vietnam War. It happened when President Nixon tried to get the CIA to cover up the involvement of the White House in the Watergate break-in. More recently, it happened when William Casey set a tone that led to the involvement of a handful of agency employees in the Iran-contra affair.

The surest safeguard against such aberrations again subverting the CIA's integrity is an institutional attitude that accepts both congressional oversight and scrutiny by the press. Not too long ago, the CIA met even the most devastating charges, from accusations of drug running to murder, with a stoic "no comment." This suggested that the CIA does not have to answer for its actions. All too often, that attitude translated into unlawful or simply stupid activities. It was an attitude that failed to take account of the fact that the CIA can explain itself without giving away all its secrets.

It is not enough for the press and Congress to be vigilant. The agency itself must recognize and understand the value of such examination. For only through responsiveness to Congress and the media will the CIA be accountable to the American people.

Epilogue

With the Cold War over, the CIA was an agency in search of a mission. Not that its role did not remain critical. It would be naive to think there would be no more Saddam Husseins or Russian coups. Nor would anyone want to rule out the possibility that rogue countries or terrorists might try to threaten the U.S. with nuclear weapons. Just as much as the U.S. needs an FBI, the country needs a CIA to warn of such threats. But given the fact that the primary threat—the Soviet Union—was gone, the CIA remained vastly overstaffed. This was despite budget cuts of up to 10 percent mandated by the House and Senate intelligence committees.

In a desperate attempt to justify its remaining budget, the CIA tried to emphasize its role in fighting narcotics and terrorism. But law enforcement agencies by and large were not impressed with the agency's intelligence on drug trafficking. CIA officers still felt uncomfortable in this arena. Nor was the threat of terrorism enough to justify the existence of an entire agency. Largely to feed their own egos, CIA officials still demanded large staffs, which often had little to do. In particular, the CIA's princes, whose reward for a distinguished career was assignment as station chief in London, Geneva, or Paris, insisted on retaining hundreds of officers beyond what they needed. By virtue of their political clout within the agency, the princes got what they wanted.

Against this background, the sensational arrests of Aldrich H. Ames and his wife, Maria, in February 1994 came as a reminder not only of why the CIA was still needed but also of how much remains to be done to make it a more disciplined, focused, and effective agency. A spy novelist could not have dreamed up more perfect positions for a mole within the CIA. The heavy-smoking, heavy-drinking fifty-two-year-old officer had worked for the CIA since 1962. By 1983, he had been named chief of the counterintelligence branch in the Soviet/East European Division within the Directorate of Operations. In 1985, Ames began working with the joint FBI-CIA squad within the FBI. Called Courtship, this squad tries to recruit KGB officers to work for the U.S. More recently, Ames had been assigned to the CIA's Counternarcotics Center, with responsibility for the Balkan area.

When he was assigned to Mexico City in 1982, Ames met Maria del Rosario Casas, a Colombian cultural attaché, and recruited her to work as an agent for the CIA. They began an affair that led to Ames's divorce from his wife and his marriage in 1985 to his former agent.

Because Ames's job in counterintelligence required him to review files and ask questions not only at the CIA but at the FBI and other sensitive agencies, he was in an even better position to help the Russians than was the director of Central Intelligence. If the DCI began asking for a lot of sensitive case files, other employees might become suspicious. But that was part of Ames's job.

The $2.5 million Ames was charged with receiving from the Russians beginning in 1985 signified the value of the information he was accused of passing. For the KGB is careful about how it spends its money. Never before in U.S. history had any known spy received anywhere near that sum. The closest figure was the $1 million received by Navy warrant officer John A. Walker, Jr., who collected the money over an eighteen-year period. By comparison, Ames received at least $2.5 million in just over eight years.

As a result of information Ames was believed to have

passed, the FBI said at least ten Soviet and later Russian agents working for the CIA or FBI had been executed. They included the two spies that Courtship and the FBI recruited within the Soviet embassy in Washington. Other sources said the number of spies compromised by Ames could be far higher. Indeed, the Ames case was the most damaging spy case in U.S. history.

Ames was caught by the joint FBI-CIA squad only because a defector who had had access to KGB files began working for the FBI in 1992. The defector provided the FBI with hundreds of leads on potential spy cases within the CIA and other agencies.* While the defector did not know Ames's name, he had enough information to allow the FBI to focus on Ames by May 1993.

Besides signaling that the Russians were not ready to be considered close allies, the case shined a devastating spotlight on the CIA's security—or lack of it. After Ames's arrest, a cavalcade of former CIA officials began appearing on television to say there was nothing really surprising about the case: Spying will continue regardless of whether the Cold War is over, and there is not much that can be done about it. This roll-over attitude was symptomatic of why the CIA got taken so badly and why so many other spies had previously penetrated the agency's supposedly airtight security.

While it is true that spying, like bank robberies, will always continue, it is not true that nothing can be done about it. The fact that a spy has succeeded is not sufficient reason to blame an agency, any more than it would be fair to blame the FBI when a bank is held up. Yet in virtually every penetration of the CIA, there had been warning signs that should have tipped off the CIA to a possible security breach, and in virtually every case when the CIA's Office of Security got involved, it botched the job.

The Ames case was a classic example. Ames was known to be a heavy drinker, a borderline alcoholic. He violated

---

*The existence of the defector was revealed in the author's book *The FBI: Inside the World's Most Powerful Law Enforcement Agency*.

agency rules by having an affair with an agent working for him in Mexico City, the woman he later married and who would be arrested with him. In 1984, Ames again violated agency rules by sleeping with her in a New York CIA safehouse, a sanctuary for the most sensitive meetings with agents working for the CIA.

After divorcing that year and remarrying in 1985, Ames complained to coworkers about his lack of money, a result of his divorce agreement. Then, in 1989, he bought a home at 2512 North Randolph Street in Arlington, Virginia, for $540,000 in cash. He spent another $99,000 on improvements. In 1992, he began driving to work in a Jaguar he had purchased for $25,000. His total credit card charges beginning in 1985 were $455,000.

After being transferred to the CIA's Counternarcotics Center, Ames continued to spend much of his time in the CIA's Soviet Division. By schmoozing with former colleagues, Ames was able to cull as much information as he had before. Ames also tried to obtain identities of covert agents whose real names were stored in CIA computers. Access was initially denied, but no one tried to find out who had been trying to pry loose information to which they were not entitled. Ames later was able to break into the database.

With all these red flags waving, Ames should have been transferred to a less-sensitive position, if not fired. Yet nothing was done—no discipline was meted out for violating agency rules, no investigators were called in to probe Ames's activities or find out how he could live so well on an annual salary of $69,843.

Looking back at previous CIA penetrations, the same pattern emerged. The CIA knew Edward Lee Howard had a drug problem but prepared to send him anyway to Moscow, where he began working for the Soviets. The agency knew that William P. Kampiles also had a drug problem but allowed him access to the top-secret manual for the KH-11 spy satellite, which he promptly sold to the Soviets. The agency knew that CIA officer David H. Barnett had left the agency, but when he reapplied, it failed to give him a new polygraph test. It turned out he had told the Soviets about

CIA operations in Indonesia. The CIA knew that Sharon Scranage, a CIA support employee in Ghana, had been having an affair with a cousin of the Ghanaian prime minister—a violation of agency rules. But the CIA did not discipline her and left her in place. She then gave her boyfriend information about virtually all the CIA's operations in Ghana.

In the case of Karl F. Koecher, the Czech Intelligence Service officer who became a CIA employee, investigators realized later that the Office of Security had overlooked his failure on a polygraph test. Thus his application should have been rejected. Yet when spies from the other side were willing to help the CIA, as when top KGB officer Vitaly Yurchenko defected to the U.S., the Office of Security treated them as prisoners, leading —in Yurchenko's case— to his redefection. It was also significant that the defector who started the FBI on Ames's trail had chosen to work with the FBI, not the CIA.

If the Office of Security consisted of Keystone Kops, it was symptomatic of the larger agency culture, which abhors security. Some have speculated that the attitude is a reaction to the fear generated by James J. Angleton, the legendary CIA counterintelligence chief who never did catch a spy but unfairly accused many patriotic CIA officers of selling out their country. While modern CIA officers have little recollection of Angleton, his amateurish methods may have contributed to a backlash. Now security is considered a nuisance, if not an affront. The Office of Security is the enemy, called in only when it is too late. There is no mechanism for communicating to the Office of Security suspicions that may or may not turn out to be well founded. In any case, no one wants to report irregularities, because the same thing might happen to them. CIA officers consider searches of their briefcases to be humiliating. Infractions of rules and heavy drinking are tolerated, and discipline, if meted out, is lax and inconsistent.

The Office of Security itself is a disaster. Consisting of roughly five hundred of the CIA's twenty-two thousand employees, it is staffed by people who generally have no security experience. Of the four who headed the office while

Ames was allegedly spying—James Lynch, William R. Kotapish, Frank Ruocco, and the current director, Robert H. Iwai—only Kotapish had any prior experience in security work. Ruocco, for example, was a CIA analyst. Having done little to improve CIA security, Ruocco was promoted to run the CIA's Directorate of Administration, which includes the Office of Security. He then hired Iwai, the director when Ames was arrested, who was previously in the satellite business.

In contrast to the FBI, the Office of Security does not know how to develop informants by gaining the confidence of employees. Unlike FBI polygraph examiners, CIA examiners routinely accept cover stories given by subjects to explain why they failed the tests. That happened when the office passed all of the thirty-eight Cuban agents who were working for the CIA in 1987. It turned out nearly all of them were secretly working for Fidel Castro. Meanwhile, the FBI had flunked nearly all the Cuban agents who were also working for Castro and had wanted to provide information to the bureau. The reason is that ultimately, the princes of the CIA's Directorate of Operations want everyone to pass to show what a good job they are doing. Because of their political clout within the agency, they can ensure that that happens by pressuring the Office of Security to look for ways to pass agents or employees who should be flunked.

"The system tends to protect people with problems," one of Ames's coworkers said.

A day after Ames's arrest was announced, Director of Central Intelligence R. James Woolsey, who had become DCI in 1993, met with CIA employees in the agency's 7,000-square-foot auditorium. After recounting what employees already knew from the press about the case, Woolsey—whose address was seen by every CIA employee on classified closed-circuit television—spent five minutes explaining why he had himself refused to take a polygraph test, as other recent directors had done. Besides the fact that he was a political appointee and thus did not have to, Woolsey said he remained "skeptical" about the polygraph's effectiveness.

Woolsey's performance sickened many CIA officers, who

pointed out that they, too, have questions about the efficacy of the polygraph but are required to take the test or lose their jobs. The fact that Woolsey would not take the examination —and then had the effrontery to defend his decision even after the revelation of the biggest security breach in the history of the CIA—tells a lot about the air of indifference that allowed the Ames case to happen. But it also underscores how effectively the CIA has covered up its own incompetence. For contrary to initial news reports and to the impression Woolsey conveyed, the polygraph was stunningly accurate in Ames's case.

In fact, after Ames passed his first polygraph test when he entered the CIA in 1962, he flunked every subsequent test. Even in 1976, when he had not yet begun spying, Ames failed when asked if he had had any unauthorized contact with foreign nationals. In 1986, a year after he was said to have begun spying, Ames took a third test and flunked again, this time on the question of whether any foreign intelligence service had "pitched" him—tried to recruit him to spy. Ames insisted then that he had flunked because he was worried that Vitaly Yurchenko—whom he had helped debrief in 1985—had given his identity to the Soviets when Yurchenko redefected. The examiner bought the story.

On April 12, 1991, Ames took his fourth test. Ames flunked again on such key questions as whether he had disclosed classified information without authorization. On April 16, he was retested and failed his fifth and final test.

On these tests, as on the others, the CIA polygraph examiners wrote on their reports that Ames had shown deception. They then recounted his elaborate stories, including claims that his worries about money had shown up as deception on key questions. For example, the examiner wrote on the report of Ames's final exam, "I don't think he is a spy, but he does have money problems." Contrary to their own findings, the examiners wrote as their final conclusion, "No deception." Yet a CIA memo in Ames's file said Ames had failed all his tests.

Thus the controversy over why Ames beat the polygraph tests was built on a deception—a deception fed by the CIA. After Ames became a suspect, the CIA specifically ordered that the damaging polygraph results not be communicated to other agencies. However, the joint FBI-CIA squad working the case had already seen Ames's polygraph reports. Early on, two polygraphers in the FBI's Washington metropolitan field office wrote a report noting that the CIA had failed Ames and saying that, based on their own readings of the tests, they agreed. Even FBI officials accustomed to the CIA's blasé attitude about security were astounded.

The fact is that polygraphs, when used by skilled operators, are right in a surprising number of cases. A 1987 FBI study asked FBI agents whether, in retrospect, they felt the polygraph administered in cases they were involved in had been wrong. Based on their responses, the FBI concluded that less than one percent of its own twenty thousand polygraph determinations since 1973 had been incorrect. While subjects can be trained to fool the polygraph by such means as developing a confident attitude and flexing muscles in response to control questions, a good polygraph operator can often penetrate even these stratagems. When subjects take drugs to calm themselves, their polygraph readings appear flat. Noticing this, a polygraph examiner can demand a urine sample, which can be analyzed for the presence of drugs.

While three of the top polygraph examiners in the country work at the CIA, most of the others at the agency are considered within the profession to be lacking in expertise. With characteristic arrogance, the CIA insists on training its own operators instead of sending them to a Defense Department school used by the FBI, NSA, and other federal agencies. The Chicago school where CIA examiners are sent teaches that their perception of a subject's body language and demeanor should override what the polygraphs tell them. Thus if subjects such as Ames or Koecher are skilled at inventing stories, CIA examiners are taught to accept them. Since spies are whizzes at making up stories, and since they receive further training from the KGB, it is no wonder the CIA's polygraph operators are no match for them.

Thus the CIA's polygraph program is a joke, one that searches for ways to ignore signs of deception. Low-level employees who may have engaged in minor transgressions but have no standing within the agency are flunked. Higher-level employees who are spies are given the benefit of the doubt. By contrast, the FBI's policy is to report deceptive results without any filtering by polygraph examiners. It is then up to investigators to determine the facts about their activities. In Ames's case, no investigators were alerted to the fact that he had failed the tests.

How the CIA could disregard its own tests becomes easier to understand when the CIA's attitude about security and its other failures in the Ames case are examined. How could the agency allow such a heavy drinker as Ames to continue in his sensitive job? The fact is that only the most public and embarrassing drunkenness results in the withdrawal of a CIA officer. In one European country, a CIA officer routinely hit a bar at 10:30 A.M. It was not until he urinated in his pants in the embassy that the CIA, after much soul-searching, reluctantly transferred him to headquarters. How could the agency have allowed Ames to have access to almost everything? The fact is that the agency's vaunted "compartmentation" is a joke. Supervisors boast of major successes at meetings, and officers exchange information over lunch or—in Ames's case—during smoking breaks outside the CIA's building.

Besides having easy access to almost any information he wanted because of his counterintelligence functions, Ames sat on two promotion boards that allowed him to learn the identities and recruitment successes of hundreds of other CIA officers throughout the world. How could the agency have ignored Ames's unexplained wealth? The fact is that even when Ames engaged in gross security violations, no disciplinary action was ever meted out. Indeed, after being caught in the CIA safe house in New York with Maria, Ames was promoted.

How could an examiner have blithely dismissed Ames's demonstrated deception as being related to the Jaguar-owner's purported worries about money? Not wanting to share their power with polygraphers, and fearful of a tool they do not fully understand, the princes of the CIA pressure examiners to pass subjects who have failed. How could an officer with Ames's demonstrated lack of ability even be allowed to work at the CIA, much less in a sensitive position? Coworkers thought Ames was not very bright. Underscoring that judgment, Ames kept notes to his Russian handlers and records of the payments he received from them in his personal computer at home. Ames was either illiterate or made a lot of typos. In one note to his Russian handlers, replicated from a typewriter ribbon, Ames said: "Besides getting cash in Carascus [sic] (I have mentuoned [sic] how little I like this method, though it is acceptable), I still hope that you will have decided on some safer, paper transfer of some sort of a large amount [of money]."

Part of the answer to how the CIA could employ someone of his caliber in a key position is that the CIA has always used counterintelligence as a dumping ground for the least competent officers. Traditionally, the way to advance has been to obtain positive intelligence that will impress the president with the CIA's capabilities. Forgotten in that shortsighted approach is the fact that without good counterintelligence and security, the best sources in the world will be executed before they have had a chance to tell the CIA anything.

Once officers become part of the exclusive club that constitutes the Directorate of Operations, they are immune from accountability to the outside world. The secrecy, the exclusivity, and the power that go with having inside information all conspire to create an unreal atmosphere that leads to unfathomable disasters such as the Ames case. Like any fashionable club, the clandestine service excludes outsiders such as women, who are looked down upon and given little chance to rise.

The CIA not only protects its own, it punishes those who blow the whistle and object to lax discipline. Such people are considered troublemakers who do not understand the system. Proposals to tighten security are met with exaggeration—that they would turn the CIA into Alcatraz.

After the Ames case broke, the CIA's inspector general began investigating what went wrong. It was typical of the inspector general's office that initially Burton L. Gerber was to be in overall charge of the investigation. Gerber was one of those CIA officials who had promoted Ames. While Gerber was later taken off the case, many of the investigators had previously worked in the Directorate of Operations and would be returning to it once their assignment to the inspector general was over. Having the CIA investigate itself was a waste of time and money.

Instead of improving security, the CIA's response over the years to embarrassing spy cases has been to try to cover them up by opposing prosecutions that would make its mistakes public. Thus the CIA's blasé attitude about security is a form of self-protection, a way of insulating CIA officers from accountability. The attitude is fueled by directors of Central Intelligence who consider the subject of security to be both dreary and beneath them.

Instead of signaling that business as usual would not do, Woolsey defended the agency publicly, minimized the damage, and misled the intelligence committees about Ames's polygraph results, saying he passed with flying colors. Only after the author's op-ed piece criticizing Woolsey for not taking the polygraph test appeared in the March 8, 1994 *New York Times* did Woolsey issue the word that he would take the test. He did not say when.

The CIA was founded to prevent another surprise attack such as occurred at Pearl Harbor. Over the years, the CIA has served that purpose well, predicting most of the changes and threats it should have predicted. But the damage from the Ames case to the CIA's credibility and to its reputation for protecting its sources and methods was devastating.

"There has been massive incompetence at the CIA," an official working on the Ames case said.

If the Ames case demonstrated that the CIA's security system is a failure, it also illustrated how easy it was for the CIA to mislead the press. Besides frequent references to Ames's passing his polygraph tests instead of failing them, the media ran stories suggesting that the Ames case meant that Yurchenko was not a real defector after all; that it was Ames's wife, rather than Ames, who had recruited him to spy for the Russians; and that it was brilliant CIA analysis and access to German Stasi files, rather than an FBI defector's information, that had led to Ames's arrest; that

Ames's spying was the fault of the FBI, rather than the CIA; and that the FBI was leaking unfavorable stories about the CIA.

In fact, electronic interception of Ames's conversations showed that forty-one-year-old Maria Ames did not know about her husband's spy activities until 1991. Rather than show Yurchenko to be a plant, the Ames case meant that still-unresolved leads Yurchenko provided about moles in the CIA should be pursued even more vigorously, which the FBI began doing. The CIA's negligence in ignoring all the warning signs that Ames was spying was akin to a bank's leaving its front door and vault door open overnight. While it would be nice if the police had spotted the open door, the primary fault lay with the institution that left the doors open. Finally, while FBI agents were livid about the way the CIA had allowed both the CIA's and FBI's operations to be compromised, many FBI officials went out of their way to downplay the CIA's blunders. Because they still had to work with the agency, they did not want to exacerbate frictions between the agencies.

If nothing else, the Ames case showed that the subject of spying was not passé. Ever since the Cold War ended, the FBI and CIA had been saying that the Russians continued to spy on the U.S. No one took it seriously. Now the mailbox where Ames was said to have made chalk marks for his KGB handlers at 37th and R Streets NW in Washington was the most photographed mailbox in U.S. history. Tour buses pointed out the location to visitors from out of town. Once out of favor in Hollywood, spy movies again became highly prized.

But the implications of the Ames case are far more serious. If the CIA is to continue to protect the U.S. from potential international threats, it must take drastic action to change the agency climate that led to the Ames case. That change has to begin at the top. By example, the director needs to show that he is ready to make a clean break with the sloppiness of the past. By initially arrogantly refusing to submit to the same security procedure as everyone else, then defending the agency's gross negligence and incompetence, Woolsey demonstrated that he not only condoned a system that placed the country at risk, he also was not up to the task of correcting it.

Besides getting a new director, the CIA needed to fire or remove to less-sensitive positions every supervisor who allowed Ames to continue in his job despite the obvious signs that something was wrong. To direct its Office of Security, the CIA needed to appoint a former FBI counter-intelligence agent. To be sure, the FBI has made its own mistakes, including allowing Richard W. Miller, who later committed espionage, to continue as an agent. But the lapses have not stemmed from systemic problems. Over the years, the FBI has compiled an impressive record for catching spies.* Since 1975, FBI counterintelligence investigations have resulted in the prosecution of more than seventy people for espionage. All but one were convicted. The security departments of most major corporations are headed by former FBI agents, who know how to pursue investigations lawfully and are likely to have good liaison with the bureau.

As it is, the CIA resists FBI investigations. Since 1991, the CIA has refused to cooperate with the bureau or has withheld information on at least ten occasions. Through Ames, the Russians already knew the CIA's most valuable secrets, yet even as the FBI gathered evidence for a prosecution of Ames, the CIA continued to block the FBI from obtaining information about what Ames knew. The reason is that the CIA does not want the FBI to know of its mistakes, just as it does not really want good security.

In many respects, the lax security is related to the CIA's other major failing: its continuing collective enmity toward defectors such as Vitaly Yurchenko.** The agents betrayed by Ames were, in effect, defectors—in spy jargon, defectors-in-place. CIA officers have contempt for defectors, whom they regard as "pains in the ass"—unbalanced traitors to their own countries. If a man such as Ames betrays them to

---

*How the FBI catches spies is the subject of the author's book *Spy vs. Spy.*

**The CIA's mishandling of Yurchenko is portrayed in the author's book *Escape from the CIA.*

the other side, CIA officers do not consider the loss to be great. To them, spying is a game. So long as the princes of the CIA maintain their own lofty positions within the agency, they win.

That judgment was borne out by the way the affair ended. Having received a scathing report from CIA inspector general Frederick P. Hitz about the Ames case, Woolsey reprimanded eleven of the twenty-three present or former CIA officers who were cited in the report for having neglected their duties by ignoring the signs that Ames was engaged in spying.

In contrast, when FBI agents failed to watch Edward Lee Howard carefully before he escaped to the Soviet Union, they were fired. Woolsey portrayed himself as a judge who had to take into account the rights of the CIA officers involved. He said no "misconduct" was involved. What was involved was gross negligence, something for which employees of private companies are routinely fired. In this case, the national security was at stake. The inspector general found Ames had compromised some thirty-six intelligence operations. Woolsey's inaction meant that at the CIA, "It's business as usual," as Senator Dennis DeConcini, chairman of the Senate Select Committee on Intelligence, put it.

As might be expected, high-ranking princes of the CIA who had lobbied Woolsey on behalf of the officers applauded his decision. They had convinced Woolsey that the officers were so special that anything more than a letter in their personnel files would ruin their precious morale and was unnecessary because they were so devoted to their jobs.

In fact, the officers in question were devoted to their own self-interest. As the inspector general concluded, CIA officers willfully ignored Ames's spying, because they did not want to blow the whistle on one of their own. In contrast, when a female CIA station chief in Jamaica broke that code of silence by reporting a subordinate for beating his wife, the full force of the CIA's bureaucracy came down on her. She became the target of an inspector general's investigation, rumors were circulated about her sex life, and her career at the agency was ruined.

Woolsey's decision perpetuated the air of indifference

that had led to the fiasco in the first place. It turned the stomachs of many CIA officers who recognized that it meant such catastrophes would happen again. To be sure, in return for leniency for his wife, Ames pleaded guilty and got life in prison without possibility of parole. But that was because his fate was in the hands of the Justice Department and FBI, not the CIA.

To fill the vacuum caused by Woolsey's lack of leadership, a presidential commission was formed to study ways to restructure the CIA and decide if, indeed, the agency was needed at all. Yet deciding such a question was like deciding whether a community needed a fire department. Because Woolsey had failed to seize the initiative and do his job, public support was so weakened for the agency that a commission was seen as the only way to salvage what was left of the CIA's declining credibility.

Ultimately, the fault lay with President Clinton, who could not manage his own White House staff, let alone the CIA. Oversight committees and commissions can go only so far in forcing change. It was up to Clinton, to whom Woolsey reported, to insist on aggressive action. What was needed was not only a series of firings but an extensive retraining program to change the culture of the agency, as well as a restructuring to bring about better coordination within the CIA.

Until a strong and competent president overhauls the agency, America will remain at risk. Indeed, because of Ames and a few other spies such as John A. Walker, Jr., the U.S. likely would have lost a war with the Soviet Union, those familiar with the Ames case say.

The CIA has come a long way since the days when it plotted with the Mafia to get Fidel Castro's beard to fall off, gave LSD to unsuspecting subjects, and spied illegally on Americans. But powerful as it is, the Ames case and the way it was handled demonstrate that the CIA still has a long way to go before it becomes the effective, disciplined agency America deserves.

Directors of
Central Intelligence

Sidney W. Souers*	January 23, 1946–June 10, 1946
Hoyt S. Vandenberg	June 10, 1946–May 1, 1947
Roscoe H. Hillenkoeter	May 1, 1947–October 7, 1950
Walter Bedell Smith	October 7, 1950–February 9, 1953
Allen W. Dulles	February 26, 1953–November 29, 1961
John A. McCone	November 29, 1961–April 28, 1965
William F. Raborn, Jr.	April 28, 1965–June 30, 1966

* The first three directors of Central Intelligence headed the Central Intelligence Group, a forerunner of the CIA established on January 22, 1946. The CIA was established by the National Security Act of 1947, which became effective on September 18, 1947. Adm. Hillenkoeter was reappointed DCI over the new agency.

Richard Helms	June 30, 1966–February 2, 1973
James R. Schlesinger	February 2, 1973–July 2, 1973
William E. Colby	September 4, 1973–January 30, 1976
George H. Bush	January 30, 1976–January 20, 1977
Stansfield Turner	March 9, 1977–January 20, 1981
William J. Casey	January 28, 1981–January 29, 1987
William H. Webster	May 26, 1987–September 1, 1991
Robert M. Gates	November 12, 1991–

DEPUTY DIRECTORS OF CENTRAL INTELLIGENCE

Kingman Douglas	March 2, 1946–July 11, 1946
Edwin K. Wright	January 20, 1947–March 9, 1949
William H. Jackson	October 7, 1950–August 3, 1951
Allen W. Dulles	August 23, 1951–February 26, 1953
Charles P. Cabell	April 23, 1953–January 31, 1962
Marshall S. Carter	April 3, 1962–April 28, 1965
Richard Helms	April 28, 1965–June 30, 1966
Rufus L. Taylor	October 13, 1966–February 1, 1969
Robert E. Cushman, Jr.	May 7, 1969–December 31, 1971
Vernon A. Walters	May 2, 1972–July 2, 1976
Enno H. Knoche	July 7, 1976–August 1, 1977
Frank C. Carlucci III	February 10, 1978–January 20, 1981
Bobby R. Inman	February 12, 1981–June 10, 1982
John N. McMahon	June 10, 1982–March 29, 1986
Robert M. Gates	April 18, 1986–March 20, 1989
Richard J. Kerr	March 20, 1989–March 2, 1992
William O. Studeman	April 14, 1992–

Notes

1. William Colby and Peter Forbath, *Honorable Men: My Life in the CIA* (Simon & Schuster, 1978), p. 338.
2. Interview with McMahon on January 25, 1991.
3. Interview on June 7, 1990, with Saunders.
4. Interview on September 19, 1990, with Polgar.
5. Interview on April 13, 1990, with Whipple.
6. CIA History Staff, *Directors and Deputy Directors of Central Intelligence* (1989), p. 11.
7. Interview on August 17, 1990, with Colby.
8. Memo of July 24, 1991, from Leahy to Joe Jamele, press secretary to Leahy; and interview on July 17, 1991, with Jamele.
9. Interview on July 11, 1990, with Simmons.
10. Interview on April 13, 1990, with Whipple.
11. *Time,* May 28, 1990, p. 50.
12. Interview on September 28, 1990, with Polgar.
13. Commission on CIA Activities within the United States

(the Rockefeller Commission), *Report to the President* (Government Printing Office, 1976), pp. 52–53.

14. Interview on July 2, 1990, with Clarke.

15. Tom Gilligan, *CIA Life: 10,000 Days with the Agency* (Foreign Intelligence Press, 1991), p. 252.

16. Interview on May 2, 1991, with Rodriguez.

17. *New York Times*, March 23, 1988, p. A-1.

18. *New York Times*, March 31, 1989, p. A-6.

19. Gregory F. Treverton, *Covert Action: The Limits of Intervention in the Postwar World* (Basic Books, 1987), p. 176.

20. "Secret Intelligence," a Public Broadcasting Service special that appeared in Washington on WETA-TV on January 17, 1989.

21. Loch K. Johnson, *America's Secret Power* (Oxford University Press, 1989), p. 64.

22. Interview on July 11, 1990, with Bissell.

23. Report of the CIA inspector general of August 25, 1967, obtained by the author under the Freedom of Information Act, p. 14.

24. Report of the CIA inspector general of August 25, 1967, obtained by the author under the Freedom of Information Act, p. 4.

25. An accurate account of the Fadlallah incident appears in David C. Martin and John Walcott's *Best Laid Plans* (Touchstone, 1988), p. 220.

26. Interview on January 25, 1991, with McMahon.

27. Interview on December 6, 1990, with Bruemmer.

28. *Washington Post*, June 14, 1991, p. A-19.

29. Interview on April 11, 1990, with Bowen.

30. Harry Rositzke, *The CIA's Secret Operations* (Reader's Digest Press, 1977), p. 20.

31. Curtis Peebles, *Guardians: Strategic Reconnaissance Satellites* (Presidio Press, 1987), p. 13.

32. William Hood, *Mole* (W.W. Norton, 1982), p. 127.

33. William Hood, *Mole* (W.W. Norton, 1982), p. 186.

34. Oleg Penkovskiy, *The Penkovskiy Papers* (Doubleday & Co., 1965).

35. Peter Wright, *Spy Catcher* (Viking, 1987), p. 208.

36. *Washington Post,* March 11, 1983, p. A-1.

37. Associated Press, April 19, 1987. Sellers, on March 20, 1988, declined comment.

38. Reuters, October 22, 1986.

39. The Associated Press, April 19, 1977.

40. See the author's book *Escape from the CIA: How the KGB Won and Lost the Most Important KGB Spy Ever to Defect to the U.S.* (Pocket Books, 1991).

41. *Washington Post,* May 6, 1990, p. A-1.

42. Interview on September 5, 1990, with Proctor.

43. An authoritative account by Steven Emerson and Richard Rothschild in the September 12, 1988, issue of *U.S. News & World Report* reported Fawaz Younis's intercepted conversation and many of the details of the CIA's involvement in capturing him. These were confirmed in an interview on August 31, 1990, with Oliver (Buck) Revell, then associate deputy director of the FBI, who directed the arrest of Younis.

44. Interviews on August 20, 1990, and on March 13, 1991, with Francis D. Carter, Younis's lawyer.

45. *Washington Post,* June 27, 1991, p. A-1.

46. Interview on August 31, 1991, with Revell.

47. Tom Mangold, *Cold Warrior: James Jesus Angleton* (Simon & Schuster, 1991), pp. 340–44, and *Washington Post,* May 14, 1991.

48. CIA memo from James Angleton to the FBI director on September 20, 1967.

49. Recounted on page 336 of the Pocket Books edition of the author's *Spy vs. Spy.* After the Soviets relinquished their control of Czechoslovakia, Koecher worked for the new Czech government but is now retired. Hana Koecher is working for a Czech firm that exports art to the West.

50. Tom Mangold, *Cold Warrior: James Jesus Angleton* (Simon & Schuster, 1991), p. 317.

51. An account of Shin Bet's feat in obtaining Khrushchev's secret speech is given by Yossi Melman and Dan Raviv in the *International Journal of Intelligence and Counterintelligence,* Vol. 4, No. 2, p. 219.

52. Webster's meeting with reporters was May 31, 1991.

53. Commission on CIA Activities within the United States (the Rockefeller Commission), *Report to the President* (Government Printing Office, 1976), pp. 173–89, 193.

54. Thomas Powers, *The Man Who Kept the Secrets: Richard Helms and the CIA* (Knopf, 1987), pp. 261, 267.

55. William Colby and Peter Forbath, *Honorable Men: My Life in the CIA* (Simon & Schuster, 1978), p. 345.

56. A subsequent report by Sheffield Edwards, director of the CIA's Office of Security, on the administration of LSD to Frank Olson created confusion about whether Olson was told he would be given LSD prior to taking it on November 19, 1953. Edwards's memo of November 29, 1953, says "it was decided to experiment with the drug LSD, and for the members present to administer the drugs to themselves to ascertain the effect a clandestine application would have on a meeting or conference." But a January 29, 1975, CIA memo quotes a December 1, 1953, memo from the CIA Inspector General's office as stating that the individuals "were not told they had been given LSD until 20 minutes afterwards."

    According to page 227 of the Rockefeller Commission report: "Prior to receiving the LSD, the subject [Olson] had participated in discussions where the testing of such substances on unsuspecting subjects was agreed to in principle. However, this individual was not made aware that he had been given LSD until about 20 minutes after it had been administered."

57. CIA memo to DCI on December 18, 1953.

58. Interview on August 17, 1990, with Colby.

59. Thomas Powers's *The Man Who Kept the Secrets: Richard Helms and the CIA* (Knopf, 1987), on pages 276–78, includes an excellent description of the state of congressional oversight in the CIA's early days.

60. Interview on July 10, 1990, with Simmons.

61. Interview on October 25, 1990, with Helms.

62. Interview on October 25, 1990, with Helms.

63. Interview on August 29, 1990, with Cord Meyer.

64. Interview on July 11, 1990, with Bissell.

65. Interview on July 11, 1990, with Bissell.
66. Interview on May 10, 1990, with Bross.
67. Interview on April 11, 1990, with Bowen.
68. Interview on August 17, 1990, with Colby.
69. Interview on September 5, 1990, with Proctor.
70. Interview on June 10, 1990, with Simmons.
71. William Colby and Peter Forbath, *Honorable Men: My Life in the CIA* (Simon & Schuster, 1978), p. 441.
72. Interview on September 10, 1990, with Miller.
73. Interview on May 15, 1990, with Saunders.
74. Interview on September 28, 1990, with Polgar.
75. Interview on December 18, 1990, with Gates.
76. *New York Times,* May 19, 1991, p. E-5.
77. U.S. Congress, *Report of the Congressional Committees Investigating the Iran-Contra Affair* (U.S. Government Printing Office, 1987), p. 379.
78. Interview on June 10, 1990, with Simmons.
79. Interview on May 1, 1991, with Shuster.
80. Interview on July 11, 1990, with Bissell.
81. Interview on September 7, 1990, with Bissell.
82. Harold P. Ford, *Estimative Intelligence: The Purposes and Problems of National Intelligence Estimating* (Defense Intelligence College, 1989), p. 192, taken from David A. Brinkley and Andrew W. Hull's *Estimative Intelligence* (Defense Intelligence School, 1979).
83. Russell Jack Smith, *The Unknown CIA: My Three Decades with the Agency* (Pergamon-Brassey's, 1989), p. 127.
84. Michael R. Beschloss, *Mayday: Eisenhower, Khrushchev, and the U-2 Affair* (Harper & Row, 1986), p. 400.
85. An excellent discussion of the National Reconnaissance Office appears in Jeffrey T. Richelson's *The U.S. Intelligence Community* (Ballinger, 1989), pp. 26–29.
86. Interview on August 24, 1990, with Lundahl.
87. William E. Burrows, *Deep Black: Space Espionage and National Security* (Random House, 1986), p. 219.
88. Interview on August 24, 1990, with Lundahl.
89. Interview on August 24, 1990, with Lundahl.

90. Interview on September 4, 1990, with Smith.
91. William E. Burrows, *Deep Black: Space Espionage and National Security* (Random House, 1986), p. 149.
92. Interview on August 24, 1990, with Lundahl.
93. Adapted from a mock intelligence estimate presented in Harold P. Ford's *Estimative Intelligence: The Purposes and Problems of National Intelligence Estimating* (Defense Intelligence College, 1989), pp. 3–6.
94. Harold P. Ford, *Estimative Intelligence: The Purposes and Problems of National Intelligence Estimating* (Defense Intelligence College, 1989), p. 16.
95. Interview on May 14, 1990, with Cline.
96. Russell Jack Smith, *The Unknown CIA: My Three Decades with the Agency* (Pergamon-Brassey's, 1989), p. 140.
97. Harold P. Ford, *Estimative Intelligence: The Purposes and Problems of National Intelligence Estimating* (Defense Intelligence College, 1989), pp. 38, 86.
98. Interview on September 5, 1990, with Proctor.
99. Interview on September 5, 1990, with Proctor.
100. Loch K. Johnson, *America's Secret Power* (Oxford University Press, 1989), p. 85.
101. Interview on December 27, 1990, with Turner.
102. Russell Jack Smith, *The Unknown CIA: My Three Decades with the Agency* (Pergamon-Brassey's, 1989), p. 54.
103. Interview on April 11, 1990, with Bowen.
104. Russell Jack Smith, *The Unknown CIA: My Three Decades with the Agency* (Pergamon-Brassey's, 1989), p. 31.
105. Interview on December 18, 1990, with Gates.
106. *New York Times,* June 13, 1991, p. A-1.
107. Harold P. Ford, *Estimative Intelligence: The Purposes and Problems of National Intelligence Estimating* (Defense Intelligence College, 1989), p. 110.
108. Peter S. Usowski, "John McCone and the Cuban Missile Crisis," *International Journal of Intelligence and Counterintelligence,* Vol. 2, No. 4, pp. 555–58; and Lewis Sorley, *The Central Intelligence Agency: An Overview* (Association of Former Intelligence Officers, 1990), p. 46.

109. Harold P. Ford, *Estimative Intelligence: The Purposes and Problems of National Intelligence Estimating* (Defense Intelligence College, 1989), p. 72.

110. Loch K. Johnson, *America's Secret Power* (Oxford University Press, 1989), p. 94.

111. Abram N. Shulsky, *Silent Warfare: Understanding the World of Intelligence* (Pergamon-Brassey's, 1991), p. 61.

112. Ray S. Cline, *The CIA Under Reagan, Bush & Casey* (Acropolis Books, 1991), p. 223.

113. Interview on September 28, 1990, with Polgar.

114. Interview on September 4, 1990, with Smith.

115. Thomas Powers, *The Man Who Kept the Secrets: Richard Helms and the CIA* (Knopf, 1987), p. 243.

116. Cord Meyer, *Facing Reality: From World Federalism to the CIA* (University Press of America, 1980), pp. 67–80.

117. John Ranelagh, *The Agency: The Rise and Decline of the CIA* (Touchstone, 1987), p: 239.

118. Interview on August 9, 1990, with Meyer.

119. Interview on August 8, 1991, with Sporkin.

120. Interview on July 27, 1990, with Bross.

121. Interview on August 9, 1990, with Meyer.

122. Interview on September 3, 1990, with Fuller.

123. Interview on August 15, 1990, with Whipple.

124. Interview on October 5, 1990, with Inman.

125. Interview on August 9, 1990, with Meyer.

126. Interview on September 3, 1990, with Fuller.

127. Interview on January 4, 1991, with Kerr.

128. Interview on December 18, 1990, with Gates.

129. Interview on January 4, 1991, with Kerr.

130. CIA chart, "USSR: Comparison of CIA Estimates of Overall Growth with Official and Unofficial Soviet Estimates, 1928–1987."

131. Interviews on August 29, 1990, with Graham, and with CIA officials.

132. William T. Lee, *Trends in Soviet Military Outlays and Economic Priorities 1970–1988* (July 30, 1990), p. 10.

133. Interview on August 4, 1990, with Lee.

134. Igor Birman, *Soviet Studies,* January 1980, p. 99.

135. *Washington Post,* October 27, 1980.
136. Interview on July 30, 1990, with Birman.
137. U.S. Congress, Joint Economic Committee study papers, November 23, 1987, p. 126.
138. Anders Åslund in Henry S. Rowen and Charles Wolf, Jr.'s *The Impoverished Superpower: Perestroika and the Soviet Military Burden* (Institute for Contemporary Studies, 1990), p. 53.
139. *The Soviet Economy Stumbles Badly in 1989* (CIA, May 1990), p. v.
140. *New York Times,* April 27, 1990, p. A-35.
141. Interview on August 20, 1990, with Bergson.
142. *Time,* November 5, 1990, p. 63.
143. Interview on December 18, 1990, with Gates.
144. Interview on January 4, 1990, with Kerr.
145. *New York Times,* July 13, 1991, p. A-1.
146. Don Oberdorfer, "Missed Signals in the Middle East," *Washington Post Magazine,* March 17, 1991, p. 40.
147. Interview on June 23, 1991, with Cannistraro; and *New York Times,* March 4, 1991, p. A-11.
148. Dr. Post's assessment of Saddam Hussein appeared on page 6 of the August 26, 1990, *Boston Sunday Herald.*
149. *Washington Post,* January 11, 1990.
150. The *Wall Street Journal*'s story on the CIA's performance during the Gulf War, written by Walter S. Mossberg, appeared on page A-10 of the March 18, 1991, edition. Headlined, "U.S. Intelligence Agencies Triumphed in Gulf War Despite Some Weak Spots," the story said, "In most respects, the Persian Gulf war was a triumph for the U.S. intelligence community."
151. Sun Tzu, *The Art of War* (Shambhala, 1988), p. 82.
152. *Washington Post,* March 18, 1991, p. A-16.
153. *The New Yorker,* June 24, 1991, p. 67.
154. Interview on January 4, 1991, with Kerr.
155. Interview on August 17, 1990, with Colby.
156. *Washington Post,* June 29, 1973, p. A-29; interview on April 27, 1991, with Colby.
157. Interview on December 12, 1990, with Baker.

158. Elizabeth Miles Cooke, *The History of the Old Georgetown Pike* (published by Cooke, 1977), p. 11.
159. Elizabeth Miles Cooke, *The History of the Old Georgetown Pike* (published by Cooke, 1977), p. 33; Nan Netherton, et al., *Fairfax County, Virginia: A History* (Fairfax County Board of Supervisors, 1978), p. 484; Louise C. Curran and William J. Curran, *McLean Remembers* (the McLean Scene Inc., 1967), p. 9; Fairfax County government, *Langley Fork Historic District* (1980), p. 8; *McLean Handbook, 1986–1987* ed. (The Handbook Group, Reston, Virginia), pp. 7, 9; John C. Mackall, *Yearbook*, Vol. 4, 1955 (Historical Society of Fairfax County, Virginia), pp. 1–2; interview on January 20, 1991, with Henry C. Mackall, a descendant of Benjamin Mackall, who acquired the Langley estate from the Lee family in 1836.
160. Interviews on April 24, 1991, with Warner and with Elder.
161. Interview on April 26, 1991, with Elder.
162. Sale and purchase agreement dated July 25, 1947, between Margaret Scattergood and the Federal Works administrator; Elizabeth Miles Cooke, *The History of the Old Georgetown Pike* (published by Cooke, 1977), p. 35; interview on January 20, 1991, with Nancy H. Blanchet, a grandniece and executor of Scattergood's will.
163. Interview on January 21, 1991, with Blanchet.
164. Interview on January 25, 1991, with Fitzwater.
165. Interview on January 23, 1991, with Sylvia Blanchet.
166. *Washington Post,* November 9, 1986, p. C-6; memorial minute read at the memorial service for Scattergood at the Langley Hill Monthly Meeting of the Religious Society of Friends, November 23, 1986; last will and testament of Margaret Scattergood, February 5, 1982, filed with the Circuit Court of Fairfax County, Virginia.
167. Interview on January 5, 1991, with Sanborn.
168. The second-largest collection of intelligence books in the United States is the Russell J. Bowen Collection on Intelligence, Security, and Covert Activities at Georgetown University's main library. This collection, donated

by a retired CIA analyst, has more than 11,000 volumes.

169. Interview on November 26, 1990, with Baker.

170. Turner said he has no recollection of the incident.

171. For a full discussion of Yurchenko's case, see the author's *Escape from the CIA: How the CIA Won and Lost the Most Important KGB Spy Ever to Defect to the U.S.* (Pocket Books, 1991).

172. Interview on March 24, 1991, with Stern.

173. Cord Meyer, *Facing Reality: From World Federalism to the CIA* (University Press of America, 1980), p. 86. In an interview on August 29, 1990, Meyer said he knew nothing about a Soviet effort to give the information to *Ramparts*.

174. Asked on June 26, 1991, why he thought the tip for the *Ramparts* article came from the KGB instead of from Michael Wood, Brown said he had no comment.

175. For a full discussion of the Koecher case, see the author's *Spy vs. Spy: Stalking Soviet Spies in America* (Scribner's, 1988).

   When asked in an interview with the author in Prague if he compromised Ogorodnik, Koecher said, "I'm deeply sorry about that. But the people who did him in were the CIA and he himself. They recruited him in such a clumsy manner. . . . I'm not denying I gave them the document [that compromised him], and I'm not confirming it. I sure do know I worked on the case. I confess it."

176. A more complete discussion of the case of Boyce and Lee can be found in Robert Lindsey's *The Falcon and the Snowman: A True Story of Friendship and Espionage* (Pocket Books, 1980, originally published by Simon & Schuster in 1979), and in the author's book *The Spy in the Russian Club: How Glenn Souther Stole America's Nuclear War Plans and Escaped to Moscow* (Scribner's, 1990).

177. Moore's case is discussed at length in the author's book *Escape from the CIA: How the CIA Won and Lost the Most Important KGB Spy Ever to Defect to the U.S.* (Pocket Books, 1991).

178. *Washington Post,* November 17, 1990.

179. Interview on November 13, 1990, with Horan.

180. The author sat in on an introduction to the Career Training Program on January 25, 1991.

181. U.S. Congress, House Permanent Select Committee on Intelligence, *Compilation of Intelligence Laws and Related Laws and Executive Orders of Interest to the National Intelligence Community* (U.S. Government Printing Office, March 1987), p. 6; and *Fact Book on Intelligence* (CIA, June 1990), p. 14.

182. Russell Jack Smith, *The Unknown CIA: My Three Decades with the Agency* (Pergamon-Brassey's, 1989), p. 167.

183. Interview on July 6, 1991, with Elder.

184. Interview on March 29, 1990, with Crowley.

185. Interview on August 28, 1990, with Hetu.

186. Commission on CIA Activities within the United States (the Rockefeller Commission), *Report to the President* (Government Printing Office, 1976), p. 170.

187. Stansfield Turner, *Secrecy and Democracy: The CIA in Transition* (Houghton Mifflin, 1985), p. 197.

188. Interview on August 28, 1990, with Hetu.

189. Stansfield Turner, *Secrecy and Democracy: The CIA in Transition* (Houghton Mifflin, 1985), p. 197.

190. Interview on December 27, 1990, with Turner.

191. Donald Rochon, a black FBI agent, won a discrimination suit against the FBI after other agents in Omaha and Chicago harassed him, beginning in 1983, for being black.

192. Employment statistics provided by the FBI's public affairs office.

193. Interview on January 7, 1991, with Bruemmer.

194. Interview on December 12, 1990, with Austin.

195. William H. Webster, introduction to *The Civil War Battlefield Guide,* edited by Frances H. Kennedy (Houghton Mifflin, 1990), p. 91.

196. Interview on December 4, 1990, with Spaeth.

197. Interview on April 30, 1991, with Bellinger.

198. Interview on December 17, 1990, with Clark.

199. Interview on November 23, 1990, with Bruemmer.
200. Interview on January 7, 1991, with Bruemmer.
201. Interview on April 29, 1991, with Bellinger.
202. Interview on December 4, 1990, with Spaeth.
203. Thomas Powers, *The Man Who Kept the Secrets* (Knopf, 1987), p. 10.
204. Thomas Powers, *The Man Who Kept the Secrets* (Knopf, 1987), p. 303–5; John Ranelagh, *The Agency: The Rise and Decline of the CIA* (Touchstone, 1987), p. 612–14.
205. Interview on October 25, 1990, with Helms.
206. Interview on April 5, 1991, with Webster.
207. Interview on June 26, 1991, with an associate of George.
208. U.S. Congress, Senate Select Committee on Intelligence, hearing on the nomination of Robert M. Gates, April 10, 1986, p. 23.
209. Interview on November 6, 1990, with McGregor.
210. Interview on November 23, 1990, with McGregor.
211. Interview on January 7, 1991, with Bruemmer.
212. Interview on December 12, 1990, with Baker.
213. Interview on December 12, 1990, with Baker.
214. Interview on July 16, 1991, with Bellinger.
215. Interview on December 27, 1990, with Turner.
216. Interview on July 15, 1991, with McGregor.
217. *Report of the Congressional Committees Investigating the Iran-contra Affair*, November 17, 1987, p. 381.
218. Tom Gilligan, *CIA Life: 10,000 Days with the Agency* (Foreign Intelligence Press, 1991), p. 187.
219. Interview on August 2, 1990, with McCurdy.
220. Interviews on November 6, 1990, with McGregor, on November 28, 1990, with Gutman, and on December 7, 1990, with Hassler.
221. Interview on August 15, 1991, with an associate of George.
222. Interview on July 30, 1991, with McGregor.
223. *Washington Post*, July 16, 1989, p. N-11.
224. Interview on August 9, 1990, with Meyer.
225. Interview on December 18, 1990, with Bruemmer.
226. Interview on December 10, 1990, with Young.
227. *Washington Post*, November 30, 1989.

228. Interview on December 17, 1990, with Lynda Webster.

229. Interview on December 17, 1990, with Lynda Webster.

230. Interview on December 17, 1990, with Lynda Webster.

231. *Los Angeles Times,* May 9, 1991, p. A-1; and *New York Times,* May 9, 1991, p. A-1.

232. Interview on December 18, 1990, with Gates.

233. White House press releases of June 28 and July 25, 1991. Originally established as the Medal of Freedom by President Truman in 1945, the medal became the Presidential Medal of Freedom in 1963 under President Kennedy.

234. Interview on July 6, 1991, with Elder.

235. "Public Affairs Chronology," CIA.

236. Memo for the record by Grogan, March 1, 1962.

237. John Fitzpatrick, ed., *The Writings of George Washington from the Original Manuscript Sources, 1745–1799,* Vol. 7 (U.S. Government Printing Office, 1932), p. 479.

238. An excellent discussion of the CIA's use of the press for spying appears in Loch K. Johnson's *America's Secret Power: The CIA in a Democratic Society* (Oxford University Press, 1989), p. 182–203.

239. Interview on July 11, 1990, with Bissell.

240. Interview on January 25, 1991, with McMahon.

241. William Colby and Peter Forbath, *Honorable Men: My Life in the CIA* (Simon & Schuster, 1978), p. 21.

242. Interview on June 24, 1991, with Colby.

243. Interview on August 28, 1990, with Hetu.

244. Interview on July 27, 1990, with Bross.

245. David Wise, *The American Police State: The Government Against the People* (Random House, 1976), p. 198.

246. Interviews on September 7, 1990, with Warner, and on September 7, 1990, with Marchetti; "The Marchetti Case: New Case Law," John S. Warner, *Studies in Intelligence* (CIA, 1977), p. 1.

247. Interview on August 17, 1990, with Colby.

248. Interview on August 28, 1990, with Hetu; and Loch K. Johnson's *America's Secret Power: The CIA in a Democratic Society* (Oxford University Press, 1989), p. 250.

249. Stansfield Turner, *Secrecy and Democracy: The CIA in Transition* (Houghton Mifflin, 1985), p. xi.

250. "CIA and the University," speech delivered by Robert M. Gates at the John F. Kennedy School of Government, Harvard University, February 13, 1986.

251. An excellent discussion of the CIA's relations with the academic world appear in Loch K. Johnson's *America's Secret Power: The CIA in a Democratic Society* (Oxford University Press, 1989), p. 157–81.

252. *Washington Post,* June 20, 1991, p. A-3; and *New York Times,* June 20, 1991, p. B-1.

253. Memo dated October 12, 1990, from Richard Vengroff, dean, the University of Connecticut, Division of International Affairs.

254. The CIA's maps and analyses are sold by the National Technical Information Service, Commerce Department, Springfield, Virginia.

255. Interview on August 28, 1990, with Hetu.

256. Interview on August 28, 1990, with Hetu.

257. *New York Times,* September 27, 1985, p. A-1.

258. United Press International, September 27, 1985, A.M. cycle.

259. Interview on December 30, 1990, with Engelberg.

260. Interview on January 3, 1991, with Lauder.

261. Interview on December 30, 1990, with Engelberg.

262. Interview on April 5, 1991, with Webster.

263. Interview on November 26, 1990, with Baker.

264. William M. Baker's speech in the Harvard Lecture Series in Boston, July 27, 1989.

265. The Intelligence Identities Protection Act of 1982 imposes criminal penalties on those who have authorized access to classified information and intentionally disclose names of "covert agents." Those who do not have authorized access to classified information—such as journalists—may be subject to penalties if they engage in a "pattern of activities intended to identify and expose covert agents . . . with reason to believe that such activities would impair or impede the foreign intelligence activities of the U.S."

266. Interview on July 4, 1991, with Gerth.

267. *Security Awareness in the 1980's,* Defense Security Institute, p. 203.

268. *Washington Post*, June 13, 1990, p. A-3.
269. *Periscope*, November 3, 1990 (Association of Former Intelligence Officers), p. 7. The CIA denied the claim that the agency had assassinated Palme, calling it "nonsense."
270. William Colby and Peter Forbath, *Honorable Men: My Life in the CIA* (Simon & Schuster, 1978), p. 312.
271. Royal Commission of Inquiry into the Activities of the Nugan Hand Group, final report, government of Australia. (Australian Government Publishing Service, 1985); and author interviews in the fall of 1985 with a number of those involved in the Nugan Hand Bank, including Colby, Erle Cocke, Jr., and Adm. Earl (Bud) Yates.

   Pages 131 and 218 of the final report say Hand met with Colby to ask about the tax consequences for Americans who invested in overseas ventures and the tax impact on Hand and Nugan if they became resident aliens in the U.S. Colby also discussed with Hand his wish to keep his U.S. passport while still an Australian citizen. Colby's then law firm of Reid & Priest received a check from the bank for $10,000 for his advice, but the check was lost, and no replacement check was ever issued. As a result, Colby was never paid.
272. *Washington Post*, August 3, 1991, p. A-1.
273. Declaration of plaintiff's counsel, *Tony Avirgan and Martha Honey vs. John Hull*, et al., Civil Case No. 86-1146, U.S. District Court, Southern District of Florida.
274. U.S. Congress, *Report of the Congressional Committees Investigating the Iran-Contra Affair* (U.S. Government Printing Office, 1987), p. 59.
275. *Washington Post*, February 4, 1989, p. A-10.
276. CIA memo of January 24, 1979.
277. Steve Weinberg, "The Mob, the CIA, and the S&L Scandal," *Columbia Journalism Review*, November 1990, p. 28; and Nicols Fox, "The Story Hardly Anyone Wants to Touch," *Washington Journalism Review*, July/August 1990, p. 10.
278. *Washington Post*, December 22, 1990.
279. *Washington Post*, August 7, 1990, p. A-5.

Notes

280. Ronald Kessler, *Spy vs. Spy: Stalking Soviet Spies in America* (Scribner's, 1988), pp. 100, 104.

281. *Washington Post,* August 11, 1991, p. C-1.

282. Interview on December 18, 1990, with Bruemmer.

283. Peter Maas, *Manhunt* (Random House, 1986), p. 278.

284. Interview on December 31, 1990, with Engelberg.

285. Interview on December 31, 1990, with Engelberg.

286. Interview on January 25, 1991, with McMahon.

287. Interview on December 30, 1990, with Engelberg.

288. Interview on December 18, 1990, with Greenleaf.

289. U.S. Congress, House Permanent Select Committee on Intelligence, *Compilation of Intelligence Laws and Related Laws and Executive Orders of Interest to the National Intelligence Community* (U.S. Government Printing Office, March 1987), pp. 6–9.

290. Commission on CIA Activities within the United States (the Rockefeller Commisssion), *Report to the President* (Government Printing Office, 1976), pp. 51–55.

291. Interview on June 29, 1990, with Houston.

292. Interviews on July 9, 1990, and on August 24, 1991, with Warner.

293. John Ranelagh, *The Agency: The Rise and Decline of the CIA* (Touchstone, 1987), p. 210.

294. *Washington Post,* December 18, 1987, p. A-12.

295. *New York Times,* July 8, 1991, p. A-9.

296. *New York Times,* July 10, 1991, p. A-1.

297. Interview on August 8, 1991, with Sporkin.

298. Interview on December 6, 1990, with Bruemmer.

299. Interview on January 7, 1991, with Bruemmer; and *Washington Post,* October 13, 1990, p. A-2, and October 25, 1990.

300. *Washington Post,* October 5, 1988, p. A-9.

301. Interview on April 5, 1991, with Webster.

302. Interview on January 7, 1991, with Bruemmer.

303. *New York Times,* June 17, 1990, p. E-21.

304. Interview on January 25, 1991, with McMahon.

305. *Washington Post,* November 1, 1990.

306. Interview on January 4, 1991, with Kerr.

Selected Bibliography

Andrew, Christopher, and Oleg Gordievsky. *KGB: The Inside Story*. Harper Collins, 1990.

Belin, David W. *Final Disclosure*. Scribner's, 1988.

Beschloss, Michael R. *Mayday: Eisenhower, Khrushchev, and the U-2 Affair*. Harper & Row, 1986.

Bittman, Ladislav. *The KGB and Soviet Disinformation: An Insider's View*. Pergamon-Brassey's, 1985.

Breckinridge, Scott D. *The CIA and the U.S. Intelligence System*. Westview Press, 1986.

Brook-Shepherd, Gordon. *The Storm Birds: The Dramatic Stories of the Top Soviet Spies Who Have Defected Since World War II*. Weidenfeld & Nicholson, 1989.

Burrows, William E. *Deep Black: Space Espionage and National Security*. Random House, 1986.

Carl, Leo. *The International Dictionary of Intelligence*. International Defense Consultant Services, 1990.

Chavchavadze, David. *Crowns and Trenchcoats: A Russian Prince in the CIA*. Atlantic International Publications, 1990.

Selected Bibliography

Cline, Ray S. *The CIA Under Reagan, Bush & Casey*. Acropolis Books, 1991.

Colby, William, and Peter Forbath. *Honorable Men: My Life in the CIA*. Simon & Schuster, 1978.

Commission on CIA Activities within the United States (the Rockefeller Commission). *Report to the President*. Government Printing Office, 1976.

Darling, Arthur B. *The Central Intelligence Agency: An Instrument of Government to 1950*. Pennsylvania State University Press, 1990.

De Silva, Peter. *Sub Rosa: The CIA and the Uses of Intelligence*. Times Books, 1978.

Dulles, Allen. *Great True Spy Stories*. Castle, 1968.

Emerson, Steven, and Brian Duffy. *The Fall of Pan Am 103: Inside the Lockerbie Investigation*. G. P. Putnam's Sons, 1990.

Ford, Harold P. *Estimative Intelligence: The Purposes and Problems of National Intelligence Estimating*. Defense Intelligence College, 1989.

Gilligan, Tom. *CIA Life: 10,000 Days with the Agency*. Foreign Intelligence Press, 1991.

Hood, William. *Mole*. W. W. Norton, 1982.

Jeffreys-Jones, Rhodri. *American Espionage: From Secret Service to the CIA*. The Free Press, 1977.

Johnson, Loch K. *America's Secret Power: The CIA in a Democratic Society*. Oxford University Press, 1989.

Kessler, Ronald. *Escape from the CIA: How the CIA Won and Lost the Most Important KGB Spy Ever to Defect to the U.S.* Pocket Books, 1991.

———. *Moscow Station: How the KGB Penetrated the American Embassy in Moscow*. Scribner's, 1989.

———. *The Spy in the Russian Club: How Glenn Souther Stole America's Nuclear War Plans and Escaped to Moscow*. Scribner's, 1990.

———. *Spy vs. Spy: Stalking Soviet Spies in America*. Scribner's, 1988.

Laqueur, Walter. *A World of Secrets: The Uses and Limits of Intelligence*. Basic Books, 1985.

Levchenko, Stanislav. *On the Wrong Side*. Pergamon-Brassey's, 1988.

Selected Bibliography

Mangold, Tom. *Cold Warrior: James Jesus Angleton*. Simon & Schuster, 1991.

Marchetti, Victor, and John D. Marks. *The CIA and the Cult of Intelligence*. Knopf, 1974.

Martin, David C., and John Walcott. *Best Laid Plans: The Inside Story of America's War Against Terrorism*. Touchstone, 1989 (originally published by Harper & Row, 1988).

Meyer, Cord. *Facing Reality: From World Federalism to the CIA*. University Press of America, 1980.

Payne, Ronald, and Christopher Dobson. *Who's Who in Espionage*. St. Martin's Press, 1984.

Peebles, Curtis. *Guardians: Strategic Reconnaissance Satellites*. Presidio Press, 1987.

Penkovskiy, Oleg. *The Penkovskiy Papers*. Doubleday, 1965.

Persico, Joseph E. *Casey: The Lives and Secrets of William J. Casey*. Viking, 1990.

Powers, Thomas. *The Man Who Kept the Secrets: Richard Helms and the CIA*. Knopf, 1987.

Prados, John. *The Soviet Estimate: U.S. Intelligence Analysis and Soviet Strategic Forces*. Princeton University Press, 1982.

———. *Presidents' Secret Wars: CIA and Pentagon Covert Operations from World War II through Iranscam*. William Morrow, 1986.

Rafizadeh, Mansur. *Witness: From the Shah to the Secret Arms Deal*. William Morrow, 1987.

Ranelagh, John. *The Agency: The Rise and Decline of the CIA*. Touchstone, 1987 (originally published by Cambridge Publishing Ltd., 1986).

Richelson, Jeffrey T. *America's Secret Eyes in Space: The U.S. Keyhole Spy Satellite Program*. Harper & Row, 1990.

———. *The U.S. Intelligence Community*. Ballinger, 1989.

Romerstein, Herbert, and Stanislav Levchenko. *The KGB Against the "Main Enemy": How the Soviet Intelligence Service Operates Against the United States*. Lexington Books, 1989.

Rositzke, Harry. *The CIA's Secret Operations*. Reader's Digest Press, 1977.

Rowen, Henry S., and Charles Wolf, Jr. *The Impoverished Superpower: Perestroika and the Soviet Military Burden*. Institute for Contemporary Studies, 1990.

Shulsky, Abram N. *Silent Warfare: Understanding the World of Intelligence.* Pergamon-Brassey's, 1991.

Smith, Russell Jack. *The Unknown CIA: My Three Decades with the Agency.* Pergamon-Brassey's, 1989.

Sorley, Lewis. *The Central Intelligence Agency: An Overview.* Association of Former Intelligence Officers, 1990.

Thomas, Gordon. *Journey Into Madness: The True Story of Secret CIA Mind Control and Medical Abuse.* Bantam, 1989.

The Tower Commission Report: The Full Text of the President's Special Review Board. Bantam Books and Times Books, 1987.

Treverton, Gregory F. *Covert Action: The Limits of Intervention in the Postwar World.* Basic Books, 1987.

Troy, Thomas F. *Donovan and the CIA.* University Publications of America, 1981.

Turner, Stansfield. *Secrecy and Democracy: The CIA in Transition.* Houghton Mifflin, 1985.

U.S. Congress. House Permanent Select Committee on Intelligence. *Compilation of Intelligence Laws and Related Laws and Executive Orders of Interest to the National Intelligence Community.* U.S. Government Printing Office, March 1987.

———. Senate Select Committee to Study Government Operations with Respect to Intelligence Activities (the Church Committee). *Final Report.* U.S. Government Printing Office, 1976.

———. *Report of the Congressional Committees Investigating the Iran-contra Affair.* U.S. Government Printing Office, 1987.

Wise, David. *The Spy Who Got Away: The Inside Story of Edward Lee Howard, the CIA Agent Who Betrayed His Country's Secrets and Escaped to Moscow.* Random House, 1988.

Woodward, Bob. *Veil: The Secret Wars of the CIA 1981–1987.* Simon & Schuster, 1987.

Wyden, Peter. *Bay of Pigs: The Untold Story.* Simon & Schuter, 1979.

Glossary

Agent—Person acting under control of an intelligence or security service to obtain or help obtain information for intelligence purposes. Also known as an asset.

Analysis—Review of collected information to determine its significance, collate it with other information in hand, and draw conclusions resulting in intelligence judgments.

Asset—See AGENT.

Case officer—A staff member of an intelligence service who is responsible for handling agents. Also known as an operations officer.

Clandestine operations—Operations carried out secretly.

Collection—Acquisition of information to be processed for intelligence.

Communications intelligence (COMINT)—Intelligence derived from intercepted communications.

Consumer—Person or organization that receives and makes use of intelligence.

Glossary

Counterintelligence—Activities undertaken to thwart efforts by hostile intelligence services to penetrate or compromise one's own intelligence service and operations.

Cover—Protective guise assumed by an individual or activity to conceal its true identity and affiliation.

Defector—Person who has repudiated his country of citizenship and may possess information of intelligence interest.

Dissemination—Distribution of intelligence to consumers via written, oral, or electronic means.

Espionage—Clandestine intelligence collection.

Estimate—An intelligence product analyzing and assessing future possible developments and courses of action.

Evaluation—Determination of the probable validity, pertinence, and utility of intelligence information.

Finding—A written determination by the president required before covert action may be undertaken.

Foreign intelligence—Intelligence concerning areas and activities outside the United States.

Human source intelligence (HUMINT)—Intelligence collected by means of agents or informers.

Imagery—Representations of objects reproduced on film, electro-optical display, radar, or other means.

Information—Unevaluated raw data not yet processed to produce intelligence.

Intelligence—The product of collection, evaluation, and analysis of information.

Operations officer—See CASE OFFICER.

Paramilitary operations—Operations undertaken by military forces separate from the regular armed forces of a nation.

Processing—Manipulation of collected raw information of intelligence interest to make it usable for analysis.

Product—Finished intelligence disseminated to consumers.

Reconnaissance—Observation mission undertaken to acquire by various means information about a target of intelligence interest.

Requirement—Statement by a consumer of an intelligence need to be filled.

Security—Measures taken to protect sensitive activities, data, and personnel against compromise.

Glossary

Signals intelligence (SIGINT)—Intelligence derived from the interception, processing, and analysis of communications, electronic emissions, or telemetry.

Strategic intelligence—Intelligence supporting national- and international-level formulation of policy, plans, and strategy.

Target—Person, place, or thing against which intelligence operations are directed.

Telemetry—Electronic signals given off by, for example, missiles or rockets during operational testing.

Excerpted by permission from Dr. Lewis Sorley's *The Central Intelligence Agency: An Overview*, published by the Association of Former Intelligence Officers.

Index

Index

Index

Index

The Bestselling Author of THE FBI and
INSIDE THE CIA

RONALD KESSLER

THE HIDDEN LIVES OF THE MODERN
PRESIDENTS AND THE SECRETS OF
THE WORLD'S MOST POWERFUL
INSTITUTION

INSIDE the WHITE HOUSE

Available from Pocket Books

POCKET
B O O K S

1011-01